Bomber Commander

Bomber Commander

A Biography of Wing Commander Donald Teale Saville
DSO, DFC

Francis Roy Chappell

Pen & Sword
AVIATION

First published in Great Britain in 2004 by
Pen & Sword Aviation
an imprint of
Pen & Sword Books Ltd

ISBN 1 84415 092 5

British Library Cataloguing-in-Publication Data
A CIP catalogue record for this book is
available from the British Library

Typeset in 10/12pt Palatino by
Phoenix Typesetting, Auldgirth, Dumfriesshire

Printed and bound in England by
CPI UK

The Publishers would like to thank Andrew and other members of the Chappell family for their help during the preparation of this book for publication. Also the many members of the Saville family who have delved into their archives to find photographs and other important reports and memories of Donald Saville's life and career.

Pen & Sword Books Ltd incorporates the Imprints of Pen & Sword Aviation, Pen & Sword Maritime, Pen & Sword Military, Wharncliffe Local History, Pen & Sword Select, Pen & Sword Military Classics and Leo Cooper.

For a complete list of Pen & Sword titles please contact
PEN & SWORD BOOKS LIMITED
47 Church Street, Barnsley, South Yorkshire, S70 2AS, England
E-mail: enquiries@pen-and-sword.co.uk
Website: www.pen-and-sword.co.uk

To the memory of
those who did not come back
and as a tribute to all who served with
Wing Commander D. T. Saville, DSO, DFC, RAFVR
in RAF Ferry Pool, 12 Squadron RAF,
458 Squadron RAAF, 104 Squadron RAF
and 218 Squadron RAF
in the Second World War.

When you go home
Tell them of us and say
For your tomorrow
We gave our today

Memorial at Kohima

Contents

Acknowledgements

In undertaking a biography one soon becomes aware of the debt owed to the many people and institutions who provide information and help of various kinds during the years of research and writing. While one may intend to acknowledge all such assistance it is almost inevitable that some people are overlooked. To anyone in that position I offer sincere apologies and thanks.

Those who were in at the beginning include Professor Michael Roe of the University of Tasmania History Department and Mr Hugh Campbell, formerly a senior officer in the Tasmanian Education Department, who kindly acted as referees in an application for a research grant from the Australian War Memorial. This application was successful in 1985, some time after correspondence with the manager of the Commonwealth Portland Cement Co. Ltd at Portland, N.S.W., had revealed that members of the Saville family, including two brothers of Wing Commander Donald Teale Saville, DSO, DFC, were alive and living in New South Wales. The manager provided addresses and the first stage of detective work was well in progress.

From this point on Mr Frank Allsopp of Taroona was most helpful as typist and manuscript reader, showing admirable patience and good temper in all circumstances!

In some approximate order of contact I wish to thank:

John and Mollie Saville, Norman and Jean Saville, Peter Phillips, Mrs Judy Bowen, Mrs Peggy de Seriere, Mr Bert Fawcett

W/Cdr Dereck French, F/Lt Harry Godfrey, Air Commodore A. E. Mather

F/Lt H. M. Fuller, F/Lt T. Howes, S/Ldr Leslie Manfield, F/Lt John Showell, F/Lt John Stanley, S/Ldr R. J. Ginn, F/Lt S. M. Boylan, F/Lt Colin Corten, W/Cdr G. H. N. Gibson, Air Commodore C. J. Mount, G/Capt Hugh Mansell, S/Ldr P. E. Mackay, F/Lt Leslie Ward, F/Lt Neil Watkins, F/Lt W. McRae

Peter Anderson, F/Lt Eric Lloyd, F/Sgt Dave Rodden

F/Lt W. K. Dunn, Professor David Gumby

John Harrison, Harry Whelan, W/Cdr F. R. Graeme-Evans, Lindsay Millar.

Captain John Presgrave, Captain Arthur Lovell, Captain Peter Gibbes, Mrs Inez Laurie, Mrs Marguerite Pixley
F/Lt W. J. Kenton, S/Ldr Ian Ryall, S/Ldr G. M. Rothwell, S/Ldr L. E. Skan, F/Lt Piper, John Brengelmans, Mrs Cedric Eyre, F. and C. Clitheroe, R. Kent, W/Cdr W. J. Smith
Mrs Margaret Alderson, Mrs I. Benedek, Karen Atherton
Martin Middlebrook, the Australian War Memorial Staff, the RAAF Museum, Point Cook, the RAAF Archives Branch, Canberra, the Air Historical Branch, Ministry of Defence, London, the RAF Bomber Command Museum and Library, Hendon, the Public Record Office, Kew, the Friends School, Great Ayton, Yorkshire.

Dusk is our dawn and midnight is our noon:
And for the sun we have the silver moon.
We love the darkness and we hate the light,
For we are wedded to the gloomy night.

'The Night Bombers', Paul Bewsher 1917

Briefing

Men in the Briefing Room
Aircrews listening laughing
At Intelligence assessment of target defences.
Pilots sensitive cynical and silent
Envisaging searchlights fighters and flak
Navigators serious and laden with 'met gen'
Bomb aimers bewildered by mission changes
Wops absorbing fresh call signs and channels
Engineers' minds switched on fuel tanks and gauges
Mentally checking each engine's performance
Gunners grim determined and restless
Eager to test guns early in flight.
Groundwork done and planning over –
War in the air and the target ahead.

FRC

Foreword

by

Air Commodore A. E. Mather,

DFC, AFC, RAAF (Retired)

As well as feeling honoured at being invited to write this foreword, I also feel a sense of unique history in that I was a contemporary of both the subject, Wing Commander D. T. Saville, DSO, DFC and also of the biographer, Squadron Leader F. R. Chappell, RAF, having seen service with both during the critical period of the war in the Middle East from the loss of Tobruk and the retreat back to the Delta area to the Allied breakthrough of the enemy-held line at El Alamein.

Don Saville I came to know both personally and professionally over a series of wartime coincidences (although I suspect he had a large hand in arranging some of these). We first met when I and a fellow Australian pilot were posted to 21 OTU, Moreton-in-the-Marsh in August 1941. Don approached us and, introducing himself, threw us the keys of his car with the words: 'I'm going away for the weekend – I guess you've got a driver's licence. Have a look around the local countryside.' This was typical of his personal kindnesses and thoughtfulness towards his subordinates. We were brand-new pilot officers and he was a squadron leader at the time; a world of difference in those days. In similar vein I knew him to bring out bags full of 'goodies' for distribution to the troops after special trips to Cairo etc. – all at personal expense and effort to himself.

I next met Don briefly at 12 Squadron, Binbrook, which was my first posting out of OTU. With the advent of Australian squadrons he was posted as Flight Commander to 458 Squadron, RAAF at Holme-on-Spalding Moor. I was subsequently posted to the same squadron in February 1942. After some operations over Europe and two ferry tours to the Middle East, I was again reunited with Wing Commander Saville as my commanding officer at 104 Squadron, RAF Kabrit. This again, I suspect, was the result of Saville's persuasiveness with the hierarchy, as he had recently asked me, 'How would you like to join me in the war in the desert?' From this period on I served under Don Saville as commanding officer of 104 Squadron with Roy Chappell (known to all of us aircrew as 'Chappie') as our intelligence officer.

Chappie was one of those rare intelligence officers who earned the respect of all by his enthusiasm, energy and sincerity towards the crews whom he was serving. His willingness to fly on an operation at any time endeared him to us all.

Don Saville is relatively unknown to present-generation Australians. For this reason I thoroughly commend this book to all who seek shining examples of courage, leadership and inspiration, all of which he typified in that generation of pioneer aviators. He was truly a great and extraordinary Australian who never let one forget that to be an Australian on overseas service was an honour and an obligation to show the best of the Australian character. He was at heart a complete individualist – a 'larrikin' in the kindest sense of the word, with a burning desire to get things done operationally as he saw the need. He had a somewhat contemptuous scorn for higher bureaucracy. He was a legend in his time, being one of the old and bold aviators with something over 8,000 flying hours when I first met him at 21 OTU.

Comparing this with my own grand total of 190 flying hours when I took part in my first night raid as a Wellington captain, on Hamburg in 1941, gives some idea of our respective levels of skill and experience. Nevertheless Don never talked down to us, but went out of his way to encourage, train and pass on any first-hand knowledge he could to all budding aspirants to professional aircraft captaincy. He also had the happy knack of seeming to get his own way with higher authority in all matters operational. This I suspect was a tribute to the high regard in which he was held for his experience and background in aviation matters generally. He also had a strong personal 'old boy' relationship with many senior officers who had been his contemporaries in his earlier career in the RAAF and RAF.

This biography is so real to me in its language and its accuracy that I immediately relive the times of which it speaks. I am sure it will be of tremendous interest and stimulate the memory of all those who lived through those somewhat hectic times. It should also serve as a great inspiration to any members of later generations who wish to know of, and aspire to, the heights of leadership and courage.

A. E. Mather.

Introduction

The need for a biography of Don Saville emerged during the writing of an earlier book dealing with the activities of the night-bomber squadrons of 205 Group RAF in the Middle East, Malta and Italy in the Second World War. Many Australians served in those squadrons, among them Wing Commander Saville, a colourful character who was a flight commander in 458 Squadron RAAF before taking command of No. 104 Wellington Bomber Squadron RAF.

Correspondence from ex-RAAF and ex-RAF personnel after the publication of my earlier book, *Wellington Wings* revealed more stories of Don Saville and much interest in him as a never-to-be-forgotten leader. His qualities and special features were often typical of his Australian nationalism and background. He was widely known and respected as an exceptionally skilled, daring and confident aviator who had flown more than eighty different types of aircraft and reputedly achieved some 10,000 flying hours.

He was fifteen years or more older than his squadron aircrews and in 1943 was probably the oldest pilot in Bomber Command still flying on operations over Germany. Although over the normal age limit, he had forced his way into Bomber Command and operational flying by his determination to make the maximum contribution to the war effort.

He carried leadership by example to its utmost limits by the unprecedented feat of compiling a full tour of operations while in command of a bomber squadron (thirty-two operations with 104 Squadron). When he was finally shot down over Hamburg he was statistically on a third tour of operations.

His command skills were such that he succeeded equally well in the diverse conditions of desert warfare, Malta tensions and the morale-testing pressures of a Bomber Command Stirling squadron in 1943.

He was proudly and obviously Australian, but was equally appreciated by British and other Allied personnel.

Such a man, such a pilot, such a leader, deserves to be remembered as an example for future Australian leaders in aviation and other fields.

It is worthy of note that only the knife-edge of fate separated mid-level commanders who were killed in action from those who survived to proceed to positions of high command with appropriate honours. But it is as a bomber squadron commander that Don Saville is to be remembered – a testing position requiring brave and confident leadership. Command of a bomber squadron was a peak in mid-level leadership; the commander controlled a group of highly trained young men at their maximum mental and physical fitness capacity, men who were aware that they might well be killed in the next few hours. A squadron was thus a powder-keg of energy which could be directed towards acts of determination, bravery and heroism – or, under a weak leader, slip into poor morale and inefficiency.

Within a good squadron the sense of camaraderie and *esprit de corps* was strong and comforting; the determination to win the war even at the cost of self-sacrifice was present and felt by all.

Wing Commander Donald Teale Saville, DSO, DFC, RAFVR, was an outstanding squadron commander and under his inspiring leadership the aircrews and groundstaff of No. 104 Wellington Bomber Squadron RAF (Middle East) and No. 218 Stirling Bomber Squadron RAF (Bomber Command) performed with valiant efficiency.

Chapter One

Tragedy at Hamburg

In clear weather on the night of 24/25 July 1943, a Stirling four-engined bomber of 218 Squadron Royal Air Force flew in over the northern suburbs towards the centre of Hamburg, which was already ablaze with fires. It was the first of the four Bomber Command mass raids, which together with two daylight attacks by the United States Air Force, would destroy half the buildings in the city and kill some 50,000 of the 1½ million inhabitants.

The Stirling, P for Peter, was in the third wave of the attack and its experienced crew, under the command of Wing Commander Donald Saville, DFC were amazed and delighted with the effects of the 'window' (short strips of metal foil) dropped by the bombers ahead of them, which had caused searchlights to wave about aimlessly and the flak to be restricted to firing barrages.

Night-fighter controllers, with their Würzburg detectors, were also unable to direct their fast cannon-firing aircraft, mainly Me. 110 and Ju. 88 night fighters, overhead, and out of the 740 attacking bombers only twelve were to be lost. Hamburg's defences were in confusion.

But, underneath Saville's Stirling, and unseen and undetected by the captain and second pilot in the cockpit and the mid-upper and rear gunners, there was a dark shape rising and falling with the plane above in the turbulence caused by so many aircraft passing through the airspace. One of the highly skilled German night-fighter pilots had made visual contact with one unlucky British bomber, in spite of the dislocation of radar by 'window'.

Two factors may have contributed to the disaster awaiting P for Peter. First Saville and his crew had the task of dropping marker flares at a given point along the route to the target and this required flying straight and level to assist accurate navigation. (The 3 Group bombing form for 24 July 1943 states that a special aircraft would drop Yellow TIs at Position A on the coast of Germany at 54°11'N, 08°50'E. Flying Officer H.C. Eyre, the survivor from Stirling P for Peter, said that their crew had a special task that night.) Secondly the success of the 'window' was such that even this experienced crew had their night vision temporarily impaired by looking ahead to the wandering searchlights, the bright Hamburg fires and the even brighter magnesium bombing flares floating over the city.

The pilot of the German night fighter peered upwards to confirm his identification of an enemy bomber flying steadily towards the target. He probably told his radar operator, toiling at his Lichtenstein set in the dark fuselage, that they were in luck and he believed that it was a Stirling because of the single tail fin and its altitude well below the main stream of droning bombers at 5,500–7,000 metres (18,000–23,000 ft).

Satisfied, the German pilot raised the nose of his aircraft and pressed the firing button of the deadly cannons. The upward-firing cannons' *Schrage Musik* had not yet been fitted to night fighters but the result was nevertheless violent and horrific. Instantly the stricken bomber was engulfed in flames and the night fighter swerved and dived away, the crew fearful of being destroyed themselves by the explosion of their quarry. Inside the doomed Stirling there was time only for the captain's quick order. 'Get away boys!'

Saville stayed at the controls, fighting to steady the blazing bomber, and by making the supreme sacrifice himself, gave time for four crewmen to drop away through the hatch. The other three were quickly overwhelmed and incinerated with their captain as the fiery wreck plunged earthwards.

Floating down by parachute the four survivors were in shock but felt a numbed thankfulness for their own escape as they watched the flaming streak that was P for Peter. However, the tragedy was not yet over.

As they landed, three of the four were seized by a mob of enraged civilians. Amidst the horrors of a city undergoing the most massive and successful bombing attack yet made by Bomber Command, the three allied airmen were, according to F/O Eyre, the fourth survivor, lynched by hanging from lamp posts. He survived because he landed on the roof of an airfield building and was captured and protected from the mob by *Luftwaffe* personnel with rifles and drawn bayonets. Wounded by shrapnel and injured in landing, he became a prisoner of war and returned to Britain in 1945 to tell his tragic story.

So ended the brave career of Wing Commander Donald Teale Saville – the highest-ranking officer to be lost that night. He was awarded the DSO on 27 July 1943 in recognition of his distinguished service as Squadron Commander of No. 218 (Gold Coast) Stirling Bomber Squadron, Downham Market.

An Australian in the RAF, Don Saville was born at Portland, N.S.W., in 1903. In his fortieth year in 1943, he was probably the oldest pilot flying on operations in a bomber squadron. Certainly he was one of the most experienced and skilful pilots in the service.

By his own daring and example he inspired the squadron crews under his command. They would follow him to any target and they know instinctively that he would never send them where he himself was not prepared to go.

Don Saville's death in action over Hamburg was the end of sixteen years of success and adventure in the world of flying. He had triumphed over nature's winds and storms and successfully tested the limits of man's ingenious flying machines. It took war weapons and annihilation to finally drive him from his beloved skies.

Chapter Two

John Saville

A biographer tends to look closely at the parents and family of his subject in the belief that they are to a degree responsible for the physical and behavioural characteristics of their children.

The relative importance of nature (inherited endowment) and nurture (the effects of environment and education) is a constant topic of academic debate. However, it is probably safe to say that both are important, although the relative contributions may vary for each characteristic. Philip Larkin, the British poet who was offered the poet laureateship in succession to Sir John Betjeman but declined it, has left us with a cynical verse on the subject of heredity:

> They fuck you up, your Mum and Dad,
> They may not mean to but they do,
> They fill you up with all the faults they had,
> And add some extra, just for you.

Donald Saville and his brothers and sisters did not suffer because of their parents. On the contrary, they benefited from having a mother and father who provided a good home environment and good education to support a sound contribution from heredity. The family background was professional with a very adequate income.

The Savilles can be traced back to Yorkshire, and to the area around Middlesbrough, at the mouth of the River Tees. Between Middlesbrough and Whitby is the beautiful region of the Cleveland Hills and the North York moors. John Saville, Don's father, was born, like Captain James Cook, the famous navigator, in the village of Marton-in-Cleveland, which today lies on the edge of Middlesbrough's urban sprawl.

Born in 1866 John was the youngest son in a tragedy-afflicted family of eight children, six boys and two girls. His father was killed in a mine accident at the Cleveland iron ore mine of Dorman Long and Co., and four of his brothers were killed in the First World War. Abraham, the eldest, survived to become a goldmining engineer in Western Australia and New South Wales. The two sisters married and brought up families in England.

After attending local schools, John Saville went to Newcastle and trained as an engineer in the engineering works and shipyard of Armstrong Whitworth and Co. He was a small, slim, active and alert young man. Donald is said by his brothers to have been much like his father in build and personality.

At the end of his training John decided to go to America, where he had no difficulty in finding work. On his return to Britain he joined Fraser and Chalmers whose engineering works on the Thames estuary manufactured mining machinery. The firm supplied and erected plant at mines all over the world. John Saville was first sent to Dolgellau in North Wales to erect milling plant at the only gold mine in the British Isles. Now largely a tourist attraction, the mine supplied the gold for the wedding ring of Sarah, Duchess of York, in 1986.

While working there, John met Thomas Russell, a fine example of a nineteenth-century British entrepreneur, who was subsequently to have a strong influence on the Saville fortunes. He and his family had extensive mining and commercial interests in New Zealand, Central and South America and Britain. He had shares in the gold mine at Dolgellau and happened to be on a visit there in 1889 at the same time as the young John Saville. The two men became friends and Russell invited Saville to call at his London office when the work in Wales was completed.

Saville agreed, but first had to instal a similar plant in a Hungarian gold mine. By the time he had completed this task and returned to London he had decided to make gold-mining his life's work. Before calling on Russell he attended the London School of Mines, where he qualified as an assayer, knowing that this would be valuable in his chosen profession.

Russell immediately offered Saville a position as an engineer at a gold mine in Brazil. He accepted and spent three years at the mine with two other Englishmen, one the mine manager and the other an assayer. The assayer had a serious accident at the mine and had to return to England, so for eighteen months Saville was both engineer and assayer. The mine was successful and operated profitably for many years.

Returning after his contract period in South America, Saville found his friend and employer very enthusiastic over the discovery of gold in Western Australia. Saville was sent out in 1894 to assess the leases and if possible to buy some of them – a task which revealed the reliance placed upon his judgment. Unfortunately he arrived at Kalgoorlie before the reef was exposed and did not recognise the potential of the area – one of the few wrong decisions in his long working career.

His next job was as manager of a gold mine in the mountains on the west coast of Mexico, reached by ship from San Francisco. The mine was small but very rich, the region wild and the populace unruly. Saville found that he had two big problems: in 1896 Mexico had so many bandits that armed guards were necessary at the mine; and the mine itself was extremely wet. On one occasion a robber with a gun rushed past the guards and approached Saville. Saville, who was always armed, did not argue with the bandit; he shot him.

For five years Saville worked the mine successfully until he received an urgent cable from London requesting his return and informing him that another manager was already *en route* to Mexico to take over.

There was barely time to catch the next coastal steamer and he reached the port only to see the boat pulling out. He did not hesitate; he knew that the steamer had to call at another port 48 km (30 miles) or so up the coast. He bought a mule, rode the distance across inhospitable country and caught the boat. He arrived back in London in June 1902.

This time Thomas Russell did not send him off immediately to another posting. Instead they sat down together and Saville listened politely to a long story.

In 1896 the New Zealand Mines Trust, in which Thomas Russell had a large interest, had sent a man over from New Zealand to investigate and buy gold mines in eastern Australia. This man was Dr A. Schiedel, a German metallurgist. The search was not very successful and the only result was the purchase of a small gold-dredging operation near Braidwood in south-eastern New South Wales.

However Schiedel also came across a small cement works at Portland, near Lithgow, that had closed. The leases and freehold land still contained everything necessary for the manufacture of cement and Schiedel persuaded the Mines Trust board (Chairman, Thomas Russell) to buy the site and build a modern plant.

At a general meeting of the Trust, however, Russell was left in no doubt as to the shareholders' feelings. They pointed out that the Trust was a gold-mining company and there was no desire to be mixed up in cement or anything else! Russell accepted full responsibility for going into the cement industry, and offered to take over the interest of any dissatisfied shareholder. In due course he found himself practically owning the cement works, which was not yet in production.

He formed a new company, the Commonwealth Portland Cement Company, which was completely independent of the New Zealand Mines Trust. He had two clear objectives: to justify to the Trust shareholders his decision to go into cement and to save his investment.

Now came the bombshell for Saville – Russell had recalled him from Mexico to send him out to Portland! Saville's reaction was similar to that of the shareholders: he was a gold mining engineer with no knowledge of cement and no interest in that industry. Moreover his earlier visit to Australia had left him with no desire to return there. He was appalled at this sudden change of direction. At the age of thirty-six he felt confident and competent in the gold-mining industry and had envisaged this as his lifetime occupation and interest. When he considered the matter carefully, however, he decided that out of fondness for and loyalty to Thomas Russell he would have to accept the position.

Arrangements were quickly made for him to go to Germany to be briefed on the operation and maintenance of Krupps mills and kilns. He saw a number of German cement plants and on his return to London also visited several British factories along the banks of the Thames and Medway estuaries.

Despite the rush of preparation and instruction, he still found time to get married. He was evidently a quick worker for in the brief weeks he could spare from his training in 1902–3 he successfully courted Yorkshire girl, Isobel Teale. Born at Richmond in 1874 and trained as a nurse at the respected Glasgow Infirmary, Isobel was an excellent nurse with the ability to organise a team of helpers in an emergency. At that time, owing to the influence of Florence Nightingale and the patriotic fervour aroused by the Crimean and Boer Wars the nursing profession had developed as a popular career for well-educated girls.

John Saville, now aged thirty-seven persuaded Isobel to accompany him on this new adventure to faraway Australia and they were married in Middlesbrough shortly before sailing early in February 1903 on RMS *China*, a P & O ship of 8,000 tons.

Thomas Russell was at the quay to see them off and he handed John the latest publication on cement manufacture suggesting that the six weeks' voyage would be ample time for him to study it.

They travelled first class with all the luxury and comfort available at the time but Isobel proved to be a poor sailor and did not enjoy the long voyage through the tropics to the southern hemisphere.

Chapter Three

Portland, N.S.W.

There was no-one to meet the Savilles on their arrival in Sydney, but John was not unduly worried. He took Isobel into the city and arranged accommodation. The next day he went to the company office with his letter of introduction, to meet Dr Schiedel, but it was immediately obvious that he was not welcome. He therefore decided to move on to Portland, travelling by train across the Blue Mountains to the place that was so drastically to change his professional career.

Portland in 1903 was no place for the faint-hearted or those too dependent on the comforts of city life. It was a tiny township clustered around the one industry, a cement mill, which was itself in doubt as a viable concern. It lay among hills approximately half way between Katoomba and Bathurst, and some 16 km (10 miles) north of the main road to the west, now the Great Western Highway. In 1903 the dirt and gravel roads connecting Portland to the outside world and to Lithgow, the nearest town 32 km (20 miles) to the south-east, were subject to flooding at two creek crossings and the place could be isolated for days at a time.

Apart from the unsightly industrial buildings, the quarry and the scattered houses, the immediate scenery was pleasant, with hills covered by trees and bushland, while the air was fresh and clean away from the white smoke from the single tall chimney stack. The place was a challenge to John Saville but no shock to him after his experience in mining settlements. But to Isabella (as she liked to be called) it must have been a great change from her previous life in Britain, and a testing time as a young wife, already pregnant.

The manager's house was occupied by a German named Grose, who showed no sign of giving up his position. The Savilles settled into rooms at the new Coronation Hotel. John walked around the works area 'getting the feel of the place' as he termed it. The German staff ignored him but it was evident that the Australian workmen were not happy working under the Germans.

Disturbed by his assessment of the conditions, Saville wrote a letter to Thomas Russell explaining the position and suggesting that he should move on to New Zealand and the important Waihi Gold Mine in which the Russell company had an interest. However, he was surprised to find that his wife was in favour of staying at Portland, which she recognised as being in an open, healthy area with a good climate. She had an obsessive fear of tuberculosis after having lost two sisters from this deadly disease. Moreover, being pregnant perhaps she felt a need for a settled home.

The year 1903 was particularly dry, and while awaiting a reply from London, Saville discovered that Portland's water supply was inadequate and promised to be a serious problem.

He became friendly with Mr Beardmore, the company secretary at the cement mill, and through contacts with him and the hotelier, Havenhand and Walter Tweedier, a local businessman and landowner, he was brought up to date with the Portland situation. Havenhand and Tweedier were both nervous about their investments because of the uncertainty about the future of Portland as a cement-manufacturing centre.

In due course Russell's reply came, enclosing a copy of a letter sent at the same time to Dr Schiedel in Sydney. Both letters were brief and to the point. Saville was to take complete control at Portland and Schiedel was to remain in charge of the Sydney office without interfering in any way with Portland. Saville was now ready to move and he quickly got rid of the German staff. He and his wife moved into the manager's house and he began to sort out the problems at the cement plant.

Cement manufacture is a chemical process, but the chemist at Portland, a Scandinavian, was an alcoholic given to disappearing into the bush for three or four days at a time. As a result the raw mix at the mill fluctuated and the cement was unsound. Saville sacked the chemist and with assistance from Sydney obtained another, a German from Batavia, who proved very capable. There was no further trouble with the mix.

The feed to the two kilns was not sufficiently finely ground, so a cable went off for another ball-and-tube mill from Krupps. When it arrived the foundations were already in and it was quickly at work. The raw meal was now satisfactory and the resulting cement up to government specifications and acceptable to the N.S.W. Public Works Department.

When extra power was required, Saville purchased the engine which had powered the Sydney cable trams from a location at Rushcutters Bay. The engine was dismantled and re-erected in the Portland power house.

When the water supply to the new boilers became an acute problem Saville solved it by buying water from the N.S.W. railway department.

The water was loaded into rail wagons at Newnes Junction with a tarpaulin in the bottom and another over the top. By the time the wagons arrived at the cement mill half the water had been lost but the plant was kept in operation. A dam was later built behind the works.

By 1905 the company had turned the corner and was making a profit but Thomas Russell barely had time to appreciate the success of his plans; he suffered a heart attack and died in his London office at the age of seventy-five. The loyal John Saville was left in sole and complete charge of the Commonwealth Portland Cement Company.

He was also now father of a growing young family. Donald and John, twins born in 1903, Norman in 1905, Hilda in 1906 and Eva in 1907. Portland was a one-company township and Saville's word was law and his status almost god-like. As the children grew up they could not fail to be aware of their father's power and standing in the community. The children were the local royalty and began to behave as such as they became conscious of their privileged position. The boys were daring in their games, including climbing the tall pines at the end of the garden adjoining the road and the works on the other side. Ensconced in the top branches they threw down pine cones and branches at passers-by and were subjects of envy and annoyance to the local children.

The three boys turned easily to their father for approval and assistance when he was available to listen and help them, while the girls tended to cling more closely to their mother. The parents wanted to retain British traditions and influences in the family and kept the children aloof from other Portland children. Isabella in particular made no effort to get on with the 'colonials'. Any friends she made were English or Scottish.

She made some use of her nursing training in arranging a healthy diet for her family and by prescribing less appreciated regular doses of castor oil and other medicines. However, she was not happy in Portland and her husband was made well aware of the fact.

In the early days at Portland Saville was also responsible for the gold mine at Mongarlowe near Braidwood, N.S.W. The dredging operation was eventually closed down as being unprofitable and the pick of the workers transferred to Portland.

There are two stories about him which may have some relevance to qualities revealed later in his son Donald. The first concerns a damaged chimney stack.

In the days when the cement works had only one tall chimney two or three men had the daily task of cleaning out the ash which collected inside at the base. One day they reported finding one or two firebricks amongst the ash and the number gradually increased over the weeks until it became obvious that the brick lining of the stack was breaking up.

As the damaged area could not be seen it must be near the top. The matter was urgent because without its stack the whole plant would have to be shut down.

Saville sent to Sydney for steeplejacks, who arrived promptly. They went about their work expertly, attaching a rope ladder as they went up the chimney. They went over the top and inspected the inside lining. They reported that some damage could be seen and they would need supplies of firebricks, cement and mortar.

Saville said, 'I'll go up myself and have a look.' The steeplejacks thought he was joking, but he was not. He went up the swaying rope ladder, hanging out as he got to the outward curve at the top of the chimney but keeping his toes in place and his grasp firm. He reached the rim and sat on the edge looking inside.

His extraordinary feat was watched by many of the workmen, who held their breath with admiration as he clambered back down the flimsy rope ladder and made his way slowly but surely to safety at ground level. A cheer went up as he reached the base – and well deserved, for few men have the nerve to emulate steeplejacks or high riggers, highly paid specialists who have special skills and iron nerves, and are accustomed to heights.

Repairs were later carried out by the steeplejacks. It still stands at Portland today although it is now second to a larger and taller chimney.

The second story concerns a quarry hoist. Associated with every cement factory there has to be a limestone or chalk quarry. At Portland in the 1920s the quarry had grown to an enormous hole some 60 metres (200 ft) deep. Limestone was removed by trucks using an incline on one side. However, mud and rubbish on the floor was removed by scraping up the debris with a steam shovel, forming heaps, then lifting the waste by means of a hoist and large box-like container. The hoist was mounted on a traveller running on steel cables stretched across the quarry between two towers on either side. A winding operator worked the hoist from one of the towers, bringing the huge bucket across to the edge of the quarry where the mud etc., was discharged into railway wagons and taken to a dump 800 metres (½ mile) away.

One day the hoist on the traveller became stuck on its cables in the middle of the quarry and could not be moved to the edge. In due course the works manager was informed and he came to see what the trouble was. He climbed the gantry or tower and said, 'I'll have to look at it.'

To the amazement of his men he climbed out on the cables, standing on the lower one and hanging on by hand to the upper one. Moving cautiously but steadily out over the quarry and not apparently bothered by the 60 metre (200 ft) drop to the rough limestone floor below he reached the hoist and inspected it carefully.

As the workmen watched – their numbers had grown considerably as word spread throughout the plant that the boss was out on the wires over the quarry – Saville calmly edged his way back to the tower and asked for a cold chisel and hammer.

He had located the trouble; a small strand of one cable had broken and bent upwards, stopping the wheels of the hoist traveller from moving towards the side. Saville went back over the abyss, cut off the broken piece of wire and returned to the operator on the tower.

'Start her up again,' he said.

The hoist was soon working again normally and the men returned to their jobs, hoping that they had not been observed by their manager while on his precarious mission. The Saville legend of leadership by example had been reinforced. It had been noted that he had not even bothered to remove his jacket and tie.

John Saville in his prime could do the jobs of most of his men and they knew it. He was a stern but considerate employer who had the complete confidence and respect of his workmen. He expected and demanded strict loyalty to the company from all workmen and staff. He recognised ability and chose men for promotion who usually performed as well as he had expected. His judgment was sound. He was firm and even ruthless in his decisions. No man who failed was ever given a second chance; he never again employed any man who had been sacked and the men knew this. He was small in stature but commanded the respect of everyone around him.

However, this fearless man, who kept such close control over the Portland workforce, was a kind, affectionate and generous father. One surviving son describes him as the finest man he ever met – a man with a ready wit and a sense of humour. These qualities were reserved for the home, however. The other son says his father was wonderful, 'but as children we saw little of him, as he was so involved in building up a new industry.' Both sons say that their father did not drink alcohol or smoke and they never heard him swear. He does not seem to have been a religious man but he helped the Anglican church in Portland by gifts of land and money. His outstanding characteristic was his complete loyalty to his company and to the maintenance of the workforce.

He was fond of telling stories to his children and they later realised that many of them were founded on fact. They were stories of his own experiences in his single days as a gold-mining engineer and manager. His main interests were gold and gold mining, early automobiles, motor and motor-cycle racing, the 'new-fangled' aeroplanes, cement manufacture and its problems – and he fitted in his family when he could find time to do so.

Nevertheless, the Saville children felt themselves to be a close-knit family living amidst an absorbing and sometimes exciting environment with a god-like industrial magnate as father and provider. Their mother Isabella also made her contribution to family stability and discipline before illness and fatigue took their toll in later life.

With a human dynamo, a brilliant and self-sufficient 'workaholic' as a husband, Isabella had a difficult act to follow!

Chapter Four

A Disjointed Education

For the Saville family, 1909 was a critical year. Superficially at least this was the result of Isabella's inability to settle happily in the small company town with its limited social life, despite having a large comfortable house and two servants. John never mixed with the staff of the cement company, nor with the people in the town, so that her activities were restricted to the family, the church and the hospital.

With John and Donald now six years old, Norman four, Hilda three and Eva only two, the house was full of noise and family incidents which had to be dealt with by the mother alone. Isabella and the children saw little of John because he was away in the office of the cement mill, totally engaged in the problems of an expanding industry with a workforce eventually in excess of 1,000 men.

Governesses came and went, but they and the servants were not always able to deal effectively with the cheeky boys. Isabella became increasingly frustrated. She was well educated for her day and wanted her children to grow up as British as she and her husband were. Eventually she decided that she must take them to England.

John was understanding and helpful. He arranged berths for them in the P & O ship *China*, the same one in which he and his wife had travelled to Australia. He took them all to Sydney, saw them safely on board and watched the ship sail and the children waving goodbye. It was a splendid adventure for the children but John was deeply worried.

The separation did not last much more than a week, however. The family left the ship at Adelaide because Isabella had become seriously ill with seasickness. They returned to Melbourne, where John met them. Warm and considerate, he spared no expense to give them all, and especially his wife, the best conditions in which to recover. He chartered the most luxurious form of railway travel available at that time – special trains from Melbourne to Portland via Sydney.

A small steam locomotive with driver and fireman, a single first class coach and a guard in his van, formed the special train as far as Albury, where a N.S.W. special was waiting on the standard-gauge line. It was arranged that Eva, Hilda and Norman would travel in one compartment with their mother and father. The noisy twins, John and Donald, were given another compartment to themselves.

Although Saville saw the guard before they left to make sure that the door to the boys' compartment was locked, for some reason it was not, and somewhere near Wodonga, with the train travelling fast along an embankment the door opened and Don, who had been playing with the latch, fell out. His brother saw him roll down the bank. Then, terrified, he rushed along the corridor to his father. By the time the train came to a halt it had travelled some miles from the scene of the accident.

John was placed in the guard's van to locate the site and the train reversed until Don was seen making for the bush. He later explained that he was running away because he thought the train would come down on him. Miraculously he suffered only a broken collarbone, bruises and loss of some skin here and there.

Later in life Isabella told her son John that had she been able to complete the voyage to England in 1909 she would never have returned to Portland.

Back at Ivanhoe, the manager's house across the road from the cement mill, she and John talked over the whole matter. They decided not to persevere with governesses but to send the children to the local primary school. John also promised to take the family to Britain a year or two hence, when he felt he could safely leave the mill in the hands of his senior staff. He probably also promised, like other husbands in a similar situation, to get home earlier from his demanding work and to see more of his family.

Perhaps John Saville succeeded where many husbands have failed because family recollections of the period 1909–12 are that it was mainly uneventful. John and Norman today recall going on picnics with the family in their father's new F.N. car, and these years of international tension and competition in building up the armies and navies of Europe passed calmly and quietly in Portland. Strong leadership from the top and steady work by a labour force unstirred by unions, meant that cement production and company profits increased.

In 1912 Saville lived up to his word. He had business to do in London and took Isabella and the twins with him in RMS *Maloja*, a new P. & O. liner of 12,000 tons, completed in the previous year. It was decided to leave Norman, Hilda and Eve in the care of their uncle, Abraham Saville, who was now manager-engineer of the gold dredge at Mongarlowe, and his wife.

The trip soon provided a reminder of world events because the *Maloja*'s radio operator picked up the SOS call from the White Star liner *Titanic* as it sank on the opposite side of the Atlantic. The passengers arrived in a Britain stunned by the tragic loss of the latest product of the shipbuilding art – a huge four-funnelled liner, four times the tonnage of the *Maloja* and supposedly unsinkable. This was also the year in which the tragedy of the Scott Antarctic expedition was to be revealed but as yet the newspapers were merely reporting anxiety and apprehension.

Isabella took her two boys to visit her relatives in Scotland at Glasgow and Gouroch. John had business in London, the Midlands and north-east England. The London board of the company approved the purchase of two steam shovels and a locomotive but turned down Saville's plans for further expansion at Portland. John was disappointed but placed the orders for the new equipment and also purchased some second-hand machinery for the cement mill.

When he was free from business matters he took his family on a tour of the area of North Yorkshire where he had grown up as a boy – Middlesbrough, Marton, Great Ayton, the Cleveland Hills, the North York Moors and the busy little port of Whitby. He explained to the boys that this was Captain Cook's country and therefore had a close association with Australia and Australians. They were interested, but the real highlight of the trip for them was having dinner in a London hotel at a table next to that of the American car manufacturer, Henry Ford.

As an engineer, John Saville was deeply interested in automobiles and fascinated by aircraft. He wanted to learn to fly an aeroplane and while in England bought a book on building one. Although he himself never became a pilot, or built an aircraft, it is possible that some of his enthusiasm rubbed off on Donald, who was destined to become an aviator.

All too soon, or so it seemed to the boys, the trip came to an end and the family journeyed by train overland and by ferry to Marseilles to join the RMS *Morea* for the voyage home to Australia. They avoided the Bay of Biscay because it might upset Isabella's delicate health.

Education was again now uppermost in the minds of the Saville parents. The time had come when the children had to move outside Portland to find suitable schools. John was now a wealthy man, owing to his own single minded efforts as manager of the cement company and also to his successful investments on the stockmarket, particularly in gold-mining shares. He loved a gamble in mining shares and throughout his lifetime used his extensive knowledge of mining to great advantage in buying and selling shares in new ventures.

They therefore agreed on a move to the larger centre of Bathurst.

John purchased a very large house called Hereford at Kelso, just outside Bathurst. It had been built for a Mr James Rutherford, an American who was managing director of the transport firm Cobb & Co.

Isabella was soon installed there with suitable servants, and it was arranged that John, Don and Norman should attend All Saints College and Hilda and Eva were enrolled at a local girls' school. John came to Bathurst at weekends and the family settled down to a new life which pleased one member rather more than the others – Isabella. For her the move represented more freedom, more congenial friends, a higher standard of living and more cultural opportunities than were available at Portland. For a while she was happy, feeling that the Savilles had 'arrived'.

The two surviving brothers, John and Norman, say that, looking back at their disjointed education, they wonder why their parents sent them to so many different schools! Their education was expensive, but for them it had little sense of unity and direction. In 1914 the three boys became boarders at the Sydney Church of England Grammar School (S.C.E.G.S.) North Sydney. They were among the youngest boys in the famous school and suffered as a result. John was never really happy at the school and went back to Portland a year later after falling sick with an attack of pneumonia. Don and Norman, with a greater talent for sports managed to survive by getting into lowly teams for football and cricket. Norman says that they were soon up to pranks in their school house. He remembers climbing down ropes of knotted sheets to go to the pictures with other boys. On their return, Don, who was good at gymnastics and games, climbed up to the windows successfully. Norman, younger and with weaker muscles, had to be pulled up by the others.

During the school holidays the boys often spent part of the time at the gold dredge at Mongarlowe, where they were allowed to pick gold nuggets out of the gravel which was too coarse to go through the screens. At the end of the holiday the gold scales were brought out and their uncle weighed the gold and paid the boys 2s 6d (12½p) per ounce.

John and Norman say that Donald in many ways took after his father. He showed this at school in the effort and determination he put into everything he did. He was popular with other boys, direct in his outlook and noted as a good sport. Throughout his career in various schools he would often be found helping boys in lower grades with subjects they found difficult.

As twins John and Don were naturally very close while Norman, two years younger, had to tag along behind. Norman says that this led to a certain amount of fighting between himself and Don – mostly as a result of his own resentment at being left out of the twins' activities.

The First World War brought trouble to Portland. The rush to volunteer caused a manpower shortage in industry, which affected even Portland with its relatively happy and settled work force. Even Saville tried to volunteer for service in the Australian Flying Corps when it was started, but the authorities refused to countenance it, on account of his age and his vital managerial role in an essential industry.

As the war progressed a whispering campaign started in Sydney that Portland was a German company. The Federal Government eventually felt that it had to take some action and Brunagle, the German chemist, and his family were interned and Dr Schiedel put under house arrest in Sydney. This brought increased strain on Saville and the rest of the staff, although a suitable replacement for Dr Schiedel was found in Sydney. He was John Symonds, who eventually worked his way up to become general manager of the company in the 1930s.

Another turning point in the Saville family history came in 1916. At a time when some wealthy and favoured British families were sending their children overseas for shelter in Australia, New Zealand, South Africa, Canada, the United States and other places remote from the war in Europe, the Savilles did the reverse. They sent them from Australia to be educated in Britain! This decision appears at first to be inexplicable, even foolish.

What possible explanation could there be for such strange behaviour by two otherwise competent and sensible parents? Apparently they were not satisfied with the progress Donald and Norman were making while John, who had been withdrawn from S.C.E.G.S., was another problem. Although now settled and successful in Australia, they were still British at heart and wanted their children to be the same. They cherished a hope that Donald might enter the Royal Navy as an officer cadet at Osborne Naval College on the Isle of Wight – he was now of suitable age for such a move.

Norman believes that his mother had a strong influence on the decision. He thinks that she was so deeply affected by patriotism and love for Britain at the time that she believed she should help the war effort by going back to the hospital in Scotland where she had trained as a nurse.

It is also probable that John and Isabella, both born in Yorkshire, still felt a strong attachment to their native county and had therefore decided on a Yorkshire school and environment for their children's education. They chose Ayton School, close to John's birthplace, and one of Britain's noted Quaker schools, opened in 1841 and originally established for the education of non-members' children. It is even possible that the parents had looked at the school on their visit to Britain in 1912 and made a decision then as to its suitability.

In retrospect the choice appears to have been a good one, because John and Norman look back with pleasure to their days at Ayton, where they all duly received the British upbringing and influences their parents wanted, while clearly remaining Australian. The girls were hardly long enough at Ayton to benefit for they were withdrawn after only one year.

The voyage on the SS *Arawa* was as dangerous and exciting as might be expected in the middle of the First World War. The family joined the ship in Sydney and this time John Saville must indeed have been worried as he farewelled his wife and children, for he well knew that merchant ships were frequently being attacked and sunk by raiders, submarines and mines.

Arawa was laden with food for Britain – Australian and New Zealand butter and cheese, and apples which were loaded at Hobart. As on all previous voyages Isabella was immediately laid low by acute seasickness and the children were left to fend for themselves. The boys skylarked and fought with other boys on board whose parents were puzzled by the absence of any parent to whom they could complain.

At Cape Town the ship was coaled and, still without escort, proceeded up the west coast of Africa. One day she suddenly began zigzagging from her course and the boys saw, some 12–16 km (8–10 miles) astern, the low profile of a following submarine. The speeds of the ship and the German submarine on the surface were similar so the enemy remained too far away for accurate gunnery and did not open fire. The *Arawa* had no guns fitted but eventually, by steering a straight course, she was able to draw away slowly until, with the sudden disappearance of the sun at the equatorial nightfall, the captain felt that she was safe. Conversation at dinner that night was subdued – the danger had been a disconcerting reminder of the reality of the war towards which *Arawa* was steaming at full speed.

As a result of the encounter they put into the port of Dakar and the ship was fitted with a gun and supplied with two naval gunners. The Saville boys made friends with these two men and raided the ship's larder to get extra food for them. The ship was, even now, not in convoy but the gun did not have to be fired in anger on the remainder of the voyage. The effect of the war on shipping was emphasised in the Channel and Thames approaches by the number of wrecks to be seen.

This time the Savilles arrived in a Britain worried by the heavy losses of men at the front and also by the number of ships lost by the Grand Fleet in the recent battle with the German fleet in the North Sea off the Jutland peninsula.

With the hazardous voyage over and passengers and luggage disembarked, Isabella took her family to King's Cross Station and caught the first available train north to Yorkshire. Education for the young Saville was about to begin amidst the beautiful and serene country scenery surrounding the extensive grounds of Ayton School. These were themselves traversed by the crystal-clear waters of the River Leven or Beck, and overlooked by the cone-shaped Roseberry Hill (or Roseberry Topping) and the flat-topped Monument Hill, so called because of its obelisk in honour of Captain James Cook, the first European to discover the east coast of Terra Australis.

The school was small, with just 150 pupils, but well organised by the headmaster, Herbert Dennis, and the Headmistress, Miss Sophia Wells, with a small devoted staff. Mrs Muriel Dennis, the wife of the Headmaster, was mistress of the household. Several staff members had been called up to the forces, or to agricultural work as conscientious objectors, so that, like other schools, Ayton had had to improvise and use some part-time assistant teachers.

Tucked away in the country food rationing was less stringent at Ayton and the boarders received a limited but adequate diet. The school curriculum was sound and sensible, with music, crafts, agriculture, gymnastics, athletics, games and religion supplementing the usual academic subjects. The school was treated as a great family by the headmaster, and in this he was aided by its co-educational make-up, which assisted the normal development of girls and boys. Most schools of the day were strictly single-sex.

Within the school, pupils and staff met together for worship on a regular basis in the Friends' Meeting House, beginning with silence. The belief was that the Quaker philosophy brings a sense of obligation to the community and encourages self-assessment and self-discipline.

The three young Australian boys prospered in the school environment and made their mark in both academic work and games. Donald (known in the school as Saville II because he was born half an hour after John, who was therefore Saville I) is in the records as being for two years the school champion at gymnastics. He was also in the school teams for soccer and cricket and was house captain of Pease House, one of the four houses named after families noted as generous school benefactors. In athletics Donald usually showed up in the first three places of events for his age and in 1919 was recorded as fourth in the School's senior cross country, on a day which was exceptionally hot and exhausting.

Saville II was also mentioned in the 1919 school magazine for a short descriptive story of a visit to Whitby Abbey and in the same year won the art picture award. He was particularly good at mathematics and was well liked by those who did not shine at this vital subject because he was always ready to explain mathematical methods and how to solve problems.

Saville I (John), owing to polio damage to one leg, was unable to compete in some athletic games but achieved firsts in several school swimming events. Saville III (Norman) was in the school football and cricket teams, and was an outstanding cricket all rounder. He won the junior cross country in 1917.

While they were boarding at Ayton School the Savilles at first found themselves left on their own at holiday times. They were often attacked by village boys, so they developed the practice of going everywhere together and fighting back as a team. One day Donald chased a boy into his home and upstairs to a bedroom to punish him. The other two stood guard outside. He was quite good at boxing although this was not encouraged at Ayton. He was extremely fit and fast on his feet, although small and light.

After the first two terms, the brothers solved the problem of loneliness during school holidays by being invited to the homes of their friends in various parts of England and Scotland. Norman has vivid recollections of the happy four years spent at Ayton.

> My memory recalls how hungry we were much of the time in the war years.
>
> Although the food was not plentiful and the conditions generally were difficult (in wartime), nothing could detract from the wonderful countryside or the kindness shown to us by the school staff, other boys in the school and people in the district – they seemed to understand that we were a long way from home.
>
> In 1916 while on holiday with Mother and the girls at Gouroch we were depressed by seeing some of the naval ships damaged at Jutland limping into the Clyde for repairs.
>
> In 1917 we watched from our dormitory windows a German Zeppelin brought down in flames over the mouth of the River Tees. We were very excited and never slept again that night. You could read a paper in the bright light of the blazing airship as it came down.

Despite his parents' hopes Don was not destined to join the Royal Navy, although he was selected for interview at the Admiralty in 1916. He made the long journey from Gouroch to London by train on his own but suffered a severe bilious attack *en route*. At the interview he had not recovered completely and was not one of those selected. Fate had other ideas.

In 1917 the restless Isabella decided to leave her hospital work in Glasgow and take her daughters with her back home to Australia. A book could be written about that journey. Soon after sailing in the *Tunisian* from Liverpool they were in collision with another ship of the convoy which sank. Although damaged, the *Tunisian* proceeded in convoy to Halifax, Nova Scatia, arriving late and thus missing by 24 hours the disastrous explosion which wrecked the port. The convoy was diverted to St Johns, Newfoundland.

They crossed Canada by Canadian Pacific Railway to Vancouver and joined another vessel for the Pacific crossing. In the Pacific the German raider *Wolf* was at large but the convoy in which the Savilles were travelling avoided trouble by going far south.

Isabella returned to Portland in time to take charge of the nursing arrangements for dealing with the influenza epidemic which swept south-eastern Australia in 1918. She was at her best in an emergency. She sent the two girls to the Sydney Girls' High School and later to Ascham Ladies' College to complete their education.

The three boys at Ayton took part in the modest celebrations to mark the end of the war in 1918 and at Whitsun in 1919 attended the Old Scholars' Reunion when peace celebrations were held and a memorial board erected with sixteen names inscribed on a roll of honour. Quakers are in some difficulty about war service and honouring those killed by any sort of memorial which may suggest acceptance of war. It will be seen later that after the Second World War the Old Scholars provided a different and more acceptable memorial for the fifteen former members of the Ayton School who gave their lives during that conflict.

In 1919 the school was inspected by a team of inspectors, two men and two women, who thoroughly examined all aspects so that it might be reported on to the Board of Education and granted recognition as an efficient secondary school under the Teachers' Superannuation Act of 1918. The report was very favourable and praised the teaching (apart from a few minor faults) and the lovely grounds, and concluded that the school was well organised and carried on in accordance with the high ideals of education of the Society of Friends.

In 1919 scholars in the top form took the Oxford Local Examination and Saville I and Saville II both passed with honours – second and third class respectively. In March 1920 the three Saville boys left Ayton and returned home in the SS *Wiltshire* via the Cape of Good Hope.

A few days out from Liverpool a sports committee was set up with a minister of religion as chairman. Lists of different events were put up, including a chess competition. At Ayton chess had been very popular, particularly in the long winter evenings. All three boys played and Donald was a little above the average. All entered the chess competition and Don was drawn to play the parson. The latter said to Don, 'As there are ten minutes before lunch we can play the first match of the competition.' Don beat the parson in about 4 moves – so they were not late for lunch! The defeated chairman was so upset that he went to the notice board, tore down the chess list and threw it overboard! From then on it was difficult for the Saville boys to get far in any ship competition!

The long voyage home was made much longer by the ship being very heavily laden with cargo, which required it to stay up to a week in each port for unloading. At Melbourne the boys watched a winch with a petrol engine being rigged up on the deck. The engine gave a lot of trouble and took several days to get going. It transpired that the cargo included a cable for the Melbourne cable trams, and the winch was to pay out the cable. When the cable reached the wharf two four-wheeled wagons, each with one horse, were tied together and a small number of loops of the cable coiled on this platform by what appeared to be a vast number of men. The wagons were then moved ahead and another two brought in, the cable passing between the two horses, and then more cable was coiled. The process was repeated and went on for days while the Saville boys began to despair of ever reaching Sydney and Portland.

When at long last they were met in Sydney by their parents and sisters they soon discovered that their father, who always planned ahead in his business, had (with some input from Isabella) done the same for his sons, planning their future careers. He had acquired a property near Bathurst and intended that Norman should be a farmer. John was to be trained as an engineer and Donald was to become a doctor. He had, however, underestimated the individual development of each boy during four years of independence at school in England.

CHAPTER FIVE

A Restless Young Man

Soon after the three boys returned to Portland in mid-1920 their father called them all into his office at the works. He wanted to make sure that they understood their position and made their own contribution towards deciding their future careers, whatever these were to be. He had already begun to appreciate that the careers he had planned might not be what they themselves wanted, and wanted to hear from them if they had any definite ideas of their own.

But first he gave them some advice: 'You've just left school and you now have to go out into the world to make a living. It's the survival of the fittest in this world – see to it that you make yourselves fit and *keep* yourselves fit! And my second piece of advice is – never work for the government!'

Saville had followed these precepts all his life and his experience of dealing with the N.S.W. Railway Department and other government departments had made him critical of government-run enterprises in general.

'Now, John,' he went on, 'you are the eldest so you start and tell me if you have any ideas about what you want to do to earn a living.'

John thought that he would like to follow his father and become an engineer. Donald admitted that he had as yet no idea what he wanted to do, but he was not interested in becoming a doctor. Norman certainly did not want to be a farmer, but had no other suggestions to offer.

Their father was amused that only John seemed to know what he wanted, and was willing to fit in with his father's plans. He told the boys he would think over the whole matter and come up with some other ideas later. All three boys were then enrolled at the Bathurst High School. This was something of a culture shock after Ayton, but the Bathurst teachers took an interest in the boys and their parents were satisfied that the school was better than the boys becoming bored at home. Home was again Hereford and, as the girls were also in Bathurst, at a private school, the family was once again united, with their father appearing at weekends.

The brothers soon became restless under the more formal routines and less imaginative teaching than they had enjoyed in England. John left first. In order to get away from school he was willing to try farming for a year to see how he liked it. His father arranged for him to move to the Saville property on the outskirts of Bathurst.

Donald and Norman lasted longer because they took part in school sports. Then their father listened to their pleas and allowed them to leave during 1921 to take up posts at Portland, Don in the cement testing laboratory and Norman in the machine shop. Norman was later transferred to Morts Dock and Engineering Company in Sydney as an engineering apprentice.

Don found life at Portland difficult and boring, working under the suspicious eye of the chief chemist. He was given the menial task of preparing sample pats of various cement mixes to test their quality. He told his brothers that he was treated unfairly by the chemist and at times humiliated in front of other workers, just because he was the boss's son. This was probably true because a Portland sectional head might well feel ill at ease with a young Saville working in the department. Work at the laboratory became more and more intolerable, but Don stayed on to please his parents.

Then one day he and his motorcycle disappeared without warning, and without leaving any message as to his intentions. His parents were worried, but held their own counsel – they expected him to contact them to tell them where he was. As the weeks went by, however, they were tempted to inform the police in case some harm had befallen him. Nevertheless, they decided not to, hoping that Don would get in touch in due course, on the grounds that if there had been an accident they would have been informed by the authorities. It was not exactly comforting but it seemed a logical conclusion.

After six long weeks without any news Don was located by a family friend who saw him driving a car in the southern suburbs of Sydney. He had obtained work as a chauffeur to a doctor. Contact was re-established, and his parents discussed what they could do to help him find congenial work and settle into a suitable career. The Saville children were indeed fortunate in their parents. Few other fathers would have had the power, wealth and concern for their offspring to try so hard to accommodate their wishes, and few mothers would have been more concerned over the welfare of their children.

Donald had always been interested in engines, in machinery of all types and in engineering generally, although he refused to study at university level. What about becoming an engineering apprentice in a firm outside Portland? His father contacted the manager of Clyde Engineering Company in Sydney, which was preparing some mining machinery and spare parts for the Portland Cement Company.

Don agreed to go back to Sydney to learn engineering on the job with one of Australia's most successful firms, producing steam locomotives, road traction engines, bridges, farm machinery and gold-mining equipment among a wide range of machinery. He was unable to share lodgings with Norman because of the distance between their workplaces. Moreover, Don's technical evening classes were at the Granville Technical School while Norman attended Sydney Technical College.

The work at Clyde was more interesting than that at Portland, but Don was still not sure that this was his future. During the year he tried to explain his feelings to his father, who listened but began to wonder if this particularly restless son was ever going to settle down to a proper career. However, Don was no fool and he had begun to realise that to progress to the top in engineering he needed further academic qualifications, either the Leaving Certificate or Matriculation. The Oxford Certificate he had obtained at Ayton was not recognised in Australia as being of sufficient standard for university entrance, or even an engineering diploma.

His parents were still ambitious that he should become a doctor and realised that he might qualify for a university medical course if he returned to school. So in June 1922 at the age of eighteen and a half Don was accepted by Sydney Grammar School, one of Australia's finest schools, noted for its academic standards. His position was quite unusual in view of his age and his entry into one of the sixth forms without having come up through the lower forms in the usual way. With his varied experience at schools and in industry, however, he must have been an interesting pupil for his teachers, and he worked hard and with determination. He had always been good at mathematics, English and science.

Perhaps he was barred by his age from taking part in school sports because in the 1923 school athletic championships his name appeared only once, as coming third in the obstacle race. This must have been galling for the Ayton School champion gymnast and athlete.

Donald and Norman were able to board together in Balmain, and went each morning to their separate destinations – Don to school and Norman to Morts Dock and Engineering Company. The brothers enjoyed being together in Sydney and settled into a steady work routine. Don did his full stint of homework at Balmain and Norman spent certain evenings at the Sydney Technical College. Some weekends they went back to Portland where in 1923 their parents moved into a fine new manager's residence, Portland House. The old house, Ivanhoe, across the road from the cement mill, became the residence for a number of the Portland schoolteachers. It was later nicknamed Harmony Hall in what was probably a cynical reference to the problems for mainly young women newly posted from training colleges to a small industrial town with a predominantly male population.

At Bathurst the magnificent mansion Hereford was first leased as a boarding house and later sold by John Saville to the Church of England to become Marsden Ladies' College. Today, Marsden Ladies' College has joined forces with All Saints (C.E.) School, which is now co-educational, while Hereford is part of the Roman Catholic Holy Family School at Kelso, Bathurst.

As 1923 came to an end, Don performed well enough in his examinations to obtain the Leaving Certificate. He passed in English, Mathematics I, Mathematics II, and Technical Drawing. Unhappily for his parents' ambitions, however, he refused point blank to apply to the University of Sydney for the medical course (it is actually doubtful if he was qualified to do so) nor did he want to study engineering there. John and Isabella argued the advantages of a university education, but Don had been in so many schools for the last fourteen years of his life that the thought of further academic learning for another four to six years was impossible for him to face immediately.

Saville Senior was not used to his plans being thwarted, and he examined alternatives. Could he find some work suitable for all three sons so that the family could again be together in Portland or Bathurst? He could have found jobs for them all at Portland but Don was firmly opposed to working again in the testing laboratory or indeed in any other department of the cement mill. John was now working there in the engineering section, having decided not to continue as a farmer, and Norman was apparently happy at Morts Dock.

Their father could recognise some of his own determination coming out in Donald, John and Norman. Each boy wanted to be independent and plan out his own career. Would it be possible to provide them with a joint business of their own? Was there any common interest to link them?

A possible solution was eventually found at Bathurst early in 1924; the common link was the boys' interest in engineering, cars and motorcycles. John Saville bought a major share in Bathurst Motors, then a large organisation holding the Chevrolet and Buick dealership for the district and open for servicing and repairs twenty-four hours a day and seven days a week. Bathurst Motors was at this time the largest motor firm in New South Wales outside Sydney, with some twenty-four employees, mainly mechanics. Saville was willing to arrange the release of his sons from their present employers and place them in positions of minor responsibility at Bathurst, where they could develop their skills and have opportunities for promotion – if they were willing to take part in their father's plan.

To his satisfaction and Isabella's delight the three young men all saw the advantages of the scheme and readily agreed to start work in Bathurst, where they could all board together at their old home, Hereford.

The work included mechanical and body repairs, servicing, spray painting, the supply of spare parts and the retreading of tyres. The three boys became mechanics, but management was in the hands of senior men, one of whom was a pilot and racing motorcyclist. Donald was put in charge of motorcycle sales and the retreading of tyres. John worked in the electrical section and Norman in the main workshop.

As an added incentive, their father bought them each a motorcycle and encouraged them to start racing at local events. At weekends, when they were racing, he would accompany them as their manager in the pits.

Donald became a very keen competitor and worked long hours on the engine of his machine raising the compression ratio to gain more efficiency. Norman has said that he was cool and clever at racing and showed good judgment in emergencies. The brothers had some successes and some spills but fortunately did themselves no serious damage. At their age it was an exciting sport and doubtless it was useful in developing their knowledge of internal combustion engines and general engineering principles.

Donald saw the advantages in having a paper qualification as a motor mechanic and took the necessary examination and practical tests for the N.R.M.A. Certificate which was established about this time with the aim of improving standards of automobile servicing and repair. The certificate was useful in later years when he owned his own garage in Sydney.

The Bathurst experiment came to an end in 1925 because of financial difficulties and problems with the management of the firm. When Saville Senior examined the first balance sheet and discovered that the garage was losing money instead of making a sound profit as he had expected, he quickly sold his share of the business and made new arrangements for each of his three sons. This time it was back to Portland and the cement works. Don was placed in charge of the company's motor transport, John went back to the engineering department and Norman into the drawing office.

In 1926 John and Isabella went off to Europe for the first time together since the family trip of 1912. John had some business to do in Britain but this time they planned to have a well-earned holiday, visiting relatives and exploring parts of the British Isles and the mainland of Europe for sheer enjoyment.

The send-off at Sydney was a family occasion, with the three sons and their sisters all present to look over the cabin, arrange flowers and gifts and see that their mother and father were bade farewell in style as the ship sailed.

Norman tells how another gentleman arrived at the ship with a gift of flowers for his mother. It was Gus Kelly, the member of parliament for Bathurst, who had never forgotten how she had nursed him and saved his life when he developed typhoid fever when he was a cement tester at Portland. 'Your mother saved my life,' he proclaimed loudly to the family. 'If it hadn't been for her, I wouldn't be here!'

The sailing of a mail steamer from the Australian ports in the 1920s and later, until the great liners gave way to airliners, were always an emotional occasion as the ship edged away from the quay and the last streamers linking ship and shore were snapped and fell into the water. The Saville children watched sadly as their parents' ship sailed away to the Heads and then they made their own way back to the Central Station and a train to Lithgow and Portland.

The three young men, now in their twenties, were enjoying life in the family home, Portland House, overlooking the town and mill, but they were also beginning to feel the urge to move away from their parents and become independent. They enjoyed the company of girls, although Don seemed more keen on his car and motorcycle than on acquiring a steady girl-friend.

His neat and tidy habits, acquired under his mother's strong regime, showed themselves in his taste for clothes. He favoured good-quality jackets and trousers, expensive shoes and a range of hats, all of which enhanced his thin, handsome face and athletic body. The overall effect concealed his lack of height. He was a very active and fit young man, ready for anything – swimming, riding, golf, tennis, athletics, climbing, ski-ing, bush walking.

Mollie Saville, wife of John, Don's twin brother, remembers an occasion when John and Don attended the opening of the Marsden School for Girls at Hereford, the former Saville home in Bathurst in 1925. After the necessary alterations a special opening ceremony was held at the new school where Mollie was a pupil and among those attending were these two young men formally attired for the occasion, complete with bowler hats. They caused some swooning among some of the girls, according to Mollie!

Mollie recalls another occasion on the beach at Manly with one of her friends, when they were escorted by Don and a friend of his. Mollie was not impressed by Don's behaviour on the beach; he was too smart and full of backchat. Among his misdemeanours, he tried to tease two girls who were sunbathing nearby. He tried to burn their toes by throwing cigarette ends at them – a silly, spur-of-the-moment, game. Mollie summed up Don's attitude to girls at that time as always being willing to have fun with them, but never being serious in his intentions.

He was a good mixer, however, and always ready to attend the local dances and other social activities in Portland. In addition to his passion for motorcycle racing he took up golf and assisted in the construction and development of the Portland Golf club, with its undulating course on the edge of the township. With his brothers he became a member of the Freemasons in Portland and aided the construction of the imposing Portland Masonic Temple by making a loan to the building fund. Their father was not a Mason – he would have nothing to do with trade unions and regarded the Masonic as such.

The Saville brothers were not teetotallers like their parents, but had to be extremely careful to avoid their strict father finding out that they drank. It was no use trying to deceive their mother – Isabella could always tell when one of the boys had been drinking. Norman remembers that she would say, 'Norman – don't overdo it!' To which he replied 'No mother, I never will.' In fact he has always been careful and describes himself as a 'one drink only' man.

While the parents were overseas Don again became dissatisfied with his life and prospects. He craved for something more exciting to do but was now sufficiently mature to realise that others were having to settle to jobs and careers which were not always exactly to their liking. However late in 1926 an unforeseen yet attractive answer to Don's wish for a colourful and adventurous career appeared in the form of an advertisement in a Saturday edition of the *Sydney Morning Herald*. The Royal Australian Air Force was inviting young men between the ages of eighteen and twenty-five to apply for cadetships at Point Cook, Victoria, where they would receive initial flying training to be followed by short-service commissions as pilots in the Royal Air Force in Britain. Applications were to be accompanied by references from prominent citizens or employers giving supporting evidence of the suitability of the candidate for flying training. Don was immediately interested and read out the advertisement to his brothers.

'What do you think of that?' he asked. 'That wouldn't be bad, would it?' and answered his own question with the slightly humorous remark, 'I think I'll give that a fly!'

He wrote for the application form and set about getting testimonials and referees – not a difficult task because of the family connections through the Commonwealth Portland Cement Company. John remembers that his brother obtained a large number of testimonials and sorted out the most suitable to send with the completed form to RAAF Headquarters.

In due course he was invited to Sydney for an interview. He was determined to do well and impressed the selection board with his alert mind and athletic appearance. After a further anxious period of waiting the RAAF notified him that he had been selected and was to join the next cadet entry into the Australian Citizens' Air Force starting at Point Cook on 2 May 1927. At twenty-three years of age, he was on the threshold of his career as an aviator, at a time when flying itself was still a new adventure.

Chapter Six

Learning to Fly – RAAF Point Cook (1927)

Generations of RAAF pilots have learned to fly at Point Cook, Victoria, the traditional home of the air force. In 1914 four Australian pilots who learned to fly at Point Cook became the nucleus of the Australian Flying Corps of the First World War. The RAAF was officially formed on 31 March 1921, three years after the RAF in Britain.

In 1927, when Donald Saville joined, the aircraft used for flying training were First World War types, wood and fabric biplanes such as the Avro 504K, DH9A and SE5. Most had been supplied by a grateful British government in return for Australia's aviation contribution during the war. The Avro 504 was designed in 1913 by Alliott Vernon Roe, the first Englishman to fly in England (1908). It was one of the most famous wooden trainers of all time and over 8,000 were constructed.

RAAF Point Cook is just outside Melbourne between the Princes Freeway and Port Phillip Bay – Point Cook being a promontory jutting into the bay. The main road and railway linking Melbourne to Geelong divide two RAAF stations, Laverton and Point Cook.

Also on the site of the Point Cook base is the RAAF Museum with hangars full of veteran aircraft, some of which are preserved in flying condition and able to make demonstration flights at air displays and pageants. Archives, models, dioramas, photographs, paintings etc., are preserved and displayed by a small and devoted staff, all members or ex-members of the RAAF.

Air Cadet Donald Teale Saville, feeling splendid but conspicuous in his new uniform, arrived by taxi from Melbourne on 2 May 1927 and was soon immersed in the routines of service life, along with some twenty other cadets. He was twenty-three years and four months old, athletic, fit, intelligent, confident, with a good practical knowledge of internal combustion engines, accustomed to high-speed motoring in sports cars and to racing on motorcycles but not as well qualified academically as some others of the young men in the group who had attended university and obtained degrees.

It was a new life, exercising both body and mind – lectures, gymnastics, games and regular hours of drilling on the barrack square under the keen eye and sharp tongue of an NCO. The cadets, however, longed to get into the planes drawn up around the airfield.

They were not kept waiting very long – Cadet Saville was standing by for his first familiarisation flight in a service aircraft on 18 May, a fortnight and two days after his arrival. He had already met his instructor, Flying Officer Shortridge, and liked him at once. Aged about 25 or 30, Shortridge was of medium height, thickset, with a round countenance and a cheerful manner.

He stood alongside the Avro 504K biplane and eyed his pupil with interest, wondering how this very confident young man would turn out. 'Climb in, Saville,' he said, 'and put your foot on this plate and not on the wing fabric! Listen carefully to everything I say and watch your instruments, which are duplicates of those I have in front of me. Don't touch the stick – let it move freely and don't interfere with my flying – you're merely a passenger this trip. We'll see how you like flying.'

An airman marched to the propeller and stood ready to swing it. 'Swing it over half a dozen turns,' ordered Shortridge. Then he called, 'Contact!'

'Contact,' repeated the airman and pulled down firmly on the propeller blade. The engine came to life with a spluttering roar and Shortridge waited while the engine and propeller settled down to a smooth and regular rhythm.

After 'Chocks away,' he slowly taxied the Avro to the downwind end of the field. There he waited until an Aldis light flashed green before opening up the engine to full revolutions. The machine ran eagerly forward, bouncing gently on the well-kept lawn-like grass, with the tail now off the ground and the plane nicely balanced on the two wheels under the wings.

Halfway across the field Shortridge gently pulled back the control stick and suddenly all vibration ceased – they were airborne. The passenger felt a thrill of excitement as he looked around him and saw the buildings grow smaller and viewed the shore of the bay underneath them and the dark outline of Melbourne ahead. Having climbed to 150 metres (500 ft) the pilot made a gentle turn to port for a full 180° and lined up with the railway line to Geelong. Don saw beneath him the flat farmland, the scattered houses, the railway line, the roads – and it was just as he had imagined it would be from the map he had studied before leaving Portland. He knew that the map of an area can be read as an accurate representation of the countryside as viewed form the air, providing that the cartographic symbols are understood and the map reader uses his imagination to construct a landscape. He was fascinated. Did a pilot find his way by map reading?

'Are you map reading, sir?' he asked the pilot through the voice-tube.

'Hardly necessary is it? You can see the coastline and the roads and towns – but of course that is the simple way of navigating in country you don't know, if you have a good map with you and orientate it correctly. But we also navigate by following a compass bearing, allowing for wind deflection, and work on dead reckoning by estimating time and distance along a given route.'

Shortridge continued climbing while following the railway towards Geelong, tucked into the corner of Corio Bay and already clearly visible ahead. They reached an altitude of 900 metres (3,000 ft) and turned out over the bay to follow the coastline back to base. The flight had lasted thirty-five minutes. Shortridge made an engine-assisted gliding approach and a perfect three-point landing. Next day, he and Don flew another short local flight for ten minutes in the same aircraft A3-17 (Avro 540K was class A3 in the RAAF and this was No. 17 out of some fifty similar training aircraft).

Don entered the flying times and details into his flying log book (A18) under the various columns provided. At the end of the week the log book was inspected and signed by Flight Lieutenant E. Stephens the officer commanding C Flight.

During the next week Don and his instructor made two flights of one hour and twenty minutes and one hour respectively in A3-17 and one of one hour and one thirty minutes in A3-51. It was all local flying but they did turns, glides, steep turns and gliding turns, and Don was allowed to use the control stick and rudder under careful instruction from F/O Shortridge. His total flying time was now four hours and thirty-five minutes and the log entries were again inspected and signed by F/Lt Stephens.

The third week of flying was again local and shared between Avro aircraft Nos. 17 and 51. He made seven flights with F/O Shortridge instructing in take-offs and landings, known in the air force as 'circuits and bumps'. Don loved it all and was allowed to do most of the take-offs and landings under the guidance of his instructor, who had to intervene only once or twice to make corrections to ensure a safe landing. Don's flying time had now reached nine hours and thirty-five minutes – and the log book was again signed by F/Lt Stephens of C Flight.

Don was beginning to feel that he would soon be allowed to go solo and was excited at the prospect but also naturally slightly apprehensive. F/O Shortridge told him that he was doing well, but that solo would come in good time, when he was ready for it.

The fourth week produced five local flights, all in A3-17, and the practice of turns right and left, landings and take-offs. On the first flight on the morning of 10 June 1927, at 08.15 hours F/Lt Stephens took Shortridge's place and Don knew that he was being considered for a solo flight in the very near future. He took great care with his take-offs and landings and Stephens was satisfied that he was ready to go solo. He said quietly, 'You're O.K. You can go solo next week.' Don was delighted and spent the weekend in a daze of excitement and anticipation. His flying hours had reached twelve hours and thirty minutes.

The morning of 13 June 1927 dawned fine and clear. At 08.55 hours F/O Shortridge went up with Don for a final check of his flying. The machine was Don's old Avro friend A3-17, which pleased him and helped his confidence. On landing, Shortridge clambered out of the cockpit and told him to take it up on his own! Don had had thirteen hours and five minutes of dual instruction – an average sort of time before going solo under peacetime flying instruction.

At 10.10 hours he taxied carefully to the end of the field, facing into wind, looked carefully at his small array of cockpit instruments and released the blip button to allow the engine to reach full revolutions (The 504K or Avro A3 had a primitive form of carburettor without a throttle control). The plane seemed much lighter on the controls without F/O Shortridge and lifted easily from the grass. It was a thrilling moment, but Don was not worried. He felt in control and in his element as he climbed steadily to 600 metres (2,000 ft) to practise turns and glides as directed before he took off. Then came the descent by a glide down and the first landing – quite a reasonable three-pointer, as he had practised over the last few weeks. He had been told to do three landings, so he took off immediately and completed the other two adequately, even confidently, after a flight time of thirty-five minutes.

F/O Shortridge came over and shook his hand, congratulating him on an excellent solo flight and told him that he would make a first-class pilot if he went on as he had done during instruction. Like any good teacher, he felt real pleasure in seeing his pupil do what he had been taught.

On 15 June Don was again flying with his instructor aboard, rather to his surprise. However, this was the pattern for the week – alternating between dual instruction and solo flights. At the end of the week his total flying time had reached fifteen hours and thirty-five minutes, one hour and forty-five minutes of which were solo.

The programme for the week after Don's first solo flight illustrates the care taken in training pilots at Point Cook. He made seven flights in five different aircraft (all Avro 504s) under the tuition of four different instructors, each of whom looked for weaknesses or faults in the new pilot's flying technique. The officers concerned were F/O Shortridge, F/Lt Wells, F/Lt Stephens and F/Lt Gardiner. When F/Lt Gardiner was satisfied with his performance, Don was again allowed to go solo. The next week followed a similar pattern, with three dual flights and one solo.

The week commencing 11 July 1927 marked further progress. On that day Don made four flights, two with F/O Shortridge and two solo. On 12 July he made six flights, four of which were solo. On this day he was also introduced to formation flying in threes and fives. On the final flight that day F/O Shortridge took him up for stunting, loops, spins etc. Don enjoyed every moment and every manoeuvre. The next day he flew solo and practised formation flying, loops and half rolls.

On 14 July F/O Shortridge went with him for target practice and later Don made two solo flights. On the 15th he was given practice as a leader in a formation of five aircraft. In a solo flight following the formation flying Don practised loops, half rolls and spins.

The Avro 504K cockpit now felt as familiar as the driver's seat of his car – the three-dimensional path of the aircraft was exhilarating to the young pilot, who controlled the manoeuvres with easy confidence and kept the discipline of straight and level flight by visual comparison of ground with map or by keeping to a compass bearing the instruments. It was all surprisingly easy yet excitingly new, and far superior to driving a car along a road. While roads and traffic determined what a car driver could do, here in the air the feeling was of freedom to go where one pleased.

Antoine de Saint-Exupery, in his book *Wind, Sand and Stars,* explains the delights and dangers of flying elegantly.

> But a cruel light has blazed and our sight has been sharpened. The plane has taught us to travel as the crow flies. Scarcely have we taken off when we abandon those winding highways that slope down to watering troughs and stables or run away to towns dreaming in the shade of their trees. Freed henceforth from this happy servitude, delivered from the need of fountains, we set course for distant destinations.

Before the training course was completed in December, Cadet D. T. Saville had two experiences which shook him. He had developed an over-confident approach to flying and was beginning to believe it was supremely easy to one as gifted as himself. Such experiences can either scar a young flier or rouse him to a greater sense of responsibility and maturity. In Don's case, it was the latter.

Low flying was forbidden on the course. All trainee pilots were warned against it, especially over the roads and railway near Point Cook. Acts of bravado or showmanship were firmly discouraged on the grounds of the danger to aircraft and pilot and the possible risks to civilians and property. Anyone found guilty of low flying could be subject to court martial and appropriate disciplinary action.

The first incident was perhaps understandable, in spite of the official warnings – young men in their twenties are full of daring and none more so than Donald Saville. He frequently saw the trains beneath him speeding along the railway line between Melbourne and Geelong, with long trails of white or grey smoke and steam stretching back or swirling away to one side in a strong wind. Trains such as the *Geelong Flier* reached speeds of 110–130 k.p.h. (70–80 m.p.h.) on the level, straight stretches parallel with the shore of Port Phillip Bay.

It was very tempting to bring the Avro down low and race with the train. Girls in the train might wave and be thrilled to see the pilot acknowledge with a gloved hand. Don thought it should be possible to allow the landing wheels to touch the roof of a coach in a really good feat of low flying. One day he tried the experiment and duly attracted much attention from passengers, both male and female, who waved delightedly at the daring young airman as he twisted and turned, following the train. They enjoyed it thoroughly and so did Don, but he found that turbulence over and near the train made it too dangerous to force his Avro wheels down to touch a coach roof. As he banked and climbed away from the train the aircraft numbers and letter were plain to read and one passenger, at least, took careful note. By appalling bad luck, Don had performed his feat in full view of the group captain, officer commanding RAAF Station, Point Cook, who happened to be on that train.

Later a full parade was called and the delinquent cadet told to step forward. Cadet Saville did so and following an inquiry was confined to the station and suspended from flying for a period of two weeks. He also received a very severe reprimand from the CO.

Don realised that he had been lucky to escape with a light punishment, but the episode also lost him his girlfriend of the moment – in somewhat amusing circumstances.

He had developed a friendship with a Melbourne girl and was due to meet her in the city at the weekend. He sent along his best friend to keep the appointment and to explain his absence. The two of them thoroughly enjoyed their outing together and subsequently went on to a courtship and eventual marriage. Don was surprisingly philosophical about losing his girl. 'There are plenty of others,' he said with a laugh.

The second incident occurred on 12 August 1927 when Don was flying solo in Avro A3-21, in which he had already flown on a number of occasions. The engine failed after forty minutes' flying and Don had to make a forced landing in a paddock near Werribee. He had practised forced landings and did all the right things, but there was a tractor and several items of farm machinery in the paddock. He could not avoid them and severely damaged the wings on one side of the Avro, which slewed round and tipped over on its nose. The young pilot was shaken but uninjured and sadly left the wreck after checking that the fuel supply was not leaking. He telephoned for transport and a salvage party from Point Cook. A court of enquiry exonerated Cadet Saville from blame for the crash and he resumed flying on 29 August.

In September there was a new interest when he was given dual instruction on a DH9A, a heavier and more powerful biplane than the Avro. On 14 September he went solo in DH9 A1-17. He liked the machine and enjoyed the controls and their response to his commands. On 26 September he was ordered to do an altitude test on the DH9 and reached 4,500 metres (15,000 ft) during a local flight of one hour and forty minutes. At the end of September he was assessed for proficiency as a pilot on Avro and DH9 aircraft. The log book states that Cadet Pilot Saville was 'average' on each type; under 'Any special faults' it records 'a tendency to hold off bank on gliding turns'. This entry was dated 3 October and signed by F/O C. Eaton, OC C Flight and also by the wing commander commanding No. 1 FTS RAAF, whose signature is indecipherable.

At the end of October a similar entry recorded 'average' but without any special faults in flying. At the end of November Don had completed 101 hours of flying with thirty-five hours and fifty minutes solo on Avros and twenty-five hours and fifty minutes on DH9As. His proficiency was now assessed as 'average' on Avro 504Ks but 'above average' on DH9As. There were no faults in flying to be corrected. Cadet Pilot D. T. Saville had completed a very thorough course of flying training with complete success.

The final entry in his log book was signed on 1 December by S/Ldr G. Jones of Flying Squadron No. 1 FTS RAAF. He and the other successful pilots from his entry were awarded their RAAF wings. Don felt that this was the greatest moment of his life so far. He realised that in aviation he had found a thrilling and completely satisfying career, which seemed to stretch into a golden future.

The pilots on the course were now given leave and Don went home joyously to Portland to be congratulated by his family and begin preparations for going to Britain to join the RAF for further training. At this time it was the practice for RAAF pilots to take short-service commissions in the RAF to gain experience in European conditions with modern aircraft, then to return to Australia, where they might be accepted into the regular RAAF if there were sufficient vacancies, or be placed on the Reserve of Officers.

As a matter of interest, F/O Travis Shortridge, the instructor who had taken such interest in Don's flying training, was himself destined to enter the tragic pages of aviation history as a result of the mysterious disappearance of *Southern Cloud* in March 1931.

Shortridge left the RAAF in 1928 and joined Australian National Airways as a pilot. On that fateful day, the three-engined Fokker designed aircraft took off from Mascot with Shortridge as pilot, a co-pilot and eight passengers, bound for Melbourne in blustery weather which quickly deteriorated into violent thunderstorms and gale-force winds.

She vanished without trace and it was not until October 1958, twenty-seven years later, that the wreckage was discovered 1,700 metres (5,500 ft) up on the Toolong Range, some 20 km (12 miles) from Kiandra.

CHAPTER SEVEN

Flying in the Peacetime RAF (1928–32)

Donald Saville and other members of the May 1927 Point Cook entry left Sydney for Britain on 18 December 1927. One can imagine that the voyage on the SS *Ulysses* would have been an extremely happy one for the young pilots on their way to join the RAF for the next stage in their training. There must have been some wild occasions on board.

Flying was barely out of its pioneer stage and airmen were then the heroes of the young just as astronauts are today. It was in 1928 that Charles Kingsford-Smith and Charles Ulm made the first air crossing of the Pacific from California to Brisbane in their three-engined Fokker *Southern Cross*. That was also the year when the Royal Flying Doctor Service was established in Australia. It was the age of air exploration and record journeys across continents and oceans. New pilots like Don felt that they were at the forefront of an exciting world of challenge and expanding knowledge in the third dimension of the air.

The RAF List of April–June 1928 records that Pilot Officer D. T. Saville was granted a short-service commission and joined the service on 14 February 1928. He was immediately posted to the Central Flying School, Wittering, between Stamford and Peterborough close to the western edge of the flat fenlands, for a refresher course.

The RAF now repeated the type of careful training Don had already received at Point Cook. Again he flew as a passenger-pupil in an Avro 504, this time with Flight Sergeant Crane as his instructor. The plane had a Lynx engine but it flew exactly like the Avros at Point Cook and Don was completely at ease with the manoeuvres, landings, forced landings and aerobatics. F/Sgt Crane recognised the skills of his pupil and did not play the heavy instructor. After approximately five hours' dual-control and two test flights with F/O Clarkson and F/Lt Soden, Don was sent solo on 6 March 1928. He flew with great confidence, knowing that he now had over a hundred flying hours behind him.

Later in March he was given dual instruction in a Bristol Fighter and then a DH9A, followed by solo flights in each type. The April assessment of his flying was 'above the average (pupil pilot)', signed by S/Ldr Robb, chief flying instructor and officer commanding, Central Flying School. He signed this assessment after a personal test flight with P/O Saville on 4 April 1928.

Restless Donald was restless no longer. Flying and learning new techniques maintained his devotion to this new way of life, and there were ample periods of leave and regular weekends to explore Britain and Europe in style.

It is worth taking a look at the air force which Don joined in 1928. In his book *Right of the Line* John Terraine writes:

> Under Trenchard as Chief of the Air Staff, the RAF confirmed its basic squadron organisation (inherited from the Royal Flying Corps): established its personnel functions and named its basic trades; set up its Apprentice School to ensure a flow of skilled technicians without whom a highly technical Service could not have carried out its duties; set up a cadet college for their further education in it; created a second-line Auxiliary Air Force imitating the Territorial Army; and most important of all, developed the short-service commission system which, recognising that military aviation is basically a young man's job, offered the necessary intake of young aircrew recruits without loading the Service with impossible numbers of candidates for higher rank.

The RAAF by sending the 1927 group of pilots to train on short-service commissions in Britain, was making sure that it, too, would have a supply of young pilots to augment the normal small intake of regular officers and other ranks. These pilots, when they could not be offered permanent commissions, would be placed in the Citizens' Air Force Reserve of Officers.

While the structure of the RAF had been established there had been little government investment in research or the development of new aircraft. The RAF in 1928 was a force of wooden biplanes like those in service at the end of the First World War. In Britain, plans for new metal monoplanes did not come until 1934. Meanwhile in Germany civil aircraft were being developed which were readily adapted as bombers and the new and secret German air force was taking shape.

However, the concerns that were to beset British politicians and service chiefs in the early 1930s were unlikely to have disturbed Don and his cheerful companions in their pursuit of flying excellence at Wittering. When the refresher course came to an end, with Don's log book showing 139 flying hours, he was posted to No. 17 Fighter Squadron at Upavon, Wiltshire with effect from 3 May 1928.

This squadron had its own training scheme for new pilots and Don was given two flights by F/O Andrews in a two-seater dual-control Siskin fighter plane. Then he was sent solo in a Hawker Woodcock biplane single-seater fighter, the standard fighter in use by the squadron. From that point on it was all flying, two or three times a day on cross-country flights, with local practice of aerobatics, landings, spins and cloud flying. Strangely, or perhaps prophetically considering the development of fighter-bombers in the Second World War, Don's log book reveals that he had bombing practice with his Woodcock on two occasions in May using small 8½ lb (3.85 kg) practice bombs.

Flying continued in June, with aerobatics and formation flying in preparation for the Hendon Pageant. On the 12th Don had a minor excitement when a seized rocker arm and broken exhaust pushrod in his engine caused him to make a forced landing at Old Sarum airfield just outside Salisbury. The engine was repaired by mechanics from Upavon and he flew back to base on the same day. On another day he reached 4,500 metres (15,000 ft) in a battle flight height test.

For a period of ten days in July the squadron was at Sutton Bridge, Lincolnshire, for gunnery practice at ground targets on the edge of the Wash. Don enjoyed these exercises and was above average in accuracy on the range. August saw 17 Squadron at Biggin Hill for altitude flying over the metropolis (Don flew at 4,900 metres (16,000 ft) for one hour) and day patrols in co-operation with searchlight units for the air defence of Great Britain.

From 12 August to 16 September Don was on leave. He had friends and relations in Britain in addition to his fellow officers in the Upavon Officers' Mess, and he probably spent time visiting them. There were Saville relatives in Yorkshire and Teale relatives in Scotland, and he probably also had a few school friends from Ayton School, with whom he could enjoy weekends or longer periods in homes well spread throughout Britain. He owned a small MG sports car and was therefore highly mobile.

Upavon, while appearing small and remote in its position on the chalk downs of Salisbury Plain was actually well placed in the centre of a district with the larger centres of Bath, Swindon, and Salisbury all within a 50 km (30 mile) radius, while pleasant market towns abounded, including Marlborough, Devizes, Frome, Calne, Westbury, Warminster and Trowbridge.

The lively company of young RAF officers was much enjoyed by the young ladies of the country estates and professional homes in the towns, so it is certain that the pilots of No. 17 Fighter Squadron were able to enjoy many opportunities for social pleasures. Don, perhaps influenced by these social possibilities, took unusual care in having his uniform tailored by a firm of specialists in Savile Row, London, who produced uniforms for HRH The Prince of Wales. There were excellent military tailors in Bath and Salisbury but Savile Row had glamour and a world-wide reputation.

The RAF in peacetime seems to have provided a stimulating, comfortable and satisfying environment for the men commissioned to serve king and country in the air. But, unlikely as war seemed at the time, it was barely ten years ahead.

On their return from leave the squadron commenced a conversion course on Siskin IIIA biplanes designed and built by the Armstrong Whitworth Company. Don flew in the dual-instruction plane with F/Lt Williams and F/O Watt before going solo in the same plane and later flying the squadron's single-seater Siskins. October was largely devoted to practice for the Hendon Pageant, with exercises using the whole squadron in formation. No. 17 Squadron flew in formation from Upavon to the Hendon Pageant on 11 October in a cross-country flight of fifty minutes. They landed there and took off again in the afternoon for Biggin Hill. On 12 October they returned to Upavon.

The month ended with further cross-country flying to Upper Heyford, aerobatics, landing practice and firing the Siskin's guns at the gun butts. October had given Don nineteen hours' flying on Siskins and he was now perfectly at home in the aircraft.

November's weather was unusually good and the squadron planes were flying almost every day. Exercises in that month included battle flight interceptions and fighting practice with camera-guns fitted.

Don's total flying hours reached 250 by the 20 December, 1928, but he was a little disappointed to be assessed only 'average' on the Siskin IIIA by S/Ldr A. R. Arnold, commanding No. 17 Fighter Squadron on 8 January 1929.

That year opened with a busy month for the fighter squadron; pilots practised cloud flying, aerobatics, forced landings and gunnery tests at the butts, plus air firing of the guns at the Larkhill ranges. At the end of the month Don was posted to an air pilotage course at Calshot, using Southampton flying boats. He flew as navigator with a number of different pilots so that his theoretical knowledge of air navigation could be complemented by practical experience as he controlled the courses flown by the instructor pilot over the Solent area and later along the south and east coast.

After nearly three months and fifty-five flying hours from Calshot, he resumed training with is fighter squadron at Upavon. He took part in night-flying exercises for the first time after a cross-country flight by day to Duxford aerodrome, which was equipped for night flying.

During the first week in May the 17 Squadron detachment practised aerobatics in formation by day at Duxford and then did night flying from 21.00 hours with a series of landings using the flarepath. Returning to Upavon they flew locally until the end of the month when the squadron sent a detachment to Sutton Bridge in the fenlands for gunnery exercises.

Apart from a few forced landings due to engine trouble, Don had so far experienced no serious emergencies in his flying. But on 11 June he flew from Sutton Bridge to Waddington on a cross-country run with F/O Turner in another Siskin. Taking off from Waddington the pair of planes flew south to Hawkinge RAF Station near Folkestone. Over Kent and nearing their destination, Don was horrified to see his friend's plane's engine catch fire (it was later found to have been due to a broken petrol pipe) with flames and smoke blowing back around the pilot.

They were at about 600 metres (2,000 ft) and Don followed the smoking Siskin down, watching for the pilot to release himself and jump or fall out and open the parachute which was now worn by all service aircrew. The stricken plane had got down to about 200 metres (700 ft) when F/O Turner left the cockpit and appeared to bump against the tail unit. He went down and then the parachute came out and Don saw him suspended beneath the umbrella-like canopy, to his immense relief. The Siskin very fortunately found itself a field to crash in without damage to property.

Noting carefully where Turner had landed, Don circled once and sped away to Hawkinge, where an ambulance team and doctor were soon organised. F/O Turner had broken his right arm in hitting the Siskin's tail and also had some severe facial burns. He was admitted to the station hospital, where Don was able to visit him some three weeks later on a cross-country visit from Upavon. Turner was cheerful and making good progress.

Also in June, near Northampton on a cross-country flight, Don himself made a forced landing caused by a broken petrol pump, but happily for him there was no fire.

Exercises in July included inverted flying and daily aerobatics and spins. At the end of the month Don's log book totalled 400 flying hours. August brought more variations in the training, when 17 Squadron fighters were attached first to No. 1 Brigade AA at Farnborough and then to No. 12 Bomber Squadron for joint manoeuvres. Don managed to fly a Fairey Fox during these exercises in order to experience the manoeuvrability of the bomber type.

In October the squadron took delivery of the first machines of the very latest RAF fighter type, the Bristol Bulldog. Don made his first flight in the new plane on the afternoon of 1 October and promptly tried it out by putting it into a spin, which he then corrected. It was of course, another biplane, fundamentally little changed from the Siskin but with a more powerful engine.

During November 1929 Don did a battle flight climb to 6,000 metres (20,000 ft) in fifteen minutes in a Bulldog. At the end of the month the squadron did a special formation flight over the local area in their Bulldogs so that photographs could be taken for *Flight*, an aviation magazine. The squadron performed aerobatics, inverted turns and did petrol consumption tests.

In December flying went on in high winds up to 50 k.p.h. (30 m.p.h.), with pilots practising landing at Upavon in these difficult conditions. On another occasion there was a cross-country flight to Upper Heyford aerodrome in poor visibility and fog so that pilots were able to practise approaches in these conditions. On 14 December Don took his regular Bulldog up to 6,400 metres (21,000 ft) and back to the ground in twenty-one minutes. On other flights he experimented with cloud flying when rain was actually falling. Aerobatics, spins and forced landings were practised almost daily.

At the end of 1929, Don's total flying time had reached 500 hours. Against 'Proficiency as pilot on type' in his log book were the encouraging words 'above the average'. The officer who signed the document on 13 January 1930 was W/Cdr A. R. Arnold, the officer who had awarded 'average' one year earlier.

Don was now recognised as a very good pilot and was given instructor duties with incoming pilots to 17 Squadron. The round of flying training went on with only a brief break over Christmas, and in January he was airborne for thirty-six flights, half on the dual Siskin and half solo on Siskins. Two flights were tests of a new tail modification on the Bulldog. Bulldog J9585 was used for most solo flights and appears to have been allotted to Don as a personal plane. On 7 February he made a forced landing with a burst oil tank on this machine.

Cross-country flights in March 1930 included one to Eastchurch, with camera-gun practice at Eastchurch and firing on targets at Leysdown, both on the Isle of Sheppey in Kent. Don's status in the squadron was indicated by the fact that in April 1930 he was responsible for testing aircraft after inspection and overhaul. During that month he practised for an aerobatics competition, dropped practice bombs and took part in formation flying. The aerobatics competition was held at North Weald on 25 April but there is no indication in the log book of how successful the 17 Squadron participants were.

May saw Don engaged in instructing and testing new pilots before they went solo on squadron aircraft. Manoeuvres were held with No. 12

Bomber Squadron in the Andover area. He tested a Bulldog which had had some wing modifications and took the same machine to Sutton Bridge for a full week of air firing at the Holbeach range.

The half-yearly report on his flying (2 June 1930) was again 'above the average', and was signed this time by S/Ldr R. Harrison now the officer commanding No. 17 Fighter Squadron.

In June the busy days of flying continued with much formation flying practice, including formation loops and other aerobatics for a civil air display at Haldon on the 21st.

Don took leave from 16 August to 5 September, and when he returned, he was involved in radio telephone practice and exercises in fighting with camera-guns fitted.

One sad occasion in October was a squadron formation flight over the funeral at Cardington of the R101 airship disaster victims. October also brought a change in Don's training. After his long period with fighters on No. 17 Fighter Squadron he moved to the larger, heavier and longer-duration aircraft of No. 207 Bomber Squadron, which was equipped with Fairey IIIF biplanes and based at Bircham Newton, Norfolk.

The Fairey IIIF was a two-seater carrying an aircraftsman or leading aircraftsman as airgunner in the rear seat. With proper caution 207 Squadron first gave Don two flights as a back-seat passenger with F/O Cook as pilot, then sent him solo with ballast in the rear seat instead of the gunner. After he had made two flights with ballast and after making a series of landings and take-offs, A.C. Atkins joined him and other gunners did so on subsequent flights.

Flying exercises included map reading, wireless tests, direction-finding tests using Orfordness Beacon, drift-indicator tests, ground gunnery from the back seat, cross-country flights, forced landings and some practice bombing at Bircham Newton airfield. Whether or not it was intended for bomber pilots to spin their aircraft is uncertain, but Don, while flying with ballast, succeeded in putting the IIIF into a spin and correcting successfully.

On 4 December 1930 a sudden fog came up and he made a crash landing in thick fog at the aerodrome with A.C. Atkins in the rear seat of J9147. However, neither man was injured and evidently the landing was skilfully performed in difficult circumstances. After Christmas leave from 20 December to 7 January Don was posted to Calshot on 13 January to join the training squadron with seaplanes and flying boats. From January until April 1931 he was flying Fairey IIIF and IIID seaplanes and Southampton flying boats.

These exercises may have been connected with the Schneider Trophy race, seven laps of a 50 km (30 mile) course on the Solent, which was due to be held in September. Both surviving Saville brothers report that Don was accepted for training with the High-Speed Flight of five pilots from whom three were to be chosen for the race.

The British team, however, suddenly found itself with no competition. The Italians were unable to produce an aircraft in time and the French entry crashed during trials, killing its pilot. Nevertheless on 13 September, F/Lt J. W. Boothman flew a Supermarine S6B around the course at an average speed of 544 k.p.h. (340 m.p.h.) while F/Lt G. H. Stainforth set up a new world speed record of 606 k.p.h. (379 m.p.h.) on the second S6B. Later Stainforth reached 652 k.p.h. (407.5 m.p.h.). With those high-speed flights the pilots and machines not only won the Schneider Trophy but also made a big contribution to the technology which led to the development of the Spitfire and Hurricane fighters of the Second World War.

Undoubtedly, as a fighter pilot of some four years training with additional experience in flying bombers, seaplanes and flying boats, Don was eminently eligible for consideration as a member of the High-Speed Flight in 1931. The posting to Calshot training squadron is evidence that he was in the running for selection as a racing pilot, but there is no indication that he was.

Don's log book for the period shows that his last flight from Calshot was on 10 April 1931. The entry is signed by the squadron leader, chief instructor, officer commanding RAF Station, Calshot. At this point in his career his log book shows that he had flown 670.20 hours solo, 60.15 hours dual and 81.50 hours as navigator – a total of 812 hours 25 minutes. In four years of flying with the two air forces, he had progressed from a cadet to an above-average pilot of maturity and skill sufficient to be chosen to instruct pilots and test aircraft. At twenty-eight he had changed from an unsettled young man to a calmly confident and fully trained aviator, determined to achieve the highest possible success in this new and expanding field.

The overwhelming impression of both the RAF and the RAAF is of thoroughness and careful attention to every detail of military flying given in the peacetime training of pilots. Backed by this training these pilots were able to perform with high efficiency and heroism in the Battle of Britain, in Bomber Command and other commands in the Second World War.

Don Saville's record of service in the RAF shows that he was posted to RAF Depot on 13 May 1931 and transferred back to the RAAF on 14 February 1932. The RAAF record of service gives 1 May 1932 as the date of his return to Australia and his appointment to the Citizens' Air Force Reserve with the rank of flying officer.

This means that there was almost a year in which he was not flying or engaged in formal service activities. His brother Norman was in the United Kingdom at this time, employed as an engineer with Vickers Armstrong Ltd., at Barrow-in-Furness. He and Don spent some time in the summer of 1931 touring around the south of England visiting a number of RAF squadrons where Don had friends. He reports that Don was referred to by his nicknames, King-Pin and Roo, and that they received an extremely warm welcome at the various officers' messes when they called. They seemed like gentlemen's clubs to Norman. These were the happy days of peace just prior to Hitler's rise to power.

Interestingly Don was said to have been aware of the early secret re-armament of Germany as a result of his many visits to Europe including skiing holidays when he had learned of underground factories and hangars for aircraft. His skiing companions included close friends in Gordon Richards, the famous British jockey, and one of the Smiths of Smiths' Potato Crisps. Don passed on his information to his commanding officers. Presumably British intelligence was aware of German rearmament but public knowledge was scanty until the warnings of Winston Churchill in Parliament in the 1930s.

At Christmas 1931 Don and Norman stayed in London at the Strand Palace Hotel, where Walter Lindrum the Australian champion billiards player was also a guest. Norman knew him from a previous meeting in Sydney and the three Australians teamed up for Christmas dinner. Lindrum autographed the Savilles' menu cards and Norman still has his copy.

Don was highly amused at his family's interest in his love life. His mother was determined to find out whether there was a woman in his life and showed plainly in her letters that she would like him to marry. When he wrote from England to say that he was going on holiday to Sweden and Norway, she asked, 'Why Scandinavia?' Donald wrote back in turn, 'To see the blondes, of course!'

The surviving Saville brothers believe that Don was so busy with his flying and his service life generally, that he felt marriage would handicap his career. Girls were for fun but marriage was out of the question. He was wedded to flying!

CHAPTER EIGHT

Flying Instructor (1932–7)

When Don returned to Australia he was placed on the Citizens' Air Force Reserve with the rank of Flying Officer. (He remained there until 30 April 1936 when he was discharged and relinquished rank on completion of his service.)

Australia in 1932 was in the grip of the great depression and also of the powerful legend of Lasseter's gold reef. The two were in a way connected. A man named Lewis Harold Lasseter had persuaded the Australian Workers' Union and other backers that he knew where there was a reef of gold 9.5–11 km (6–7 miles) long which was rich enough to end Australia's economic problems. He was believed to have discovered it some thirty years previously while prospecting in central Australia.

In 1930 an expedition set off from Alice Springs with high hopes. Lasseter's story was accepted implicitly and the expedition members were obsessed by the lure of gold in unbelievable quantity. However, drought conditions and the loss of their accompanying aircraft in a crash near Ayers Rock forced the party to return to Alice Springs. Lasseter, however, went on alone with two camels and a share of the rations.

He never returned and his body was discovered in 1931 by an experienced bushman, Robert Buck, who buried his remains close to the dry bed of the Docker River near the Western Australian border. The mystery of the fabulous gold reef, however, inspired many more expeditions.

John Saville had not lost his deep interest in gold mining. The story of Lasseter's reef intrigued him immensely and the return of Don from England seemed to provide a heaven-sent opportunity to organise an expedition to locate it. Don himself was very interested and made enquiries for an aircraft capable of carrying two people and the necessary equipment into the desert region where the borders of Western Australia, South Australia and the Northern Territory met.

Unfortunately (or perhaps fortunately in view of the dangers) he could not find a plane before his own business commitments prevented him pursuing the intriguing adventure – much to his father's regret. He decided to purchase a garage in Sydney, within easy reach of his new home at 1 King Avenue, Balgowlah, where he was living with his mother.

Isabella had come to Sydney on her doctor's orders to live near sea level. She had a heart condition which was affected by the altitude of Portland. Her husband had purchased what at first was a perfect house on the waterfront of North Harbour with a superb view over moored yachts to Manly and North Head. However, later on, even the steps down to the house were too much for the invalid and the Saville family moved to a level site in Steinton Street, Manly.

While Don was living at King Avenue with his mother, his brother John was working in the engineering section of the cement works at Portland and living with his father at Portland House. He was courting Mollie Tweedie of Portland and they were delighted to have Don available as best man for their wedding in November 1932 at St. James Church, King Street, Sydney. Don had known Mollie as long as John and was prepared to run the whole show. He decided that John needed building up before the wedding and organised a stag party, but John says that he managed to keep control. Norman was still in England, working at Barrow-in-Furness.

Don's garage sold petrol at a discount price because he bought it from one of the smaller oil companies. However, the business was more than a petrol station for it had a modern workshop equipped with electrical machinery and did major repairs such as cylinder reboring, valve refacing, brake relining and general overhauls. As a further investment he bought two cottages in Manly and made various improvements with the help of two capable tradesmen. These properties were still in his possession when he rejoined the RAF in 1939.

Don did not allow his flying skills to deteriorate. He let it be known that he was an experienced ex-air force pilot able to fly private planes on his B licence. He soon found himself sought by amateur aeroplane builders who wanted him to test and fly their home-made and kit-assembled aircraft from Mascot Airfield.

John reports that it became a regular weekend outing to accompany Don to Mascot and watch him take off in some crazy little plane driven by a motorcycle engine. The plane would eventually buzz across the green field and stagger into the air with the owner-constructor watching with wide eyes and a madly beating heart. Then the spectators would clamber into their cars and pursue it in case it came down in some remote paddock – as indeed it often did.

Don enjoyed the excitement of the experiments. He frequently made suggestions for improvements for the next flight. He was the test pilot

Don Saville in 1932. Having ended his period of enlistment with the RAF in England he returned to Australia and became a Flying Officer in the Citizen's Air Force Reserve.
(Saville Family)

Passport photographs taken in 1926 of Don's parents, John and Isabella Saville.
(Saville Family)

The first Saville family home in Portland, 'Ivanhoe', close to the cement works.
(Saville Family)

A young Donald Teale Saville taken at the first family home. *(Saville Family)*

The Saville boys Donald, Norman and John photographed in 1916. *(Saville Family)*

A photograph taken of the 'A' Course, Royal Australian Air Force during 1927 at Point Cook. Cadet Saville is second from the left on the bottom row. *(Saville Family)*

An Avro 504N, fitted for instrument/blind flying. This type was flown by Don during his training at No.1 Flying Training School, Point Cook. *(Philip Jarrett)*

DH9As of No. 39 Squadron RAF seen here seen here during 1923 were also flown extensively by Don during his flying training. *(Philip Jarrett)*

During Don's service with the Royal Air Force between 1928 and 1932 he flew many aircraft that were designed during World War I. Seen here, the Bristol Fighter is a typical example of an obsolete design still in service at that time. *(Philip Jarrett)*

This photograph was taken when Don was serving with No. 17 Squadron RAF and flying Hawker Woodcock fighter aircraft. He had written on the reverse 'Two other chaps and myself (centre). The long chap ruined the engine of the machine behind my machine through flying with no oil pressure'. *(Saville Family)*

Another photograph from Don's Woodcock days with No. 17 Squadron. This one is captioned 'My machine getting the engine taken out at Sutton Bridge on the Wash - our summer camp - under canvas in war conditions, only canvas hangars'. *(Saville Family)*

A Hawker Woodcock MkII of No. 17 Squadron RAF. *(Philip Jarrett)*

These Bristol Bulldog MkII fighter aircraft of No. 17 Squadron RAF entered service during 1928. *(Philip Jarrett)*

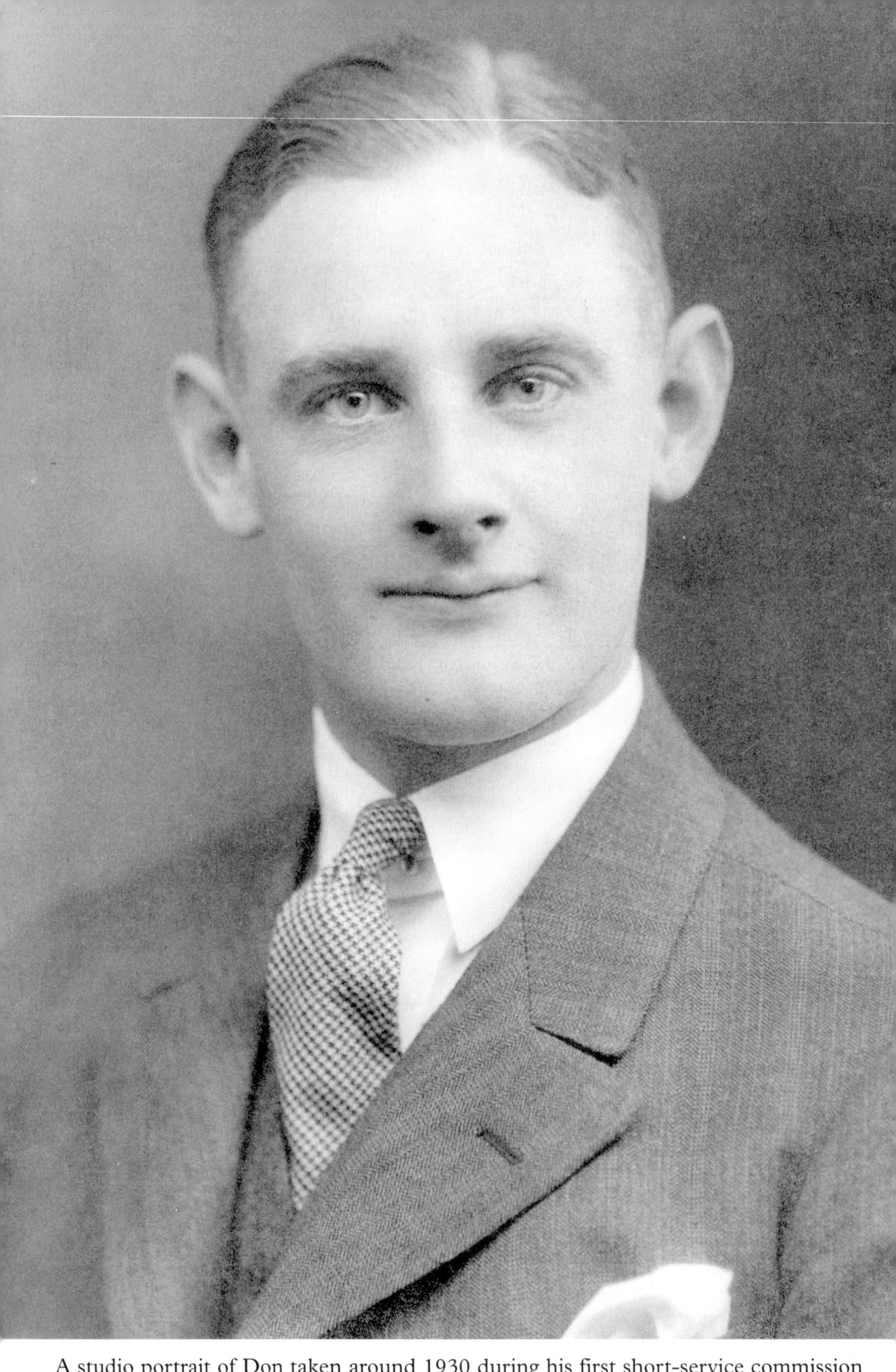

A studio portrait of Don taken around 1930 during his first short-service commission with the RAF. *(Saville Family)*

Bristol Bulldogs of No. 17 Squadron. *(Philip Jarrett)*

A line of Armstrong Whitworth Siskin fighters of No 17 Squadron RAF. Don notes on the reverse of the original 'Machines being filled up. Dual control Siskin in middle'. *(Saville Family)*

Don's Siskin 'being run up in the morning'. *(Saville Family)*

This photo of Don was taken during his first tour with the RAF 1928 - 1932 and is captioned 'Self outside the hangar - the dog belongs to one of the chaps I have in the flight'.
(Saville Family)

Don takes a break in the English Lake District during 1930. *(Saville Family)*

A dual-control trainer version of the Armstrong Whitworth Siskin belonging to No. 17 Squadron RAF. *(Philip Jarrett)*

Flying instructor Don Saville relaxing with his pipe at the Tasmanian Aero Club. The club's flight engineer is seen to Don's right in this photograph taken in 1936. *(Saville Family)*

Don when he was an Airline Captain for Australian National Airlines circa 1938.
(Saville Family)

The ubiquitous Avro Anson. This was truly the RAF's maid-of-all work throughout World War II. The aircraft operated as a light transport, Coastal Command bomber, reconnaissance aircraft, navigational and aircrew trainer and general squadron hack. Over 11,020 were built and Don spent many airborne hours in Ansons during his period with the Ferry Pool early in World War II. *(Philip Jarrett)*

A Hawker Hurricane fitted with long-range fuel tanks. *(Philip Jarrett)*

Two photographs of No. 12 Squadron Vickers Wellington Mk IIs. The 'Wimpy' was the cornerstone of RAF Bomber Command until the arrival of the first heavy bombers.
(Philip Jarrett)

Mk IV Wellington 'B' for Betty named 'Southern Cross' of No. 458 Squadron RAAF seen during the winter of 1941/2 at Holme upon Spalding Moor. Don Saville can be seen second from the left in front of the aircraft. *(Saville Family)*

as he had been on No. 17 Fighter Squadron at Upavon, but with very different aircraft and engines. Instead of controlling a large modern engine of some 150kW (200 h.p.) he might be urging a tiny four-cylinder Henderson motor-cycle engine to lift a light airframe of dubious design and efficiency. But it was still a form of flying and his experience of forced landings and quick decisions was being further developed with each weekend.

In 1933 he was asked to take part in the 1934 MacRobertson Centenary Air Race from London to Melbourne as pilot of an all-Australian plane to be built in Sydney by a group of enthusiasts led by Mr T. D. J. Leach, a lecturer in civil engineering and aeronautics at the University of Sydney. Others involved were Mr L. J. Lynch, lecturer at Sydney Technical College and Mr L. J. R. Jones, also a lecturer in aeronautics at Sydney, who was to be co-pilot.

An All-Australian Aeroplane Fund was set up to accept subscriptions to finance the project. Associations such as the Royal Aeronautical Society and the Royal Empire Society became interested, the press were more than enthusiastic, a women's auxiliary to the fund was set up and the fund-raising activities included teas and cocktail parties held at the university. The first estimates for the cost of the new plane were as low as £2,000 but this was highly optimistic because two engines were necessary and a great deal of special equipment, while the race itself would require fuel and food to be available *en route*.

A later newspaper report said:

> Including cash and labour value contributed by the designers of the plane (Messrs T. D. J. Leech, L. R. Jones and D. T. Saville) and craftsmen, the value of the subscriptions received and acknowledged by the committee now stands at £4,357. Approximately £2,200 is still required.

The *Australian Women's Weekly* announced at the end of June that it would contribute £500 to the All-Australian project and open a fund to raise further finance.

The Saville family report that their father John Saville, was extremely interested in the project and in fact provided two engines and had them delivered to the committee.

The Australian entry for the race was to be a two-engined low-wing monoplane with two seats, fitted with two Harkness Hornet (Sydney-built) four-cylinder engines, each developing about 190 kW (250 h.p.) which seems high, and in fact the engines were eventually not available. The machine's main structure was of steel and particular features were the placing of the engines as far as possible within the wings, the absence of external bracing wires and the provision of retractable undercarriage and automatic pilot. Variable-pitch propellers were not possible because of the high price and the time factor. The building of the plane was undertaken in a shop window of Grace Bros to generate interest, but later transferred to the Tugan Aircraft Company hangar at Mascot.

It was expected that the aeroplane would cruise at 320 k.p.h. (200 m.p.h.) and with fuel tanks of 545–640 litres (120–140 gal), it would have a range of ten hours' continuous flying or stages of some 2,500 km (1,600 miles). The design incorporated powerful electric lights in the wings to assist night landings.

More than fifty years after the Centenary Race it still seems an amazing feat for this aircraft, which was advanced for its day, to be fully designed and built in Australia, even though it was not completed. Moreover, in that same year, 1934, another somewhat similar aircraft was built at Cockatoo Dockyard for Sir Charles Kingsford-Smith, under the supervision of W/Cdr Wackett. This was the *Codock*, a high-wing monoplane with two engines of 130 kW (175 h.p.). It was tested at Mascot and subsequently flown to New Zealand. Kingsford-Smith himself planned to fly a plane in the Centenary Race but was eventually forced out by delays on the flight to Britain in the Lockheed Altair *Lady Southern Cross*.

While the building of the plane at Mascot and the fund-raising activities were proceeding apace, Don Saville and his co-pilot, L. R. Jones, studied the race rules and planned their route. The Australian plane was allotted forty-third place out of sixty-four entries and was entered for both the speed and the handicap sections. In the list of entries its engines were shown as Cirrus Hermes Mark IV, not Harkness as originally planned.

Unhappily, after all the efforts, the plane, called the *Centenary Racer* could not be finished in time. The failure appears to have been attributed to difficulties in the welding of the fuselage but one suspects that financial problems also played a part.

In fact only twenty out of the original sixty-four entries took off from Mildenhall Aerodrome in England on 20 October. The race was won in just under three days by Scott and Campbell-Black in their scarlet De Havilland Comet with the KLM Douglas DC2 of Parmentier and Moll winning the handicap section.

Don must have felt that his flying was being haunted by bad luck. He had missed selection for the Schneider Trophy Race, missed flying a plane on an expedition to find Lasseter's Reef and had now missed taking part in the Centenary Race, which could have made him world famous as an aviator.

However, his luck was about to change; he was soon to return to full-time flying as a career, and not far ahead lay the air war for which he was well prepared by his RAAF and RAF training.

In February 1935 he saw an item among the classified advertisements in a Sydney newspaper. There was a vacancy for a flying instructor with the Australian Aero Club (Tasmanian Section) stationed at Brighton in southern Tasmania. He applied and was appointed with effect from 1 June. He sold the Neutral Bay garage and moved to Tasmania, where he took up residence in the Imperial Hotel in Collins Street, Hobart. He took with him his French Ballot sports car which is well remembered by club members as being very fast when it was going but which often seemed to be in pieces at the club hangar.

The move to Tasmania and the aero club was nearly a disaster, as Don's brother John recounts.

> The day before sailing Don had his car loaded on *Zeelandia*. The next morning I drove him to Darling Harbour from Manly in plenty of time to catch the boat and we got his luggage aboard. He then decided he needed a flying helmet so off we went up the street to a shop opposite Sydney Town Hall. He took longer to buy the helmet than it would have taken me to buy a complete rig-out. I watched the time on the Town Hall clock and tried to get him moving, without a great deal of success. Eventually we got back to the wharf to see that the ship had cast off, with the bow well out in the stream but the stern still within two or three feet of the wharf and a rope ladder hanging over the stern. Don flung the helmet package onto the deck and took a flying leap to clutch the ladder and climb on board.
>
> Fortunately I was the only one of the family to see this dangerous effort, but the passengers and those on the wharf gave him a cheer!

The period with the Aero Club (renamed in 1935 the Tasmanian Aero club, with branches at Launceston and Hobart), was a happy interlude in Don's life. He was an excellent instructor, with a lighthearted personal approach to flying which appealed to both men and women club members. After his arrival it soon became obvious that there was no reason why flying clubs could not be operated profitably in Hobart.

Don engendered great enthusiasm for flying in southern Tasmania and trained many pilots, some of whom proceeded on to commercial flying with airlines. He took to Tasmania and to Tasmanians as they did to him. In writing to his family in New South Wales he said, 'I love this little island and flying over it, but when I'm driving a car on the ground I get this feeling I've got to be careful not to drive off the end!' this view was based on his upbringing amidst the limitless space of the Australian continent.

His stay on what was then rightly termed the 'Apple Isle' was a relatively brief nineteen months, but he made many friends and created an impression as a first-class pilot and a likeable young man. Harry Whelan of Sandy Bay, Hobart, says:

> Everyone loved Don Saville – he had the ability to get on with people. We were all keen on flying and he was the boss! He could be a bit wild at times but he was a good companion and a real character. Because he had been in the services he was something of a disciplinarian, took his job seriously and inspected and signed our flying log books at regular intervals. We admired and respected him as an expert pilot with great experience of flying and skill at aerobatics.

Harry was among the club members who had a close friendship with the new flying instructor and he recalls with amusement the enjoyable social occasions after flying, when they all called in for a drink at the Granton Hotel or at the Horseshoe Inn near Cambridge Aerodrome. In those days, Harry says, most young men were too hard-up to booze very much. 'When you had paid for two beers the hotelier would stand you the third!'

If it was a midday lunch break Don would insist that they had only two shandies to drink. He would say: 'We don't want to draw any unpleasant attention to ourselves, and we want to keep the planes in one piece!' But at a weekend party Don would let his hair down with the others. It was just as well that the aero club had a good relationship with the police and that there were no breathalyser checkpoints in those days as the boys loved to race each other back to Hobart or the Bellerive Ferry Terminal.

Jack Boyes, the owner-manager of the Imperial Hotel, played a trick on Don and Harry on one occasion. It was late at night, and there was a loud hammering on the front door. He came back to tell Don and Harry it was the police, and they took cover quickly in the hotel laundry among the tubs. They had been enjoying a drinking party long after the bar's six o'clock closing time and it was not until some considerable time had elapsed that they realised there was no police raid – it was a joke.

Don's own sense of humour showed up in a note in the club magazine *Plane Torque* for July 1935. 'Southern lady members may not like the look of the new instructor as they have not shown up as yet.'

In October, he commented: 'Mrs F. Jackson and Betty Hogarth are seen at Brighton quite frequently now. Mrs Jackson will be pleased when we go to Cambridge as she lives on that side of the river.'

Of one of the club aircraft which had been newly painted, Don wrote: 'All the old paint has been removed and a fresh coat applied. I believe the engineering staff decided that if any more paint was put on she would have difficulty in climbing at all, but now she simply leaps into the air.' In November 1935 he wrote:

> We want to see more members enrolled next year, especially a few more ladies. The social committee hope to run several functions and without the co-operation of the ladies these are rather difficult. The enthusiasts ought to make it their business to enrol their wives or girlfriends (or someone else's girlfriend for that matter).

In June 1936 *Plane Torque* reported of two of its club members: 'Professor Shatwell of the University of Tasmania has married Miss Betty Hogarth (they have joined up for dual control) – honeymoon in Brisbane.' Don must have thought this a good omen, and of some assistance in encouraging more young ladies to join the club.

Harry Whelan says that about this time Don was complaining about the inadequate salary paid to the flying instructor, which was £7.10.0 (£7.50) a week. Harry and Max Roach, then club secretary, told him that they were not inclined to sympathise, because they themselves earned far less and in those days £5 a week was a good average wage. Harry believes that the reason behind Don's complaint was that Captain Francis, the club's chief flying instructor at Western Junction Airfield near Launceston, was earning £10 a week. Don wanted to be on top in everything he did!

In 1936 dual instruction cost £2.10.0 (£2.50) per hour. Solo flying was £1.10.0. (£1.50) and a pilot taking a passenger was charged £1.15.0. (£1.75) per hour.

Club members quickly became aware of Don's complete confidence in the air and his ability to demonstrate all manoeuvres and aerobatics. Harry Whelan recalls one day when he was sure that his last hour had come because Don was not satisfied with Harry's mild side-slipping coming in to land and showed how it should be done. He violently side-slipped the Moth straight down almost to ground level and then landed so gently that the plane ran only 20 metres.

Most instructors would say, 'Watch,' and then proceed to execute a manoeuvre which would sometimes have to be repeated to ensure success. Don said firmly, 'This is the way to do it,' and promptly did it – perfectly! As a fighter pilot of five years' experience he knew it all – how to correct spins, how to land in crosswinds, how to loop or fly inverted, how to make emergency landings, how to follow another plane and turn inside it to line it up as a target, how to dive down on a ground target. He had done it all and handled his aircraft far better than he handled his sports car!

In April 1936 the club aircraft took part in a search for a missing plane, a Fox Moth on charter from Holyman Airways. Piloted by Alec Barlow, it was taking a party of three or four mining company employees to make a survey of a tin mining claim near Port Davey. It was eventually located in the Melaleuca area where it had landed on softer ground than expected, tipped over on its nose and broken its propeller. Nobody was injured.

Don lashed a spare propeller to the side of a club Moth and flew down to the south-west, where he landed on the beach of Cox Bight. From the beach a party carried the propeller to the scene of the accident. The plane was repaired and Captain Barlow flew it out successfully.

A report in 1936 by a visiting northerner referred to the remarkable results being achieved in the south by Mr D. T. Saville using VH-VAU, an old Cirrus Moth better known as *Clever Mary*, *Rickety Ann* or *Rickety Kate*, for dual instruction. Pageants at both Western Junction and Cambridge were assessed as successful, and both made a small profit.

Aero club members from the 1930s remember a number of amusing stories about Don while he was their flying instructor. On one occasion he was returning from a party at New Town in his French Ballot car and finding his way home by following the tramlines when the police noticed him weaving and stopped him. The policeman recognised Don and offered to drive him home to the Imperial Hotel but he was argumentative and refused. As a result, he spent the night in Hobart Gaol, was fined next day on a drink-driving charge and made the headlines in *The Mercury* newspaper.

In Hadley's Hotel at the time there was a small metal statue which was a great attraction to Don when he was in his cups. He developed the habit of absconding with it on various occasions. The hotel manager noticed its disappearance from its place at the foot of the stairs and if it was not returned would ring up the Imperial Hotel and ask, 'Have you got the statue, Don?' An amicable agreement was then reached for its safe return.

The famous Ballot sports car and its exuberant driver had a serious accident in February 1936 while returning from a party in the Tea Tree area. Don failed to negotiate a bridge near Brighton and broke through the wooden railing, finishing upside down in a creek bed. He was lucky; he was found and taken to the Royal Hobart Hospital with lacerated arms and no bones broken. Another piece of luck was that in the next bed was a gentleman recovering from an operation who turned out to be Mr Ivan Holyman, chairman of the Holyman Shipping Company and Holyman Airways.

Don and Holyman got on well together and Don was offered a pilot's position with Holyman Airways, which was about to be renamed Australian National Airways – the second air service to be so named following the failure of the first A.N.A. of Sir Charles Kingsford-Smith and Charles Ulm and the subsequent death of both in separate flying tragedies. However, his appointment to A.N.A. was delayed until 1937, and in the meantime he continued instructing, demonstrating and organising air pageants at Cambridge, with marked success and enthusiasm.

An indication of the easy friendly atmosphere in the Tasmanian Aero Club during the Saville regime is given by a photograph taken in 1936 of the flying instructor and ground engineer (Mr Eric Nation) sitting together on a cane settee outside the club's hangar at Cambridge. Don, in battle-dress type jacket, sporty tie and fashionable wide-bottomed trousers (Oxford bags) has a pipe in his mouth, sunglasses in his right hand and a half-smile softening his clean-cut features. He looks extremely relaxed, calm and confident, with a strong impression of a pleasant personality. The club engineer, in working overalls, also faces the camera, with no attempt to be anything but himself. This photograph, coupled with one of a club aircraft would have formed an attractive advertisement or part of a brochure for the Tasmanian Aero Club of 1936.

W/Cdr F. R. Graeme-Evans, RAF (Retired), who now lives in Tasmania, south of Hobart, remembers meeting Don Saville as flying instructor in 1936 and being impressed by him as a polite, gentlemanly man with quite a presence about him. Graeme-Evans says that it was evident that Don was doing a job beneath his qualifications but was glad to be back flying again after a break of several years.

Don seemed more like a business executive than a flying instructor in that he was well turned out with neat hair and clothes – in fact, immaculate! Graeme-Evans approached this smart young man with some caution befitting the occasion. The conversation he remembers clearly: 'Excuse me, sir,' he said, 'are you the flying instructor?'

'Don's the name,' said Don.

'Well, can you give me a bit of dual? I already have an A Licence but haven't flown for some time and want to brush up my flying ready to join the RAAF next year at Point Cook.'

'Delighted to help you,' replied Don. 'I was in the RAAF myself in 1927 and haven't long been out of the RAF.'

Graeme-Evans says he was not sure at the time whether Don was an Englishman or an Australian from his speech, but he found him a charming chap and a first-class instructor.

They got into an old Gypsy Moth and Don let Graeme-Evans take off. They flew around the Cambridge area for a while and then the pupil was allowed to make a couple of landings on the gravel runway. Graeme-Evans says that the second landing was rather bumpy and he apologised to Don.

Don was reassuring and joked: 'Oh, that wasn't too bad for a start – when you can walk away, the landing's O.K.!' They later had a drink together at the Horseshoe Inn and it was arranged that Graeme-Evans should come back for two days just before Christmas to continue the retraining.

On the second of these two flights they went south-westwards over the Wellington range to Federation Peak and Port Davey, where Don suggested they look in at Lake Pedder on the way back, a remote beauty spot then accessible only to airmen and bushwalkers. They landed on the beach of firm pinkish-white sand and together, in glorious isolation, enjoyed the views over the lake and the Franklin range. This beach and lake are now submerged beneath the waters of the enlarged Lake Pedder.

At the end of the flight, Don said, 'That's a better landing – the best of luck in the RAAF.' Graeme-Evans asked if he had any special faults to correct, but Don answered, 'No, go on as you are – but remember that you have only just started!'

W/Cdr Graeme-Evans went on to serve in the Lysanders, Tomahawks and Hurricanes of army co-operation squadrons in the Second World War. He was shot down several times and eventually became a PoW in the Western Desert and was transferred to Germany. He was the sole survivor of a group of thirteen Australian pilots serving in the RAF army co-operation squadrons.

CHAPTER NINE

Airline Captain (1937–9)

The Tasmanian Aero Club members said farewell to their Hobart flying instructor on 9 January 1937 with warm tributes to his prowess in the air and on social occasions. He received a farewell gift of a travel clock in a leather case with the inscription: 'To Mr D. T. Saville (Instructor) from Members of the Tasmanian Aero Club (S.S.) Farewell 9-1-37.'

He completed three hundred and thirty-six flying hours with the Club on January 10 when he instructed a pupil on the DH Moth VH-ULM. His total flying time had now reached 1,154 hours 50 minutes, so Ivan Holyman was employing an experienced pilot with both RAF and RAAF training, probably the best in the world, paid for by the taxpayers of Great Britain and Australia. The appointment was good business for A.N.A. and a forward move for Don at a time when there were more pilots than aircraft and airlines requiring their services.

On 12 January Don made his first flight with A.N.A. as an instructor at the company's flying school in Melbourne. He was employed for a fortnight on pupil instruction, flying Moths and a Percival Gull.

On 25 January came the big moment: his first flight as co-pilot of an A.N.A. DC2, with passengers, from Melbourne to Hobart. In those days the Bass strait crossing had a flavour of adventure about it, owing to the recent loss of two DH86 airliners and also to the fact that very varied weather conditions, including turbulence, could be expected on the run to Hobart over the mountainous island. It seemed fitting to Don that his first passenger flights should be to and from Hobart, which he had left only a fortnight previously. The new airline pilot, in his smart A.N.A. uniform, felt some pleasure in his promotion to a more structured life of routes and schedules. He had not yet become aware of the boredom of long flights over monotonous terrain which resulted from the low cruising speeds of airliners in the 1930s. The Hobart flight took the DC2 two hours and twenty minutes, compared with less than one hour by jet today.

The return journey to Melbourne next day, took two hours and thirty minutes, and again it was uneventful in the summer weather. Don resumed instruction for two days and then received a solo assignment on 30 January 1937 to fly the Percival Gull to Adelaide to pick up press photographs of the Fourth Test Match and bring them back to Melbourne. These two flights took eight hours and Don enjoyed some personal satisfaction when the photographs appeared in the Melbourne papers next day.

In February he received further training as an airline pilot by making a number of solo test flights in a DH89, a twin-engined biplane designed for one pilot and up to eight passengers. After the regulation take-offs, circuits and landings, Don received an endorsement to his pilot's licence, allowing him to fly with passengers in this type of aircraft. Thus equipped he was promptly placed as regular pilot on the DH89 'island run': Essendon (Melbourne Airport)-King Island-Wynyard-Launceston-Flinders Island and back to Launceston for the night. Next day the route was flown in reverse back to Melbourne. This route took between five and six hours' flying time in each direction.

Flying as a captain with responsibility for his own eight passengers in a DH89 (Dragon Rapide) marked a new stage in Don's career. He had a slight feeling of power and satisfaction as ground staff and passengers treated him with deference. It did not turn his head because he knew only too well that the air, like the sea, can be a treacherous element and that the safety of his aircraft and passengers depended upon him and his mastery of the skills of aviation. In the 1930s flying aids were few – pilots were largely dependent on their own resources and they were still learning while they flew. To some extent airline pilots were still pioneers in aviation and the wise and sensible aviators knew this and survived. Others, less fortunate or less skilful, had accidents. Don was totally positive in his outlook and he was determined that he would continue to develop his skills and enjoy the challenge of natural forces in the atmosphere.

At the end of February he flew his DH89 and passengers to Hobart where an engine change became necessary during the weekend. Don did not waste time. He rang up Harry Whelan and invited him to help entertain two A.N.A. air hostesses. Harry was happy to do so!

In mid-March Don was transferred to Adelaide for the Broken Hill run. At Parafield Airfield he made take-offs and landings for licence endorsement on three aircraft types which he would be flying on the local routes. These machines were a DH84 (Dragon), a Short Scion and a Monospar.

Using these three aircraft types and sometimes a DH89 Don flew passengers to Renmark, Mildura and Broken Hill, and also to Kangaroo

Island, with two longer return trips, Parafield-Mt Gambier-Melbourne, involving flights of eight or nine hours for the round trip.

April brought new destinations and longer hours, with a Douglas DC2 trip as co-pilot from Adelaide to Ceduna and Forrest, spending the night there and flying next day to Kalgoorlie and Perth. The DC2s carried an air hostess as well as the captain and co-pilot, so that passengers were beginning to be looked after in their flights as they are today. The air hostesses were not supposed to be chosen for their looks but in fact they often were and this added something to the glamour of flying.

In the Western Australian capital Don spent ten days as a spare pilot for the east-west run across the continent but was not required to fly. May brought a return to Adelaide and flights on a variety of routes from Parafield, then a move back to Melbourne and the 'island run' to Tasmania.

June 1937 brought a very special and enjoyable job. He and the A.N.A. Monospar were chartered to Australian Aerial Medical Services for an aerial survey flight with a doctor to examine new bases and routes for the Flying Doctor service. This work was interesting, for it meant flying over new scenery, landing at remote cattle and sheep stations and meeting interesting people in the outback. Don and the doctor enjoyed the informality and variety of their flights together.

When he flew the Monospar back to Adelaide after the survey had been completed, he was placed again on the Adelaide-Melbourne route via Mt Gambier or on one occasion via Renmark, Broken Hill and Mildura to Essendon.

A.N.A. Pilots were not lulled into over-confidence by remaining on one aircraft type or on one particular route for too long. In mid-July Don was sent to Sydney to gain experience and licence endorsement on the DH86, a four-engined passenger bi-plane developed in Britain for use by Qantas on the Royal Mail international air route from the UK to Australia, on the section between Singapore and Sydney. Ivan Holyman had bought several DH86s. This plane had a rather doubtful reputation because in spite of its comfort and relative quietness in flight, several had disappeared or crashed with loss of life, notably *Miss Hobart* of Holyman Airways in October 1934 off Wilson's Promontory and *Loina*, also of Holyman's, in October 1935 near King Island.

After some modifications, however, Qantas and A.N.A. continued to operate these aircraft successfully without further trouble and during the Second World War they were used as Red Cross aircraft in the Middle East before and after El Alamein. An ex-A.N.A. pilot (later Ansett senior captain), Captain John Presgrave, was one of the team of pilots flying the DH86 as an air ambulance in North Africa.

Captain Harry Purvis, writing in *Outback Airman*, says that the wings of the DH86 used to flex when lateral control was used, but it was much more alarming when the wings iced up badly and flexed with it. Captain Presgrave, who probably knows the DH86 better than any other man living today remembers that the wings moved quite a bit and the whole fuselage would twist under stress. The brakes were inefficient as the brake shoes tended to glaze and lose grip. Bad weather could cause wing flutter and ailerons had to be used delicately – engines preferably were used instead.

However, Captain Presgrave considers that the plane flew reasonably well at the time and because airfields were of grass it was always possible to take off or land into wind. If it was loaded too heavily it would swing to the right. If it was loaded properly and flown well, however, it was fine. But he did not like flying it at night.

The DH86 Gypsy engines were reliable and safety was improved by having four. Captain Peter Gibbes flew as co-pilot with Don on DH86s in 1937, and says that after the modifications they regarded the aircraft highly. It could maintain flight at about 1,200 metres (4,000 ft) on three engines. However, the DC2 was a giant step forward and the DC3 even better because the undercarriages could be raised and lowered automatically and feathering propellers enabled the machine to fly on one engine in an emergency.

Captain Gibbes found Don a good friend and companion in the air and on the ground. In the air he remembers that Don smoked incessantly and was fond of telling somewhat outrageous stories. He was a natural as a pilot and generous in giving the co-pilot opportunities to take off and land on suitable occasions. Gibbes describes him as convivial, one of the boys – a short, handsome and jovial man who loved booze and girls and was a great raconteur.

When asked if Don had any air hostess friends, John Presgrave pointed out that a captain cannot play with a hostess in the evening and then crack the whip next day on the aircraft. But he added that with other ladies it was different – the world was Don's oyster!

Don flew the DH86 with confidence and made a series of flights during July on the Melbourne-Sydney route via Canberra and/or Wagga. He apparently took the DH86 in his stride and made no complaints about it.

In August he was flying DH89s on the 'island run' to northern Tasmania, and at the end of the month was co-pilot on DC2s on the Melbourne to Launceston and Hobart route. During September 1937 his log book reveals that he was then based regularly at Melbourne and flying Melbourne (Essendon)-Mildura-Broken Hill and back with a Dragon Rapide carrying up to eight passengers.

The 'Remarks' column in Don's log book for 17 and 18 September shows three words: 'Dust storm effort'. In fact, for those two days he hit the headlines in the national newspapers and in *The Barrier Miner* of Broken Hill. The latter announced in a large headline: 'Air Liner Missing – Fails to Reach Broken Hill – Big Dust Storm!' The report went on to say:

> In a terrible dust storm, the Australian National Airways plane *Marika*, flying between Melbourne and Broken Hill, disappeared this morning. At a late hour tonight it is still missing.
>
> The machine, a DH Rapide, was due at Broken Hill at 11.00 a.m. It carried one pilot – Mr D. Saville – and there were no passengers.

The plane had left Essendon at 07.30 hours and called at Mildura fifteen minutes late after being delayed by headwinds. The weather at Broken Hill at the scheduled time of arrival was hurricane-force winds, which bent some galvanised iron telephone posts, and whipped up a dust storm which brought zero visibility. The wind was so violent and solid with particles that it blasted the paint off the sides of cars in Broken Hill.

The A.N.A. flying superintendent in Melbourne hoped that the pilot had been able to make a landing near some isolated homestead and was remaining on the ground until the weather cleared. Meanwhile a dozen cars left Broken Hill to check a report that the plane had been forced down 13 km (8 miles) north-east of the town. A search by air was arranged for next day or when the weather moderated. The search machines were to be an aero club Moth piloted by Mr Collins and a Fox Moth piloted by Mr Annear, an A.N.A. Flying Doctor pilot, who had been trained in Tasmania at the aero club and knew Don personally.

The missing plane and pilot were found early next morning. Don had encountered blinding dust storm conditions from 27 metres (90 ft) above ground to 2,700 metres (9,000 ft). Unable to see Broken Hill he wisely flew away and made a landing on the edge of the storm to check his position at the Topar Hotel on the Topar Flats. From there he made a fresh attempt to reach Broken Hill by following the railway line but this proved impossible in the conditions. He decided to make a second landing when he glimpsed a water hole and sent a radio message to Adelaide that he believed he was 16 km (10 miles) south-east of the Broken Hill aerodrome. The message was not received but when he was found by rescuers in cars at 03.00 hours Don and the DH89 were 24 km (15 miles) south-east of Broken Hill and near Redan Station. He had made a successful landing in hazardous conditions of violent wind and 100 metre visibility.

Don was taken to Redan Station and made welcome by Mr and Mrs Colley. At 08.05 hours he took off again in clearing conditions and landed twenty minutes later at Broken Hill aerodrome. He told reporters that he had not been in danger and had ample fuel. The machine was equipped for blind flying and could be flown blind until the petrol was exhausted. The only trouble was that a forced landing in open paddocks could not be perfectly safe because of the risk of potholes. He said that if he had had passengers he would have returned to Mildura.

When asked what he now hoped to do, Don said, 'Be back in Melbourne in time for the football final.' He was to be disappointed in this as he left on schedule at 11.30 hours and was not due in Essendon until 16.30 hours.

He made light of a very serious situation, in which he had saved the plane and himself by a second skilful landing during the dust storm to avoid running out of fuel. He had correctly stayed with the plane rather than risk getting lost in a search for a farmhouse or a road. He was not amused by one report in the press, however, which said that the rescue party had found the pilot asleep in the plane, as though this were a fault instead of the natural result of exhaustion after flying for some hours in a terrifying dust storm, isolated from the ground and in peril of being unable to land before the plane's fuel ran out.

Early in October Don did circuits and landings on a DC2 for senior pilot endorsement on this type of aircraft and then flew as captain with a co-pilot on the long Brisbane-Adelaide run via Sydney and Melbourne. This route involved some eight or nine hours' flying time, and with stops on the ground for refuelling and changing passengers it made a very long and tiring day for the aircrew. Don told his family that on one occasion he was so tired on reaching Brisbane that he could not summon the energy to work the brakes. He allowed the plane to come gently to a halt at the far end of the runway before taxiing to the passenger terminal and the comfort of a night's rest.

There was another side to the long journey by air. Don had now recognised the problem of boredom in flying and occasionally wrote letters to his parents and family while the automatic pilot was engaged. In good weather he could sit back, relax, listen to the regular drone of the engines and leave the co-pilot in charge. He had the ability, when he wished to do so, to switch from flying and leave the job to the co-pilot. It was perhaps an illustration of his own complete confidence while in the air, or an instinctive way of giving others the experience of command.

On 29 December 1937 Don encountered bad weather while flying DH86 VH-VSW from Sydney to Wagga. Wind gusts caused a heavy landing, which damaged the undercarriage. He obtained another DH89 to continue the flight to Canberra with his passengers but on landing the weather forced them to spend the night there before completing the route schedule to Melbourne.

After a week's leave he resumed his duties in January 1938 flying DH86s on the Melbourne-Tasmanian islands-Launceston run with an occasional Melbourne-Launceston-Melbourne route on the new DC3 aircraft developed from the DC2. This was to prove the most successful twin-engined passenger or freight monoplane in the world; some examples are still flying fifty years later. Don enjoyed piloting both the Douglas aircraft types – which in fact had very similar flying characteristics.

In February 1938 he had his annual leave of three weeks. It was a chance to visit Eurella, his brother John's property in the Capertee valley south-east of Rylstone and adjoining the tiny settlement of Glen Alice. It comprised 1,400 ha (3,500 acres) of rich volcanic and silt soils, set in a valley with beautiful scenery and steep sandstone cliffs as natural boundaries. With an average rainfall of 635 mm (25 in) and the Nile creek running into the Capertee, the land also had good-quality underground water readily available less than 6 metres (20 ft) below the surface. John and his wife Mollie had two baby girls, a herd of Hereford cattle and a flock of Corriedale sheep to show off to uncle Don, who revelled in the tranquil beauty of the farmland and took part eagerly in any jobs he was given to do.

One day when they were stripping lucerne (alfalfa) there was a violent thunderstorm with drenching rain. John and a farm worker struggled back to the homestead, soaked to the skin, but Don was not with them. After the storm was over he arrived home perfectly dry – never lacking in initiative he had got inside the stripper itself to escape the torrential rain.

The holiday passed all too quickly. He was always a favourite guest at Eurella, and was fond of spoiling his nieces with gifts but they were too young at the time to remember their airman uncle later in their lives.

In March Don was reminded of his missed opportunity back in 1932 to seek the elusive Lasseter gold reef with his father. A.N.A. DH86 *Loila* was chartered by another mining expedition (led by a Mr Cutlack) and the plane was flown by Captain Harry Purvis with Dick Probyn as co-pilot. Don would have dearly liked to be chosen for the trip but in the event the expedition did little more than photograph a long ridge of sandstone in the supposed area of the gold reef and no mining development took place.

June gave Don further experience in making emergency landings with a civilian passenger plane. On Sunday, 5 June, he took DH89 UXZ with passengers from Melbourne to Sydney without incident. However, on the return journey he and a mechanic in the same Dragon

Rapide encountered exceptionally bad visibility near Melbourne and decided to make a landing outside the blanketed area. He radioed Essendon before landing and then put the aircraft down in a paddock in flat farmland at Dalmore, 10 km (6 miles) from Kooweerup. It was a sound precaution to do that rather than risk searching for Essendon with the Dandenong Range to be avoided amidst the cloud cover, hills which later caused the loss of DC2 *Kyeema* in October while the pilot was seeking Essendon and flying in dense cloud, unable to get bearings from the aerodrome. Don and his mechanic spent the night at the farm of a Mr Burhop, close to Kooweerup, and took off safely next morning for Essendon.

July was notable for bad weather conditions on the 'islands run', and the four-engined DH86 VVB met gales over Bass Strait, which caused some delays to flight schedules. Don enjoyed fighting the elements and his jovial confidence in turbulent conditions spread to his crew and passengers. If the captain is cheerful and says his multi-engined plane is just made for this bumpy weather it certainly takes away some of the tension from anxious passengers. A few years later some anxious aircrews in Don's Wellingtons and Stirlings were to feel the same relief in bad weather or amidst enemy flak because of their skipper's calm confidence, which somehow spread throughout an aircraft, civil or military.

In July and August the log book shows that Don was now more frequently scheduled to pilot the DC2s on the Melbourne-Adelaide route (between five and five and a half hours return) and DH86s on the Melbourne-Wagga-Canberra-Sydney route and back (taking between eight and nine and a half hours flying).

Early in August he had a well-earned week of skiing at Mt Buffalo in the Victorian Alps. He had had little skiing practice since the RAF leaves spent in Switzerland with Gordon Richards and other friends.

September 1938 brought a change of base and routes. He was transferred to Perth, and arranged to go there by ship from Melbourne. This allowed him a relaxing sea voyage of nearly a week and he was able to take as much luggage as he wished. His flying hours had now reached the 3,000 mark and the impending war in Europe was just a shadow in the background to dampen his enthusiasm for his civilian flying career and the future. However, A.N.A. pilots and crew were becoming dissatisfied with their pay and service conditions, which were far worse than in some other airlines, particularly international lines such as K.N.I.L.M.

Ivan Holyman, the skilful administrator of A.N.A., was said to be out of touch with the practical side of flying, and to regard pilots as little different from bus drivers. This did not endear him to his aircrews, who also were conscious of friction between ground engineers and themselves over relative salaries. Comedians on the staff were apt to refer to the Holyman company flag as representing the 'white flag of starvation on the red flag of slavery'. The pilots had additional concerns in that they rightly believed that the navigational aids at Melbourne and Sydney were totally inadequate for bad weather conditions and they were concerned that the railway line taking coal to Bunnerong power station actually went across Mascot aerodrome and delayed air traffic.

It took an accident involving an Ansett aircraft with a coal train at Sydney and the *Kyeema* disaster at Melbourne in October 1938 before the problems were urgently attended to by the authorities. The railway was rerouted outside the Sydney aerodrome area and Lorenz radio beacons and ultra-short-wave radio were installed at major Australian airports. The A.N.A. Douglas aircraft were already equipped to deal with these new navigation and communication aids.

During September Don commenced operating from Perth by flying the long route through Kalgoorlie and Ceduna to Adelaide, returning the next day. These flights took eight to nine hours each way – a long day for pilots and passengers even on the DC2s which were used for flying over the Nullabor Plain, although stops for refuelling and meals helped break the monotony.

In December 1938 Don's father, the redoubtable John Saville, works manager of the Commonwealth Portland Cement Company, retired after thirty-five years' service to the company and the Portland community. He was the guest of honour at a dinner on 6 December 1938 attended by forty-five members of the staff and his successor, Mr McAskill. Mr J. Symonds, the general manager of the company, proposed the toast. The following extract is taken from the *Lithgow Mercury* of 8 December.

> Mr Symonds said that in its early days the company experienced great difficulties and it was not until Mr Saville took the reins that it began to forge ahead. From the day he took control of the Works thirty-five years ago it had never looked back. His success had been due to his sound knowledge of the work, his good judgment, his extraordinary capacity for hard work, and his ability to lead men.
>
> Mr Saville's career was a lesson in patience, perseverance and resolution that might well be learned by anyone who desired to achieve something worthwhile. Mr Symonds hoped that the years to come would be happily spent by Mr and Mrs Saville; that they would live long to enjoy the years of his retirement. One of the

finest examples that had been set by Mr Saville, concluded Mr Symonds, was his loyalty to the company.

Eight other speakers added their tributes and one with many years of service to the company said, 'I have never seen a more cool-headed man in a breakdown than Mr Saville, and the ability he invariably displayed on those occasions won the admiration of everyone concerned.' Don and his brothers could well have taken inspiration and encouragement for their own lives from these deserved tributes to their father.

From October 1938 to January 1939 Don was stationed at Perth to fly the DC2 run to Adelaide and back. He took three weeks' leave from mid-January to 14 February and then resumed the long flights.

On 18 May 1939 he had engine trouble on his DC2 and returned to Adelaide after only fifteen minutes. The repairs to DC2 VH USY gave him the opportunity of flying another DC2 on an unusual flight from Adelaide to Tennant Creek, a gold mining centre in the Northern Territory, and then back to Melbourne – a journey involving seventeen hours and fifteen minutes' flying.

After a few trips between Melbourne and Adelaide he was again back on the trans-Nullabor route from Perth to Adelaide, each through trip involving between eight to ten and a half hours flying.

On 15 July Don piloted DC2 VH USY for his last flight as an A.N.A. captain from Adelaide to Perth on a route taking ten hours and fifty-five minutes. He then resigned from A.N.A. His log book was certified correct by C. H. Scott, operations superintendent for Australian National Airways and by A. B. Corbett for the Director General of Civil Aviation.

Chapter Ten

Ferry Pilot and Test Pilot (1939–41)

It is known from his statements to his friends that Don Saville left Australia for Europe in August 1939 with the original intention of joining the Dutch airline K.L.M. and continuing his career as a commercial pilot under better conditions of salary and service than those pertaining in A.N.A. However, the inevitability of war was in his mind and he was determined that if it came he would be in it from the outset as a pilot in the RAF now that he was no longer in the RAAF Citizens' Air Force Reserve. The outbreak of war on 3 September 1939 resolved this issue and on landing in Britain he applied immediately to the Air Ministry for a commission. His official record of service in the RAF shows that he was granted a commission as pilot officer (on probation) in the General Duties Branch of the Royal Air Force Volunteer Reserve for the duration of hostilities, with effect from 27 September 1939.

As he had previously held a short-service commission from 1928 to 1932 with the final rank of flying officer, it seems somewhat ungenerous of the RAF to have appointed this very experienced volunteer as a pilot officer. Nevertheless, his posting to No. 2 Ferry Pool, RAF Station Filton, near Bristol was obviously a sensible use of his experience and recognition that at thirty-six he was too old for service as a fighter or bomber pilot on operational squadrons.

Flying duties started immediately and on 28 September 1939 he flew from Filton in a Wellington bomber with F/Lt Jackson, commanding officer of No. 2 Ferry Pilots Pool as pilot, to view the local district and camouflage. The buildings of the Bristol Aircraft Company and Filton Aerodrome were already disguised by camouflage so that they would be difficult for enemy eyes to recognise from the air. The camouflage was equally difficult for friendly eyes until they were thoroughly familiar with the locality.

Later that day Don flew the same Wellington from Filton to Hullavington – a short flight of forty-five minutes. He flew alone in the aircraft, as was the usual custom in ferrying by a ferry pool pilot.

On 30 September he was navigator in a ferry pool Anson on three flights to deliver and collect ferry pilots: Filton-Southampton, Southampton-Little Rissington and Little Rissington-Brooklands. The old Brooklands Motor Racing Track at Weybridge had been taken over by the Vickers firm for its factories, manufacturing and assembling the Wellington bombers equipped with two Bristol Pegasus engines. Don was landed at Brooklands to fly a new Wellington from the factory to Mildenhall. His delivery task completed, the Anson collected him from Mildenhall and returned to Filton – still on the same day. This was typical of a day's work in the ferry pool at that time.

On joining the ferry pool Don had been issued with a new RAF log book, and the summary for the two days in September 1939 shows that he had a total flying time of six hours. The entry was signed by J. S. Young, Flying Officer, and F/Lt Jackson, OC No. 2 Ferry Pilots' Pool. On the same page was this note in Don's handwriting:

> Note: Flying log books, Nos. 1 – 2 – 3 covering all flying from 18-5-1927 to 15-7-39 deposited at Bank of New South Wales during period of hostilities for safe custody after being inspected by the Air Ministry and CO, No. 2 Ferry Pilots' Pool, Filton.
>
> (Signed) D. T. Saville P/O.
> 1-10-39.
> Total to date 8046.35 hours.
> Flying only in RAF since 28-7-39: 6.00 hours.

In 1939 the Ferry Pilots' Pool was staffed mainly by experienced pilots who were too old for operations. Later it included many pilots from operational squadrons who had completed a full tour of operations with Bomber, Fighter or Coastal Command. In 1940 it began to include survivors – the very few pilots returning from squadrons decimated or wiped out completely in France or Belgium in the Battle of France.

Ferry pilots acquired high flying skills, even when they did not possess them at first. Within their ranks were various grades, denoting those who could fly a few types, many types and all types of aircraft. They usually flew alone in planes which were required to be moved from A to B, with maps on knees or in one hand, control in the other, map reading their way across and around the British Isles or flying across the Channel to France without maps. (When ferrying to France in 1940 aircraft were stripped of maps at Tangmere.)

At the end of 1939, No. 2 Ferry Pool included fifty-one pilots, of whom twenty-seven were qualified to fly all types of aircraft and were referred to as the 'hotshots'. P/O Donald Saville was very clearly a 'hotshot'! Thirteen of the pilots were from Air Transport Auxiliary (ATA), the civilian organisation set up in 1939 by Gerard d'Erlanger. Throughout the war the ferrying of service aircraft was done by both the RAF Ferry Pilots' Pool, later formed into Ferry Command, and the ATA using both men and women civilian pilots.

During October 1939 Don was flying almost every day and on some days made up to ten flights. Taking 11 October as a typical example, the day's work was as follows:

1. Don flew a Henley from Filton doing local landings.
2. He then flew a Spitfire from Filton to Shawbury and then on to Cosford. The same Spitfire was then flown back to Shawbury.
3. From Shawbury he was flown in a Blenheim piloted by S/Ldr Washbrook to Woodford.
4. At Woodford he flew another Blenheim by himself back to Shawbury.
5. S/Ldr Washbrook flew him from Shawbury to Hullavington in a Blenheim.
6. At Hullavington he was pilot for an Anson with passengers (probably ferry pilots) back to Filton.

Most of these flights were short, varying from ten to fifty-five minutes, with a total flying time of three hours and thirty minutes. However, they involved making at least sixteen take-offs and landings while flying four types of plane – Henley, Spitfire, Blenheim and Anson.

Life was never dull for ferry pilots and the flying of different aircraft types was extremely demanding of their physical and mental skills. In Britain the weather proved to be one of the most serious hazards for ferrying work, and accidents also took their toll. By the end of the month Don had flown sixty-three hours and thirty-five minutes overall while at the ferry pool and handled twelve different types of aircraft, from fighters to medium bombers and transport planes.

November 1939 saw some extension in the ferry programme, with further types of aircraft to be mastered – Hereford, Oxford and Lysander – in addition to the delivery of four new Wellingtons to an operational squadron at Marham and one Wellington to Honington.

But the delivery which Don found most interesting was taking a Hurricane to a fighter squadron in France. He flew first from Filton to Tangmere, where his maps were removed and he received instructions to fly towards Selsey Bill on the south coast just south of Chichester, and thence on a calculated bearing to cross the French coast at Le Treport.

Another pilot who was ferrying in 1940 recalls that the verbal instructions were:

> If you can see chalk on your left turn to the right and if you see sand on your right you are to turn left until you reach the point where the chalk cliffs and the sand meet – that is your crossing point and you then fly up the River Somme until you see a tall cathedral spire. This is Amiens, and adjoining this some three miles distant is your first destination at Amiens-Glisy (airfield).

Don spent the night at Glisy and next day flew to another airfield further inland, which was the base of 73 Squadron RAF, a Hurricane squadron, which with No. 1 Fighter Squadron, provided the fighter cover for the bomber squadrons (Fairey Battles) of the Advanced Air Striking Force (AASF). Eight other fighter squadrons were attached to the British Expeditionary Force as an air component. While this was the period of the phoney war between the armies it is not always realised that the opposing air forces, were engaged almost daily in actual fighting and probing each other's defences with reconnaissance aircraft. The Hurricane flown in by Don was a replacement for one of the fighters being lost daily by the RAF fighter squadrons. Don was able to sense the thrill of action and talk to some of the young pilots who were frequently engaged in dog fights with Me.109s. 'Cobber' Kain, the New Zealand air ace, was one of the fighter pilots with 73 Squadron. On 28 November Don returned on a 24 Squadron Dragon Rapide from Reims to Amiens, and then by a British Airways Electra 10A from Amiens to Hendon.

He tackled his ferry work with renewed zest in December after experiencing the atmosphere of air warfare in France. On the first six days of the month he was extremely busy flying mainly Whitleys, Wellingtons and Blenheims to and from maintenance units and operational squadrons as well as two Hurricanes and a Spitfire, which he delighted in for the change they provided.

Unfortunately he developed a stomach ulcer and was off flying duties from 8 December to 13 March, receiving treatment at Southmead Hospital, Bristol, and then in the RAF hospital at Torquay. He returned to a period of intense activity for the ferrying services of the RAF and ATA.

The year 1940 was one of crises for Britain and her allies, with the RAF suffering disastrous losses among the Battle and Blenheim bomber squadrons and the Gladiator and Hurricane fighter squadrons. The main disasters occurred on 10–15 May when the RAF lost more than half its available aircraft in Europe. The Dunkirk evacuation followed and with it the controversy over whether or not the RAF had done a proper job in defending the ships and boats engaged in the withdrawal.

Don's log book for March, April, May and June 1940 is an exciting record of the accelerated movements of service aircraft throughout Britain in reaction to the final collapse of the armies and air force units in France and Belgium. Replacement planes were flown to the continent and to the fighter squadrons and medium and heavy bomber squadrons in Britain, which were brought up to full strength by tremendous work in the factories and maintenance units, and by the ferry pilots. It can be accepted that what Don was doing was typical of what was being done by scores of other ferry pilots.

On 15 March Don flew a Hurricane replacement across the Channel to Glisy airfield near Amiens again, returning to Hendon as a passenger on a British Airways Electra. The rest of the month was spent mainly in moving Hudsons, Whitleys and Blenheims from Speke M.U. near Liverpool to other airfields in central and southern England.

April followed a similar pattern, until the 7th When Don was sent by rail to Helensburgh at the mouth of the River Clyde in Scotland to pick up a Lerwick flying boat. This twin-engined reconnaissance aircraft from 209 Squadron (Oban), a type with an unenviable reputation for poor handling characteristics, was probably being returned to the makers Saunders-Roe for repairs. Don flew it with some crew members from Scotland to Cowes, Isle of Wight, in two hours and fifty minutes. Not many ferry pilots were qualified to deal with flying boats but Don had had considerable experience flying Southamptons while on his short-service commission from 1928 to 1932, and the Lerwick did not worry him! It failed under service conditions, however, and was withdrawn from squadron use.

On 17 April Don again went over to France, this time with a Lysander for the army co-operation squadrons in the air component. He flew direct from Andover to Amiens-Glisy without the usual call at Tangmere. The return journey was to Hendon with a DH86 of 24 Transport Squadron – one of the four-engined biplanes with which he had been so familiar in A.N.A.

At the end of April Nos. 1 and 2 Ferry Pilots' Pools amalgamated to become No. 4 (Continental) Ferry Pilots' Pool and the base was moved from Filton to Cardiff. The number of aircraft types flown by Don since the war began had now reached nineteen.

May 1940, the month of the heaviest losses in RAF history, opened well for Don, with an enjoyable flight in a Gladiator biplane fighter from Brize Norton to the Isle of Man for refuelling, then further fuel stops at West Freugh and Prestwick, before finally landing almost regretfully at his destination Turnhouse (near Edinburgh), where the aircraft was to join 603 Squadron, equipped with both Gladiators and Spitfire Is. Although Don was long experienced in flying multi-engined airliners and bombers, like most pilots, he revelled in the quick response of a fighter and the Gladiator is known to have been a delight to fly. A few days later on 7 May he had a complete contrast – another flying boat! He flew in a ferry pool Anson from Cardiff to Rochester, landing on the small airfield looking down on the River Medway and Short Brothers aircraft factory, above Rochester Bridge. Moored in the river opposite the works was a massive Sunderland flying boat – the military aircraft developed from the famous Empire flying boats of the early 1930s.

Transport was provided from the airfield to the riverside factory, where Don collected the necessary papers and some crew members. He was taken by launch to the Sunderland and then went through the full cockpit drill and the starting and testing of each engine. When he was satisfied he sent the crew to take-off positions and ordered the line attached to the buoy to be released. With engine and propellers turning over slowly he took the ship of the air to mid-river and proceeded upstream towards Maidstone because the wind that day was from the north-east and take-off would be over the bridge.

Just south of Cuxton and its cement works and chalk quarries, the Sunderland was turned into the wind for the take-off run towards Rochester Bridge along this conveniently straight section of river. Gathering speed it slapped into the low waves and then got slowly up on to the steps of the hull and lifted off imperceptibly almost opposite the Short works. Those crew members who could see ahead looked somewhat anxiously at the bridge, which was soon revealed as three bridges close together – a road bridge and two railway bridges – as the great machine banked slightly left and swept safely over, passing the adjacent ancient Norman castle and cathedral on the right-hand side. Don had time for a quick glance only at the city and then turned the plane to follow the River Medway eastward to its estuary with the River Thames, keeping well away from the naval dock-yard and barracks at the adjoining Medway towns of Chatham and Gillingham.

Taking a route just off the east coast they journeyed northwards and turned inland to cross between Edinburgh and Glasgow. Don made a quiet and safe landing on the River Clyde after a flight of four hours and forty-five minutes. He returned from Glasgow to Cardiff by train and did his next ferry duty on 10 May, the opening day of the German *blitzkrieg* against Holland, Belgium, Luxemburg and France.

The ferry pool pilots' day started with an urgent request for Fairey Battle reserves to be flown from Brize Norton and Andover to France.

Don flew an Anson from Cardiff to Brize Norton and then to Andover, where they received instructions to proceed to Reims. A pool Anson also went to Reims and collected the ferry pilots, returning in darkness with Don as pilot to Tangmere, where they spent the night.

The party returned to Cardiff on 11th May knowing already that momentous and terrible land and air battles were taking place on the continent. Early on the 12th Don flew from Cardiff to Cosford in preparation for taking further reinforcements to France.

The same morning he flew a Blenheim to Andover and on to Reims. Later that day he flew a pool Anson with a party of ferry pilots from Reims directly back to Cardiff. This flight was made after dark for security reasons and took two hours and forty minutes. That was the day when five volunteer crews of No. 12 Battle Squadron were sent to destroy two bridges across the Albert Canal west of Maastricht. All five planes were lost but F/O D.E. Garland and Sgt T. Gray were posthumously awarded the Victoria Cross for damaging their objective. The third man in the crew, L.A.C. L. R. Reynolds, wireless operator/air gunner, received no award but should be paid equal tribute.

On 13 May Don made a long flight in a pool Anson, delivering and collecting ferry pilots *en route*: Cardiff-St Athan-Cardiff-Kemble-Shawbury-Tangmere, thence direct to Reims. From Reims he returned to Amiens-Glisy and picked up pilots to return to Cardiff; this section was night flying. The total flying time was seven hours and ten minutes.

The mad pace continued on 14 May but the news made it obvious why such all-out efforts were necessary to support the squadrons in France. The Battles and Blenheims were suffering losses on single operations in excess of 50 per cent while the Hurricane squadrons were in action constantly against superior numbers, with consequent heavy losses. On that day Don was flown by an Anson to Hullavington, whence he and other pilots flew replacement Hurricanes to Tangmere and then across the Channel to Amiens-Glisy for some of the ten fighter squadrons. As the most experienced pilot he again handled the return night flight direct to Cardiff by Anson.

On the 15th he again flew an Anson from Cardiff to Little Rissington and Andover, where he snatched some sleep. The next day, he flew another Anson from Andover to Glisy, then to another forward airfield and back to Glisy. The return flight was to Andover and then to Cardiff.

On the 17th he flew from Cardiff to Tangmere by Anson to deliver ferry pilots, then back on the 18th to Cardiff and again to Tangmere for the night. The 19th meant a Hurricane delivery to Scotland via Whitchurch, Sealand and Prestwick to Drem, 24 km (15 miles) from Edinburgh.

The evacuation of some fighter squadrons from France began on the same day, but it was not the end of Don's trips to France because on the 23rd he took an Anson from Cardiff to Andover and then with fellow pilots to Rouen and Paris, spending the night in a city already in fear of possible occupation by the Germans (it fell on 14 June). On the 24th Don flew the Anson back via Andover to Cardiff.

It is impossible to know whether or not he was on a mission to collect some important personages to avoid their possible capture by the German army. The sudden emergency situations in which ferry pilots sometimes delivered planes, however, account for two stories of pilots delivering Hurricanes opening fire on enemy bomber aircraft. Claims were made of two bombers damaged and one shot down. While there is no evidence that Don himself shot down any German aircraft while delivering Hurricanes, it would have been very much in keeping with his style!

Operations were normal between 24 and 28 May, when Don flew an Anson from Cardiff to Hullavington and then north to Prestwick. On the return journey he experienced bad weather conditions at night and asked Squires Gate aerodrome, Blackpool, for permission to land. He landed in heavy rain, with no night flying facilities and ran into a fence, damaging the plane but not himself or his passenger. The subsequent inquiry found that the Squires Gate flying control had mistaken the Anson for an enemy aircraft and purposely given no landing signals. P/O Saville was cleared of all blame for the crash, which occurred at the end of flights totalling nine hours and ten minutes in a twenty-four-hour period.

June brought new tests and responsibilities. On the 2nd he flew an Anson with three pilots as passengers from Cardiff to Shawbury. There they each picked up a new Hurricane fighter and flew via Tangmere direct to Reims to deliver the planes to operational squadrons of the stricken RAF in France. This delivery seems to have been even more risky than usual as the AASF bases had already shifted from Reims to the Troyes area and a day later on the 3rd were shifted further west to airfields near Le Mans.

The Dunkirk evacuation was almost over and it was difficult to envisage anything but further withdrawals and final evacuation for the AASF and air component squadrons, or what remained of them. The return journey by Anson gives an impression of confusion and perhaps of efforts to collect personnel, since the route was Reims-Ponan-Reims-Paris-Amiens-Cardiff, and the flight occupied five hours and thirty minutes, much of it at night.

On return Don was given three days' leave – well deserved and necessary after the events and tensions of May and early June. Tribute must be paid to the bravery and determination of the ferry pilots taking reinforcement fighters and bombers to France at this time – they were in effect on active operational duties where *Luftwaffe* fighters were dominant and could pounce at any time.

Returning to Cardiff on the evening of 5 June, Don discovered that he had been chosen for a most interesting, exacting and potentially dangerous duty – to deliver a long-range Hurricane fighter to Egypt, stopping only at Marseilles and Tunis, a feat never attempted before. Replacement aircraft normally went by sea through the Mediterranean or flew by easy stages via France, French North Africa, Malta and the Western Desert. With the fall of France and Italy in the war, however the Mediterranean route would become more difficult.

The Air Ministry and the ferry pool had chosen the right man for the job, because Don was not only an expert pilot but a fully qualified navigator and an airman of experience and maturity likely to make wise decisions in emergencies.

On the 6th he was flown by Anson to Hullavington where he checked over Hurricane P2406, which had been fitted with long-range tanks. Later in the day he flew it to Tangmere, taking careful note of the fuel consumption *en route* and in a series of local flights. On the 7th he took off for Marseilles via Rouen and Nantes. This section took six hours and fifteen minutes' flying.

The flight was delayed for three days at Marseilles, as the French were at first unwilling to refuel the fighter or help in any way. Don was determined and eventually the Hurricane was serviced and refuelled for the Mediterranean crossing to Tunis in French North Africa on the 11th; the journey took three hours and thirty minutes. He spent the night at El Aouina aerodrome, refuelled and was ready on the morning of the 12th for the longest leg of the operation, from Tunis to Mersa Matruh. Hostilities between Britain and Italy had commenced the day before, 11 June 1940, with an attack by the RAF on El Adem, the main Italian air base in Cyrenaica, so Don was flying through a war zone as he followed his planned route just south of Malta to hit the coast of Cyrenaica between Benghazi and Derna, keeping well away from that port and from Tobruk. This was indeed wise because only a few days later the Tobruk batteries shot down their own commander-in-chief, Air Marshal Italo Balbo. Don then followed the line of the coast slightly south of eastwards, reaching Mersa Matruh after a flight of six hours and forty-five minutes.

The next day, 13 June, he flew on and landed at Amriya aerodrome, west of Alexandria. The first Hurricane to be seen in the Middle East had arrived safely and was to become 'Collie's battleship', the one and only Hurricane under Air Commodore Collinshaw's command. He moved it rapidly about from landing ground to landing ground to impress the enemy with his strength in modern fighters. It was the end of September before a further five Hurricanes arrived via the newly formed Takoradi-Kano-Khartoum-Cairo route, which became the main aircraft supply route to the Middle East forces after the fall of France.

Don remained in Cairo for the rest of June and all July, awaiting transport back to the United Kingdom. When his travel arrangements were finally made he found that they involved an enjoyable blend. He started with a sea voyage to Mombasa, then went by train to Nairobi and then to Johannesburg and Cape Town. A ship took him from the Cape via Ascension Island and Freetown to Glasgow, arriving on 17 September.

Returning to his unit, he found that it had moved from Cardiff to Kemble. He was promoted to flight lieutenant and officer commanding No. 8 Service Ferry Squadron at Hullavington – his first command and a belated recognition of his ability.

Before moving to Hullavington and his own command he was heavily engaged in replacing Hurricanes and Spitfires lost by Fighter Command squadrons in the Battle of Britain – now in its final stages. In September he flew seven Spitfires and two Hurricanes to 415 Squadron at Coltishall and 19 Squadron at Duxford, together with some bomber movements. At Hullavington the ferry pilots included Sgt/Pilot (later F/Lt) W. J. (Ken) Kenton, a survivor from two Blenheim squadrons, 101 and 82, which had been wiped out in recent operations. He remembers Don Saville well and said in 1986 that he was a decent, quiet commanding officer and a respected and expert pilot who was always friendly and cheerful. He did not know that Don had been killed in action during the war and wrote that men such as him and W/Cdr Guy Gibson should not have been allowed to stay so long on operations. He added, 'I am grieved to know of Don's fate and please let his brothers know that Don is not forgotten and I, for one, am proud to have served under him.'

Ken recalled that the Hullavington ferry unit suffered two fatalities while Don was CO, both Blenheims and both involving young sergeant pilots. One was due to fog and the other to engine failure. Don had the sad task of telling the two young wives, who lived nearby in Hullavington village. The ferry pilots as a group were billeted at Steinbruck House, Kingston Langley, just north of Chippenham.

Hugh Bergel, in his book about ferry pilots *Fly and Deliver*, has laid down how he thinks a good CO of a ferry unit should behave.

> I am sure that the most important job a CO had to do was to go out and ferry lots of aircraft of all types in all weathers. If he could not, or would not do this, he would find himself at a considerable

> disadvantage when it came to building and maintaining high morale and a strong sense of duty among his pilots. It was clear to me that the happiest and hardest-working pools were those whose CO's loved flying and did it reasonably well.

This is a perceptive statement, and Don matches the formula – he certainly loved flying, and he did it exceptionally well! He flew many aircraft of all types and in all weathers. He was obviously an excellent CO of an enthusiastic and hard-working unit. Moreover, his experience at Hullavington was laying a foundation for his future operational commands.

In October 1940, the first month of his new command, the balance in aircraft flown by the pool's pilots changed from fighters to bombers. Don himself flew two Hurricanes and one Spitfire but thirteen bombers to various destinations in Britain and Northern Ireland.

On one of the days when Don was not flying, but was in charge at Kemble, he had a visit from an Anson piloted by P/O Geoffrey Rothwell (in 1943 a flight commander on No. 218 Stirling Bomber Squadron but at this time a pupil at FTS Grantham). Rothwell was on a solo navigation exercise to South Cerney, but it was covered by a morning mist, so instead he landed at Kemble, which being on top of a hill, was above the ground fog. He was met by a smartly dressed F/Lt Saville, who asked where he was from. The young pilot, trained to call all instructors 'sir', addressed Don as such, but Don put a stop to this and said his name was Don Saville. Rothwell was invited into a makeshift office in one of the hangars and provided with tea and biscuits. Then another FTS Anson landed at Kemble. Don hit the roof and said that pupils should not have been sent off in such conditions. He put through a call to Grantham and lambasted someone at the other end, probably the flight commander, another Australian in the RAF. 'It was refreshing,' writes Rothwell, 'to meet an officer senior in rank with such a friendly and informal manner, particularly to a pupil such as I was at the time.'

In November and December the regular delivery and collection of planes continued, while in January 1941 there were two flights for Don in Hurricanes in very bad weather, including one of four hours and thirty minutes from Hullavington to West Fruegh in Scotland. He also flew two Hudsons on test flights from Hullavington indicating a new use of his experience – as a test pilot. February was marked by flights in two very new aircraft, a Stirling four-engined bomber and a Whirlwind two-engined fighter from Westlands of Yeovil. He made other test flights from Hullavington in seven planes: Hurricane Is and IIs, a Blenheim IV and two Wellington ICs. March saw further test flying: eight flights testing Blenheim IVs and Wellington ICs. In that month he also made two interesting deliveries of Wellington bombers to 104 Squadron which was now being reformed at Driffield, Yorkshire, and which he joined later in his career.

On 26 March 1941 No. 8 Service Ferry Squadron moved from Hullavington back to Kemble and with Service Ferry HQ was re-formed into Nos. 10 and 11 Service Ferry Squadrons.

After a short leave at the end of May, Don returned to duty in June as full-time test pilot in Maintenance Command. For the entire month he tested Hurricanes from Sealand, Chester, Donibrooke, Fifeshire and Abbotsinch, near Glasgow for special movement of long-range aircraft. This involved test flights of one hour and forty-five minutes for each of thirty-four Hurricanes. In July he was back at Kemble as an acting squadron leader (paid) with effect from 1 July. He did further test-pilot work with Halifax bombers and various fighters.

Don's log book (No. 4) shows that on 2 August 1941 he flew a Monarch aircraft from Kemble to Hendon to visit the director of postings at the Air Ministry. He had decided he had done enough ferrying and testing of planes and he wanted to become an operational pilot in Bomber Command. He must have been very determined to influence the ministry because he was now approaching his thirty-eighth birthday, and the maximum age to enter operational flying was normally thirty-two judging from advertisements at the time.

The log book reveals that he returned from Hendon to Kemble on 4 August. On the 7th he again flew in the Monarch to Hendon and again went to the Air Ministry in London. It is reasonable to assume that his first request had been turned down and he was trying again. The next day he returned to Kemble. Had he been successful in persuading the director that he should join Bomber Command?

Two days later he flew an Anson from Kemble to 41 Group HQ at Andover, the maintenance group for whom he had been a test pilot. He flew back to Kemble the same day, having presumably arranged his release. Two days later, on the 11th he flew a Hurricane to Moreton-in-the-Marsh and 21 Operational Training Unit (OTU), then back to Kemble. His record of service shows his appointment on that day to 21 OTU.

By sheer determination and perseverance Don had overcome the handicap of his age and persuaded the Air Ministry to allow him to give up a post as squadron leader, a test pilot and CO of No. 11 Ferry Pool Flight and join an operational training unit for entry into an operational squadron of Bomber Command. This would mean starting as a beginner and becoming a bomber pilot/captain at flight lieutenant rank. It meant giving up the strenuous, sometimes dangerous work of a ferry and test pilot for the constant danger of life as a bomber pilot at a time when few bomber crews were completing a tour of thirty operations over enemy territory.

He knew all the facts, however, and was therefore fully conscious of what he was doing. As a daring man in his late thirties he felt a challenge to do more, to take greater risks to win the war, even if this meant further risking his own life.

Chapter Eleven

Joining Bomber Command (1941)

In log book No. 4, S/Ldr Saville noted against the date 11 August 1941 that he was posted to No. 21 OTU for a short operational training course (No. 12 Course) at Moreton-in-the-Marsh. His rank did not last long because the 21 OTU records show that Acting F/Lt D. T. Saville arrived on 11 August 1941 on posting from HQ Service Ferry Squadrons. He arrived with squadron leader stripes on his uniform and did not remove them until requested to do so by the adjutant.

The course was indeed short for there are details of only two flights. On 29 August Don took off in Wellington E for Edward with his crew for a night cross-country exercise lasting four hours and thirty-five minutes. Like other captain pilots Don selected his own crew at the OTU and they were: Sgt McGillis (second pilot), Sgt Weatherly (navigator), Sgt Chittenden (wireless operator), Sgt Heap (front gunner) and Sgt Page (rear gunner). The following day he and his crew did a day cross-country flight in the same Wellington for two hours and fifty minutes.

During his four weeks at Moreton Don attended lectures and demonstrations with the young aircrew from the flying training, navigation, signals and gunnery schools, now formed by self-selection into bomber crews. It was probably difficult for him as a very experienced pilot and navigator – and as the oldest man on the course – to settle into the conditions at the OTU. However, the acquisition of his own crew was interesting for him and confidence-building for the young sergeants, who acquired a respected pilot as their captain.

Form 540, the monthly record of operations at 21 OTU indicates an uneventful month while Don was at the unit, except for the loss of one pupil who flew into a mountainside near Pennal in the Dovey estuary in Merionethshire, (killing the crew of six). The weather was poor, with only twenty nights suitable for flying.

Thirty-seven pilots were posted in and thirty posted out, two having been killed and five having failed the course. Thirty Wellington aircraft

Wing Commander Donald Saville (3rd from right) and his crew in Lagos 1942 during his command of No 104 Squadron. (Saville Family)

A Wellington Mk II having been converted to a cargo-carrying aircraft seen at El Kabrit, Egypt in 1942. (Philip Jarrett)

No 104 Squadron flew Vickers Wellington Mk IIs. These aircraft were powered by Rolls-Royce Merlin X engines that gave them increased speed and greater bomb load over the Mk I Bristol Pegasus powered model. *(Philip Jarrett)*

The Wimpy could carry two tons of bombs and had a range of about 2,200 miles. Although the aircraft was fabric-covered, its geodic structure allowed it to survive battle damage in excess of most other aircraft of the period. *(Philip Jarrett)*

A Short Stirling Mk III, the type of heavy bomber flown by No. 218 Squadron. This was a development of the Mk I, the RAF's first four-engined heavy bomber of World War II. The Mk III was first introduced into service with the RAF in 1942. When Don Saville assumed command of 218 the aircraft was on the verge of obsolescence and did not have the ability to reach the altitude of the later Avro Lancaster and Handley Page Halifax. The result of this was that in an attacking bomber stream, the Stirlings were nearer the flack and under the bombs being dropped by other types. 'Twixt the Devil and the Deep Blue Sea' - so to speak. *(Philip Jarrett)*

The Short Stirling had a maximum speed of 260mph and a service ceiling of only 17,000 feet. It could carry a bomb load of 14,000 lb and had a range of 2,330 miles. It was defended by 8 machine guns and carried a crew of seven or eight. This was the type of aircraft in which Saville perished. *(Philip Jarrett)*

Write the address in large BLOCK letters in the panel below.
The address must NOT be typewritten.

TO: JOHN. SAVILLE
GLEN. ALICE
RYLESTONE
AUSTRALIA N. S. WALES.

513851

Write the message very plainly below this line.

12/7/43. Sender's Address: W/O. Saville 74788.
Downham Market Norfolk.

Dear John & Molly: Well here goes for an airgraph which is something new in mail services to Australia I hope it proves better than the other types of mail as they have been pretty poor for a long time now.

As you probably read in the news things really seem to be going very well for us over here and as long as we can keep hammering at the Hun we should have this show over with the next year or so

Life generally in England is very good [illegible] get plenty to eat and there is lots of amusement in fact I think the general standard of living is far better than it was in 39 and especially at this time of the year with new vegetables of all sorts every one is well fed I have plenty of strawberries & other small fruits every day

The position of Australia is really still rather obscure over here but every one feels that if the forces can hang out for a while we can bring so much stuff out in a short while that the Japs will not have a show. Well paper is short so I must close down wishing you all the best of luck Yours Sincerely Don.

Don's last letter home to his brother John. *(Saville Family)*

FUNDS MAY BE QUICKLY, SAFELY AND ECONOMICALLY TRANSFERRED BY MONEY ORDER TELEGRAM. (PLEASE TURN OVER.)

COMMONWEALTH OF AUSTRALIA.—POSTMASTER-GENERAL'S DEPARTMENT.

RECEIVED TELEGRAM

The first line of this telegram contains the following particulars in the order named.

Office of Origin. Cable 63378 Words 23 Time Lodged. 9th No.

OFFICE DATE STA[MP]
Sent at......
Ch'nl No......
14 7[illegible]
By......

Remarks. Sch. C.2233.—11/1938.

This message has been received subject to the Post and Telegraph Act and Regulations.
The time received at this office is shown at the end of the message.
The date stamp indicates the date both of lodgment and of reception unless otherwise shown after the particulars of time lodged.

To John Saville
Glenalvie
Rydstree[illegible]

Best wishes and good health
please dont worry.
Best wishes to all at home

Don Saville

The final telegram sent on 14 July 1943. *(Saville Family)*

The first memorial to Don and his crew at the British Military Cemetery, Hamburg. *(Saville Family)*

25-7-43

74738 W CDR. D. T. SAVILLE DSO. DFC.
147921 P.O. W. J. BRIGHTON
113849 F/LT. T. A. STANLEY DFC.
116801 F/LT. J. L. BIRBECK DFC.
979354 FSGT. A.B.S. HOWAT
51686 P.O. T. D. FAIRGRIEVE
R.A.F. 25-7-43

25-7-43

A photograph of the war memorial at All Saints' College Bathurst in 1990.

(Saville Family)

The final tribute. Don and five of his crew lie in Row B, Plot 4 at Hamburg, Ohlsdorf, Military Cemetery. *(Saville Family)*

were available, but some of these had been discarded from operational squadrons and were not in the best of condition.

On 5 September the former 'hotshot' ferry and test pilot was posted with his crew to No. 12 Wellington Bomber Squadron at Binbrook, Lincolnshire.

Things had not all gone Don's way at Moreton-in-the-Marsh. P/O 'Mick' Mather, RAAF, saw Don paraded in a crew room by a pompous and officious flight commander after Don's aircraft had blown a tyre on landing. The squadron leader loudly berated the fools who sent him sprog pilots who hadn't enough flying experience to master the task of flying a Wimpy. He turned to Don and asked sarcastically, 'And how many flying hours does my latest recruit have in his log book?' Most pilots at OTU had less than 200 hours at this stage. Mather says that Don stood to attention, looked the flight commander in the eye and said, quietly but very clearly: 'Nine thousand six hundred and forty-two hours, forty minutes, if I am allowed to count this last landing!'

A few days before leaving 21 OTU. Don went over by car to his former ferry base at Kemble and arranged a flight in a Havoc (AH 510), which he had flown previously in demonstrations. This American fighter-intruder or light bomber with modern nose-wheel type landing gear performed far better than the old Wellingtons at Moreton-in-the-Marsh.

With impish humour and disregard for protocol, he took off from Kemble alone and did a demonstration of its flying capabilities and his own superb skills over Moreton in a flight lasting one hour and thirty-five minutes. Clearly it was Don's Australian way of showing what he thought of Moreton. He had not enjoyed his stay there!

The incident was seen by the chief flying instructor of 21 OTU, or must have been reported to him because he did not sign Don's log book entries for the period.

No. 12 Bomber Squadron at Binbrook, 16 km (10 miles) south-west of Grimsby, was equipped with Wellington II aircraft with Merlin engines, distinctly better aircraft than those at OTU. The squadron badge, with a fox's mask in the centre, had the motto 'Leads the field', and the squadron itself was famous within the RAF.

In 1930, as a pilot in No. 17 Fighter Squadron, Don had practised manoeuvres with 12 Squadron, then equipped with Fairey Fox single-engined biplanes. Since that time the squadron had been through several vicissitudes including moving to France in 1939 with their Fairey Battles as part of the AASF commanded by Air Marshall Barrett. It had experienced the full force of the German attack in 1940 and lost almost all its aircraft and crews in costly attacks on bridges and enemy columns.

Since conversion to Wellingtons for night-bombing, it had again suffered heavy losses and F/Lt Saville and his young crew were joining at a time when morale was under strain and the whole strategy of Bomber Command was being questioned because photo reconnaissance and intelligence sources had revealed that only a small percentage of the bombs dropped were hitting their targets.

On 6 September 1941 Don and his crew reported at the 12 Squadron office, where they were welcomed by the squadron adjutant and W/Cdr Roger Maw, who had been CO since 9 April. Don was pleased to find that despite the tensions of an operational station the atmosphere was cheerful. With W/Cdr Maw in charge – labelled 'Whiz-oh Maw' in the RAF – this was understandable, as he himself was always full of irrepressible good humour.

The next day, the 7th, the squadron's spirit was again tested. The target was Berlin and ten Wellingtons were required from 12 Squadron. The CO and all his three flight commanders operated that night; two of the four did not return. W/Cdr Maw reached Berlin, saw his bombs burst and observed fires, then, he and his crew returned safely. S/Ldr Fielden (B Flight) failed to return but later all the crew were reported as PoWs. S/Ldr Edinger (C Flight) failed to return; all were killed except the navigator, P/O McCarthy, who became a PoW. S/Ldr Roberts (A Flight) returned early with engine trouble.

Of the other six crews only three reached the target while others bombed alternative or emergency targets and one jettisoned and returned early. Two planes and twelve aircrew including two flight commanders, were missing from ten that set out – 20 per cent in one operation. Don saw that even experienced captains and crews could be shot down and that with loss rates like that it would be statistically impossible for anyone to survive a tour of thirty operations.

However, ever optimistic, he looked forward to his first operation with his own crew. It came four days later on 11 September. The target was Le Havre; and only four aircraft were on that target, eight other Wellingtons were sent to Rostock. First came the normal process of a night-flying test in the morning followed by briefing and a meal, then a truck to the waiting Wellington C for Charlie at dispersal, the checks and the wait for take-off amidst mounting tension, and finally the green light from an Aldis lamp. Then it was throttles open and the roar of the Merlins as the heavy plane gathered speed down the flarepath and slowly lifted off into its element. They were off and now it was up to the crew to work together and make the operation a success.

Don called up each crew member on the intercom; each sounded calm and ready for the adventure. But the weather worsened the further they went and at their estimated time of arrival the cloud was a solid 10/10 cover with no breaks. This was a French port, so they brought the bombs back as instructed and landed safely at base, where the weather was better. It was all very disappointing but it was useful experience, and the plane and crew performed well. Only one crew from the four sent claimed to have seen Le Havre and bombed the target. No one was missing from either Le Havre or Rostock.

Operations were scheduled and a night-flying test carried out on 13 September but bad weather caused cancellation of the raid after briefing.

The next operation was therefore on the 15th, and the target this time was Hamburg. This well-known target gave some extra meaning to the briefing and Don and his crew watched and listened intently as the route was put up and explained in relation to the known defences. This was a 'hot' target and flak and searchlight opposition was expected to be severe. Ten squadron crews were detailed and Don had Wellington B for Beer with his usual crew of Sgt McGillis as 'second dickey', Sgt Weatherly as navigator, Sgt Chittenden as wireless operator, and Sgt Heap and Sgt Page as gunners.

This time they saw their target and released the bombs, but they could not see the bursts because of the glare of searchlights. The flak was as expected but B was not hit and returned safely, although Don had to make a forced landing at Wattersham because he was short of fuel. As a former test pilot, Don watched his petrol consumption carefully and wisely took no unnecessary risks.

Next morning they flew back to Binbrook feeling well pleased with their first successful operation, although they were impressed by the German defences at Hamburg. The raid had been directed at railway stations and shipyards. Eight bombers had been lost out of an attacking force of 169, but all ten Wellingtons of 12 Squadron had returned.

On the 18th and 22nd Don's crew were detailed for operations and carried out night-flying tests on Wellingtons A and F. Again operations were cancelled because of bad weather expected *en route* or over the targets. Cancellations after the tension of testing aircraft and attending the briefing were a let-down to crews but they were part of bombing operations in the weather conditions of western Europe. Sometimes crews were already in their aircraft waiting for take-off when the cancellation came through. Some felt a glorious sense of relief, but most felt cheated and deflated after all the nervous energy expended in the preparation for another operation. It all had to be gone through again next time!

On 25 September Don and his crew had a pleasant interlude by flying from Binbrook in Wellington A for Apple south to Old Sarum aerodrome at Salisbury to collect W/Cdr Maw, their CO. The flight was treated as a navigation exercise for Sgt Weatherly and was enjoyable for Don in particular as he was visiting what had been very much his territory both in his short-service commission days at Upavon and his ferry pilot period at Hullavington and Kemble. Don and Maw were becoming good friends and they had mutual friends in the RAF, being of much the same vintage and previous common experience. The return to Binbrook completed a flight of two hours and thirty minutes.

The next day was another useful experience for Don's crew as he took part in formation flying practice with two other planes, flown by W/Cdr Roberts and P/O Barnes. Afterwards Don practised flying on one engine which was quite feasible with the Mark II Wellingtons, although much less so with the Mark ICs which had less power.

On 27 and 28 September there were night flying tests on Wellington A, and Don gave the second pilot, Sgt McGillis, experience as pilot in charge of take-off, flight and landing. On both days the operations were subsequently cancelled.

Sgt McGillis also took charge of the night-flying test on the morning of 29 September, which went on to become a genuine operation against an enemy target. The crew were again flying Wellington A, which seemed to have become their aircraft judging by the number of times it was allotted to them. This third operation was to attack Stettin, a distant target – farther than Berlin. Nine Wellingtons operated from the squadron and Don eventually bombed Rostock, the alternative target, because of engine trouble and petrol shortage. Two other squadron crews did the same and only P/O Heyworth claimed to have reached Stettin. Sgt Tothill had engine trouble over Denmark and flew back safely to base on one engine after jettisoning the bombs over the sea – a considerable feat of flying.

Don's fourth operation was to Cologne on 10 October, and this sortie brought home to him the dangers of operational flying. Their Wellington was hit over the target by an accurate burst of enemy flak, which shot away the hydraulics while they were making a fourth run to ensure accurate bombing. The weather had become worse as they approached the target, where cloud was 8/10 to 4,500 metres (15,00 ft) with severe icing. They saw their bombs burst and two small fires while attacking in a dive from 4,500 metres (15,000 ft) to 3,800 metres (12,500 ft).

On landing back at Binbrook Don's undercarriage collapsed, causing him to crash land, but none of the crew were injured. Overall, however, it was another tragic night for 12 Squadron. Two Wellington crews were lost out of nine operating. F/O Faint (who had just returned from a period in hospital) and his crew did not return, while the unfortunate Sgt Tothill again had an engine failure, on a different Wellington. He again succeeded in flying back over the North Sea down almost at sea level on one engine but the plane crashed at Caister on the Norfolk coast and the entire crew were killed. Later news from the Air Ministry indicated that P/O Wise and Sgt Morton from P/O Faint's crew were wounded and PoWs – the other four were killed.

Don's next operation followed swiftly on 12 October. The target was Nuremberg marshalling yards and station. Eight Wellingtons were involved and Don and his crew, with S/Ldr Sargeaunt, who had recently joined 12 Squadron but was posted out to 458 Squadron, RAAF on 14 October, as second pilot in place of Sgt McGillis, bombed from 2,750 metres (9,000 ft). Their bomb bursts started two small fires. There was only slight flak and other sticks of bombs were observed across the presumed target. All 12 Squadron aircraft returned safely.

Middlebrook and Everitt's *The Bomber Command War Diaries* indicates that this particular raid was centred on a village on the Danube some 100 km (65 miles) from Nuremberg and on the town of Schwobach 16 km (10 miles) south of the target. Navigational errors and inaccurate identification of targets were common during Bomber Command attacks in 1941.

On 13 October, the day after the Nuremberg fiasco, Don and his crew were sent on leave. He combined business and pleasure by piloting Wellington L to Tangmere to pick up P/O Barnes and his crew from 12 Squadron, who had force landed after the Nuremberg operation. Then on the return journey he set the bomber down at White Waltham, the HQ of the ATA where, of course, he had many friends from his ferrying days. Don left the plane and P/O Barnes and crew flew back to Binbrook. White Waltham was within easy reach of London by train from Maidenhead to Paddington.

On 14 October there was a change-over in the command of 12 Squadron; W/Cdr Maw handed over to W/Cdr Roberts, the former flight commander of A Flight. W/Cdr Maw had been in command of the squadron for six months, and had kept morale up through a most difficult period of heavy losses, including that of his predecessor, W/Cdr Blackden and three flight commanders. He later received a special commendation from Bomber Command for his splendid effort. Like most good COs he had operated on the most difficult targets.

Also on the 14th there was excitement at Binbrook when P/O Heyworth, returning from another raid on Nuremberg, crash landed at base with one engine on fire. The crew got away safely.

A week later Don was back at Binbrook and doing a night-flying test on Wellington L for London with his crew in preparation for their sixth operation – target Bremen. His log book records that the target was located after a thirty-minute search and bombed from 3,600 metres (12,000 ft) on flak and searchlight concentrations after a correct run up. This raid suffered because of poor visibility, attributed to industrial haze. One hundred and thirty-six aircraft from bomber squadrons took part, with losses of two Wellingtons and one Hampden. Sgt Millar and four crew were killed in a crash approaching to land on their return. The rear gunner was saved.

Don and his usual crew were again on duty on the night of 22/23 October, for an attack on Mannheim by 123 aircraft. The crews encountered thick cloud and haze over the target. Don and his crew tried to locate the target for forty minutes and then saw their bombs fall in the town, causing fires. A lot of flak immediately came up. Only fifty-eight crews claimed to have reached the Mannheim area and forty-two bombed alternative targets. Four bombers were lost but none from 12 Squadron.

On 28 October Don and his crew carried out airfiring practice at the Mablethorpe Range and on the 30th did a special test flight for T.R.9 radio requested by the station signals staff, one of whom came on the flight as a passenger.

On the 31st a briefing revealed that 12 Squadron was again to be involved in an attack on Hamburg – always considered a tough target. Ten Wellingtons were required including L for London, with F/Lt Saville as captain, P/O Langley as second pilot, in place of Sgt McGillis, and the usual air observer, wireless operator and front and rear gunners. It was a perfect trip in clear weather until they were within 16 km (10 miles) of Hamburg. Then suddenly they met 10/10 cloud with tops to 6,000 metres (20,000 ft). Don returned to the Elbe estuary and carefully set course from the last land seen and bombed at the ETA over the target. Soon after the stick of nine 225 kg (500 lb) G.P. bombs went down from 5,000 metres (16,000 ft) flak came up but Don took L for London safely away to the east before turning for home.

On the return journey across the North Sea the port engine developed an oil leak, but Don nursed the plane back to base. All 12 Squadron Wellingtons returned from the force of 120 sent to Hamburg but four other attacking bombers were lost.

From 2 to 7 November Don and his crew flew five night-flying tests, with Don giving P/O Garlick dual instruction and demonstrating single-engine flying. Sgt McGillis does not appear in the battle order with Don after the operation against Mannheim; he had probably taken over another crew as captain. P/O Langley appears to have become the regular second pilot in Don's crew. Don was now being used by S/Ldr Jackson of A Flight as a deputy flight commander in training for that office. As a flight lieutenant with great flying experience and skill, he was obviously now a key figure in No. 12 Bomber Squadron.

The next operation, on 7/8 November to Berlin, is recognised by RAF historians as a crisis point in the war for Bomber Command. It was to be carried out as a maximum effort by nearly four hundred bombers. In fact there was opposition by some group commanders to sending aircraft to Berlin in weather which was forecast to be bad over Europe, so the effort was divided among three targets: Berlin, Cologne and Mannheim. According to *The Bomber Command War Diaries* all three targets received only scattered bombing. This was the last raid on Berlin until January 1943; at this stage in the war the losses in aircrew and aircraft were not justified by the poor results in terms of damage inflicted. The weather was in fact a serious hazard, with storms, 10/10 cloud to 3,700 metres (12,000 ft) over Berlin and icing conditions *en route*. Thirty-seven bombers (9.4 per cent) were lost out of a total force sent to the three targets of 392, probably mainly owing to the weather. At Berlin only seventy-three claimed to reach the area and losses were twenty-one bombers from 169 despatched (12.4 per cent).

The heavy losses led to Sir Richard Peirse, commander in chief of Bomber Command, being summoned to meet the Prime Minister, Winston Churchill. The war cabinet decided to impose limited operations upon Bomber Command for a period of three months. In February 1942 Air Chief Marshal Sir Arthur Harris was appointed to lead Bomber Command and a new directive came from the Air Ministry which gave emphasis to attacking the morale of enemy civil population, in particular industrial workers – i.e. area bombing of German cities.

Don and his crew flew through the terrible weather conditions of that fateful night to find the target obscured by cloud and the temperature –35°C at 8,000 metres (16,000 ft). This was Don's ninth operation and he himself must have realised that most of the attacks he had taken part in had been ineffective in the appalling autumn and winter weather conditions of 1941. He was determined to try something different and told his crew he was going down through the cloud to locate the target. When they broke cloud at possibly 600 metres (2,000 ft) they immediately attracted searchlights and light flak on the outskirts of Berlin. They were flying fast from the descent, and quickly opened up to full power to escape back into the cloud, but not before suffering some damage to the aircraft.

Don decided to bomb the alternative target of Magdeburg and climbed back to 4,250 metres (14,000 ft), which brought the Wellington above the thick cumulus and cumulo-nimbus clouds. Conditions were no better and the bombs were released 'in the area of Magdeburg', with no flashes seen for obvious reason.

Proceeding homewards, they were fired on from the defences of Wilhelmshaven and again hit by shrapnel from accurate flak. It was becoming 'a night to remember' and Don decided to seek the nearest airfield rather than try to reach Binbrook. He landed safely at Docking,

Norfolk, after an exhausting eight hours and fifty-five minutes' flying. When the WAAF on duty in the control tower asked him where he was from (meaning which station and squadron) Don replied absent-mindedly, 'From Berlin,' and swears that the girl passed out!

Next day they returned to Binbrook, where the place was found to be more seriously damaged than expected. Don received a tongue-lashing from his commanding officer for endangering his crew and aircraft by flying low over Berlin. He later admitted to friends that he had been a 'bloody fool' and deserved the rebuke from authority. However, it did not prevent him taking somewhat similar risks in the future!

After a number of night-flying tests and aborted operations due to weather, Don and his crew were posted to RAF Mildenhall for a week's instruction on standard blind approach procedure. This involved six flights of approximately two hours each and various beam approaches and landing procedures with cockpit covered, which Don took very seriously. Anything to do directly with flying received his full attention!

On his return to Binbrook Don received a posting, on 2 December, to a newly formed Australian squadron, No. 458 Wellington Bomber Squadron, at Holme upon Spalding Moor, Yorkshire. After his valuable and sometimes exciting experiences with the long-established 12 Squadron, RAF, he was again promoted to squadron leader rank as flight commander in a brand new bomber squadron, with all its own traditions to establish.

Before he left 12 Squadron he arranged a farewell evening at a local tavern with his first bomber crew, who had shared his apprenticeship in becoming an experienced Wellington bomber team by completing nine operations. He and his crew of P/O Langley, Sgt Weatherly, Sgt Chittenden, Sgt Heap and Sgt Page parted reluctantly in mutual respect and friendship.

CHAPTER TWELVE

Flight Commander No. 458 Wellington Bomber Squadron, RAAF (1941–2)

The squadron crest of No. 458 Torpedo Bomber Squadron, RAAF, shows a winged torpedo descending into the sea and the motto '*In Venimus et delemus*', which means 'We find and destroy'. One of the founding officers of the squadron at Holme upon Spalding Moor, W/Cdr L. L. Johnston, DSO, has recorded that the squadron badge was rejected by the College of Heralds and he himself preferred 'We acquired and built' as a motto.

Whatever its badge and motto, 458 Squadron quickly developed a fine sense of cohesion and today has its own history, *We Find and Destroy* by Peter Alexander, and a very active squadron association in Australia.

The squadron came together on 1 September 1941 at Holme, which is equidistant from York and Hull, about 25 km (15 miles) from each. During a cold December it was a shock for Don Saville to move across country from Binbrook, a permanent RAF station to the wartime emergency starkness of Holme upon Spalding Moor, but he was delighted to be joining an Australian squadron.

The area has been described as flat country of some farming value but little beauty. It was at its worst in winter, and this was a particularly cold winter, with heavy frosts and snow. The nearest stand-down facilities for aircrews and ground staff were three public houses at Holme and others at Market Weighton and Howden. However, both Australians and Britons are at their best in adverse conditions and the newly formed squadron was splendidly led by two Australians in the RAF, in W/Cdr N.G. Mulholland, DFC, and S/Ldr L. L. Johnston, together with an Irishman, S/Ldr K. J. Mellor, DFC, a very experienced operational pilot known as the Maestro.

When S/Ldr Mellor left to take command of No. 150 Wellington

Bomber squadron at Snaith, Don took his place on 2 December, 1941. He was to command A Flight, and 458 Squadron's leadership was now indeed Australian. Mulholland, from Brisbane and not so young himself at thirty-three years of age (Don turned thirty-eight years in December), also had a background of civil flying before joining the RAF in 1933. He had already had considerable operational experience and been awarded the DFC in January 1941 for skill, courage and leadership in operations over enemy territory. In March 1941 he had suffered severe facial injuries in a Wellington crash, which permanently affected one eye and his nose. Although the damage to his face was obvious, it did not affect his enthusiasm for flying, and the new squadron was conscious of the drive of their commander in the build-up towards operations. By an extremely good effort 458 Squadron did their first bombing operation on 20 October 1941 and received a congratulatory signal from Group HQ.

W/Cdr Mulholland was sometimes an impatient disciplinarian, but like all successful leaders he was considered to be 'a good bloke', able to mix well and to lead by example. P/O (later F/Lt) Eric Lloyd, also from Queensland and one of the raw recruits to 458 Squadron straight from OTU, had been made squadron navigation officer because he was the first navigator to arrive. He recalls an incident when his crew, who gained experience with S/Ldr Mellor, was awaiting the arrival of S/Ldr Saville. Mulholland was a very kindly man off duty and enjoyed drinking with 'the boys'. On one such night Lloyd's wireless-operator and one of the gunners challenged him to a tarmac sprint next morning. If he lost he was to take the crew on operations for a trip. Mulholland lost and agreed to take the crew on the first available operation, to Aachen on 8 December.

Lloyd recalls that it was 10/10 cloud over the target and even the searchlights and flak were lying low. The CO decided to bring the bombs home. Most captains would have dropped their bombs indiscriminately in the circumstances, but not Mulholland. He would not drop bombs on an innocent or unidentified target. The navigator continues:

> On the way back from the bomb aimer's hatch the CO asked me for the course home. Without thinking I gave him 138 degrees. Back at the navigation table I realised what I had done and checked the compass – sure enough we were flying on 138 degrees (the reciprocal of the required course of 318 degrees).
>
> As casually as possible I called through to him to alter course to 318 degrees. Not a word was said until next morning when the wing commander called me into his office and said, 'You know,

> there were two silly bastards in that kite last night: *you* for giving me the course and *me* for flying it.' Nothing else was said.

Don took over A Flight and S/Ldr Mellor's crew of Sgt Ted Anderson (second pilot), P/O Eric Lloyd (navigator-bomb aimer), Sgt 'Buck' Peters (wireless operator), Sgt 'Flogger' Howlett (front gunner), and Sgt 'Tubby' Fuller (rear gunner). Their first operation together was to Cologne on 11 December. Cloud made the target invisible so Don went down to 2,100 metres (7,000 ft) and bombed what appeared to be factories in the vicinity.

F/Sgt Dave Rodden RAF was a wireless operator air gunner on 458 Squadron in 1941 and in 1986 wrote of W/Cdr Mulholland and S/Ldr Saville:

> Aussie officers were more easy-going and approachable, with little rank or class consciousness but still able to command admiration and respect.
>
> I remember S/Ldr Saville as an officer who was only interested in results and had the interests and wellbeing of his squadron uppermost in his thoughts. He couldn't be bothered with petty complaints.
>
> I was crewed with F/Sgt J. Bond from Queensland and our rear gunner was Sgt Alf Taylor from Brisbane. Alf Taylor and I were reported (wrongly) by the 'Red Caps' for being in York in battle dress. The matter came to Holme upon Spalding Moor and was considered by S/Ldr Saville, who questioned us about it in his office. On hearing our denial of the charge he immediately, without any more comment, threw the letter into his waste-paper basket.

On Christmas Day the festivities at Holme were interrupted by the CO, accompanied by the 'Barber of Saville' (Don Saville) on the tannoy, announcing that the squadron was on stand-by because the German battle cruisers Scharnhorst and Gneisenau had steam up in Brest and it was thought they might be preparing to escape up the Channel. Celebrations ceased immediately but 458 Squadron crews were not required.

Because of the bad weather, Don and his crew did not operate again until 27 December when the target was Düsseldorf. Again the cloud cover was frustrating and Don spent an hour searching for a break without success. His log book says 'Bombed a railway station in a small town from 8,500 ft [2,600 metres] – very fed up. Shot up Heinkel III – train – gasworks. Flew home at low level. Interesting trip – Ruhr covered in snow and looked lovely in moonlight.'

Eric Lloyd gives a more detailed account of that night and says that after bombing Don converted the Wellington B for Bertie into a slow cumbersome intruder.

> We were flying at 3,000 ft [900 metres] when we spotted a flare-path with a plane preparing to land. Don drew the attention of the gunners to the lights and cut the throttles, gliding down to within a hundred yards of a Heinkel III. The German pilot probably never knew what happened. Our front gunner opened fire and the enemy plane crashed off the runway while our rear gunner made sure of the victim.
>
> The skipper opened the throttles, the engines spluttered and then caught at a few hundred feet. The two gunners sprayed the airfield and we were away before the surprised ground defences could open fire.
>
> It was now a beautiful night and we flew low at 1,000 ft [300 metres] over Ghent, the moon casting light and shadow on the spires and buildings of the darkened city. The gunners had tasted blood and again fired their guns at a gasometer and at a moving train.
>
> Next day there was talk of decorations for our crew but Air Ministry in 1941 did not approve of attacks on trains and civilian targets in Belgium and France.

No medals were awarded in spite of the audacious destruction of an enemy aircraft.

On 5 January 1942 Don's crew again flew in B for Bertie on operations – this time an attack on the enemy warships and docks at Brest. The weather forecast was 'clear over target' but B had to stay thirty-five minutes in the area before seeing the docks and bombing from 3,600 metres (12,000 ft.) The Bomber Command report of this raid by 154 aircraft says that a smokescreen prevented accurate bombing but several large fires were claimed. No bombers were lost.

By unhappy contrast, on 9 January three Wellingtons of 458 Squadron were sent against Cherbourg and only one, Sgt Holmes and crew, returned safely. Sgt Garland was hit by flak over the target and crashed in Dorset with four killed and two hospitalised. P/O Hickey and crew were not heard of again and eventually were 'presumed dead'.

Eric Lloyd remembers that in January and February 1942 some tension developed between himself and his skipper, Don, because of his navigation officer duties, which sometimes prevented him from flying. Don was strict with his crew on training exercises and much of the time

Eric was grounded with lectures. He had the commanding officer pressing him to give lectures to the crews, some of whom were more experienced than him. This required the young navigation officer to do a lot of homework before giving lectures on astro-navigation and preparing notes to circulate to navigators.

In 1941 and 1942 wireless navigation was unreliable, and often jammed by the enemy. In really bad weather at night, dead reckoning relied on forecast wind velocities and these could quickly change. This left astro-navigation when possible, and the occasional wind-drift estimate.

Later, when they were socialising in the Middle East together, Don apologised to Lloyd and admitted that his attitude had been wrong. Apparently he had read Eric's essay on astro-navigation and been suitably impressed. Eric appreciated Don's gesture and they became good friends again.

On 12 January 458 Squadron received a visit from Air Marshal Williams, the senior RAAF officer in Europe. Then on the 18th it was notified that it was to be withdrawn from operations. The reason for this sudden change in policy was believed to be a war cabinet decision to reinforce the Middle East by sending out two operational squadrons (458 and 99) to avoid the ferrying losses suffered on the reinforcement route by inexperienced crews.

On the night when the news of the move came through, Eric Lloyd had just returned to Holme after attending a bombing leaders' course. He says:

> It was a quiet night in the officers' mess, with the newly appointed Australian adjutant leading the usual game of lie dice, the older admin. officers sitting round the fire and the younger aircrew types gathered at the bar.
>
> The 'wingco', furiously blinking his bad eye (afterwards known as his tropicalised eye) interrupted the proceedings to make a short statement of policy. 'We are to fly two lots of Wimpys to Egypt. After the second trip we may stay there or go on to India.' The announcement was dramatic!
>
> There was a stunned silence and then revelry started with a cushion fight. We packed into Don Saville's flight van to continue the night at an inn 7 miles [11 km] from the drome, called the Seven Sisters. Actually it was run by seven sisters but Don had another name for the inn – the Fourteen Tits!

From 22 to 31 January W/Cdr Mulholland was in hospital at St Albans, probably for further treatment of his damaged eye. In spite of this disability he was the leader of the first four Wellingtons to leave for the Middle East, flown by himself, P/O MacKellar, P/O Clark and P/O Moore – all Australians. P/O Moore had to return to Holme with electrical trouble.

The Wellingtons to be sent to the Middle East were Mark ICs with Bristol Pegasus engines 'tropicalised' to keep the oil cool and exclude dust and sand. The squadron Mark IVs with Wasp engines had to be given inspections and transferred to maintenance units or to other squadrons. The ICs had to be inspected and test flown by the crews so that they became accustomed to them and their long-range tanks.

Because of the work involved and delays caused by the weather the first group of planes did not take off from Stanton Harcourt until 15 February. They flew to Malta by a direct route over Le Havre to the island of Galite between Sardinia and Tunisia and thence to Luqa. P/O MacKellar and P/O Clark arrived safely at Luqa but the commanding officer did not.

A tragic but brave story emerged after the overdue Wellington was discovered to have been shot down over an Italian convoy 50 km (30 miles) east of Malta. F/O J. Willis-Richards, the British rear gunner and gunnery officer of 458 Squadron, miraculously survived the combat with three Ju.88 long-range fighters protecting the convoy but the wing commander and the other members of the crew were killed, although only after fierce resistance down to sea level. Willis-Richards shot down one of the attacking fighters before his own plane disintegrated and also plunged into the waves. The rear gunner's turret was detached from the fuselage and he managed to get out and into the dinghy, which had floated clear of the wreckage. An Italian destroyer picked him up and landed him at Messina to become a PoW.

The unfortunate Wellington had come down through clouds to look for Malta in the dawn light only to find itself close to this very large convoy of merchant ships and tankers supported by battleships, cruisers and destroyers, with fighter cover overhead. At first Mulholland and his crew were not sure whether the convoy was friendly or an enemy force. Flak and fighters supplied the answer before the Wellington could regain the shelter of the clouds.

The loss of their CO was a severe blow to 458 Squadron, which was about to be divided by the ferrying operation, with ground crews *en route* to the Middle East by sea and aircrews spread from Malta and Egypt to Lagos and Holme upon Spalding Moor or Moreton-in-the-Marsh. Perhaps the finest tribute to him was the fact that the excellent spirit he had engendered in 458 Squadron lived on and was eventually renewed in the re-forming of the squadron at Shallufa in August under W/Cdr Johnston.

That spirit and the drive, and the leadership of Don in A Flight and S/Ldr Sargeaunt, who took over B Flight when S/Ldr Johnston became the squadron commander, sustained the crews in the successful ferrying operation, in which thirty-six out of thirty-seven Wellingtons arrived safely as reinforcement aircraft for the hard-pressed 205 Group night bomber squadrons.

Don and his crew left for Portreath Cornwall on 27 February to prepare for the first flight to Egypt by a different route from that taken by W/Cdr Mulholland. A signal had arrived on 22 February reporting Mulholland's loss. Eric Lloyd says that their crew and others in the squadron then expected Don to become the CO. He thinks that Don also probably expected the promotion and was secretly disappointed. However, he made no comment and congratulated the newly appointed W/Cdr Johnston, who may have had air force seniority as a regular officer – Don's commission was in the RAFVR for duration of hostilities. In fact, Don had to wait only six months before being appointed commanding officer of No. 104 Wellington Bomber Squadron, RAF, and in the meantime he became CO of the Middle East detachment of 458 Squadron, RAAF while W/Cdr Johnston remained at Holme to organise the departure of the squadron ground staff.

Eric Lloyd, reveals the first flight as a dangerous operation demanding high skills from the whole crew. The route was Portreath-Gibraltar-Malta-Egypt.

> On 28 February 1942 at 06.05 hours in Wellington N501 we left Portreath for Gibraltar. Normally the flight was eight hours but we ran into heavy rain squalls and headwinds. Don decided to use the cloud cover for protection during the daylight hours against fighter attack. Hours later we were flying at 500 ft [150 metres] a few miles off the Portugese coast. The neutrality of Portugal stretched 20 miles [30 km] from the coast but Don kept flying within sight of land against the freshening winds and rain. On reaching the Spanish coastline he climbed to a few thousand feet and handed over to the second pilot, Sgt Ted Anderson, for the easy leg along the coast to Gibraltar. He came back for a yarn and I commenced to pack my gear ready for landing. I automatically looked at the compass and we were heading almost south when suddenly we had an escort of Free French Blenheims. In these overcast conditions it was easy to jump the narrow strait to North Africa.
>
> Don took over the controls and turned back to Gibraltar. We had almost created an international incident and it was just as well that the Free French were not hostile. It was late afternoon when we

landed somewhat overdue, on a flight which had taken us eleven hours in foul flying conditions.

Don had been to Gibraltar before and next day we wandered round the Rock and the small shops opening on to narrow streets. The shops were still stocked with their wares of laces, trinkets and foods while the cosmopolitan population rubbed shoulders with the navy, army and air force. It was an entertaining exercise ending with olives for Don and cheap export Craven A cigarettes for me.

Spain was in the circuit area of the landing strip – a strip of gravel less than 1,000 yards (914 metres) long and built in the shadow of the Rock on the narrow isthmus connecting with the mainland of Spain. There was a graveyard of crashed aircraft to one side and an airman placed at the point where landing planes should touch down, to signal pilots to go round another circuit if they were overshooting. Numerous planes had gone over the edge of the runway into the bay and this was a wise precaution. There were tales of our aircraft being shot at in the landing circuit by Spanish guns.

The weather forecast for the next leg to Malta was bad but next evening, 2 March, at 19.45 hours after an argument with the met. officer about the terminal forecast for Malta, we left Gibraltar with dire warnings of bad weather and air raids. Don either had supreme confidence in my navigation or in his own ability to get to Malta.

At nightfall we were flying at 1,000 ft [300 metres] with the moon barely showing through closely knit patches of higher cloud. The coastline of North Africa was not visible but occasionally we saw flame floats on the Mediterranean beneath, indicating the company close ahead of two other squadron aircraft flown by Sgts Jack Bond and Len Laver. Despite the forecast, weather conditions were good and with little danger yet from enemy fighters, Don handed over to Sgt Anderson.

Five hours from take-off the light of Cape Bon shone out of the darkness with now imminent danger from night fighters from the Italian island fortress of Pantellaria. Don took over again as the mass of cloud thickened overhead and he reduced height to 500 ft [150 metres] as protection from fighters on the last leg to Malta.

After seven hours of flying we saw the white wash of breaking waves, the red flashing beacon and the dark smudge indicating the 20 miles [30 km] coast of the main island. We crossed the coast and circled Luqa but searchlights came on and guns started firing at us. Don flew out to sea again and instructed the wireless operator to identify us. He had been flying so low that we had not been plotted in as friendly by the ground defence and the guns had been firing 'at a strange aircraft'. Don was such an experienced pilot and had such tremendous confidence in his own ability that low flying at night and under such conditions did not seem to him, or to his crew, to be a risk – rather it was a necessary safety strategy against fighter attack. After half an hour the all-clear was given and we came in to the Luqa flarepath, which was put on briefly for our landing.

The full force of the blitz on Malta had started and two hours after our crew had got to bed about 08.00 hours the daylight bombing attacks commenced. Sleep was impossible with Bofors guns crashing just outside. Don and I got dressed and did the only thing possible – went out to watch a raid on the Grand Harbour at Valletta.

Nowhere was safe on the island and the most dangerous place was the aerodrome, Luqa, where all aircraft were dispersed in sand-bagged pits.

F/Sgt Peters, the wireless operator in Don's crew, told a newspaper interviewer:

We saw eight daylight raids while we were grounded for twelve hours. We attempted to sleep but the barrage concussion shook our beds and shrapnel pounding on the road drove us into the open. We jumped into a gun pit and watched Jerry getting a taste of ack-ack. The bombers never lost their formation despite shell bursts resembling a pepper-pot shaken in the sky.

The way the Germans flew through this hellish barrage apparently unscathed was an object lesson for us night bombers. We were fascinated to watch the bombs released at 10,000 ft [3,000 metres] and were able to watch their flight until they reached the earth.

Don's instructions were to get away as quickly as possible and as he was now the senior officer of 458 Squadron it was imperative that he should go on at once. Some squadron crews had their Wellingtons commandeered for other crews to fly them out from Malta. Members of the civilian population were also being evacuated in transitting aircraft. Don had to wait for his quota of passengers to arrive in the evening before taking off during an air raid on the harbour on 3 March.

It was to be a very uncomfortable trip for the four passengers – a mother and baby and two other evacuees – but it proved to be a beautiful night with a moon and a canopy of stars – perfect flying conditions.

Eric Lloyd continues:

> The Wellington gave the illusion of being motionless. At times like this there is an awesome feeling of being suspended in time and space. Don called our passengers up to the cockpit and they later told us that they had felt the absolute beauty of the night. It was one of the most peaceful flights I have ever made.
>
> At midnight we made landfall at Ras el Kenayis after seeing Mersa Metruh with its searchlights. As Don flew inside the Egyptian coastline there was a gradual darkening and the moon became a copper ring behind the black shadow of the earth – a total eclipse which brought on complete darkness. They had omitted to tell us at Malta briefing and one of our three crews landed in the middle of the eclipse and were puzzled by the extreme darkness.
>
> Just before dawn the flashing beacon of L.G. 224 came up over the front gun turret. We landed at 02.30 hours and waved goodbye to our passengers, who were suitably grateful and still awed by the beauty of the flight.
>
> Later that day we delivered the Wellington to the maintenance unit in Luxor. Don and I spent the night in a luxury hotel in Cairo at the expense of HQME (Headquarters Middle East), who weren't too keen on paying my board but Don wangled it somehow. As officer commanding the squadron he spent some time at headquarters.
>
> The squadron crews were united at Almaza Transit Camp near Cairo. A few days were spent happily touring the pyramids, at the Gezira Sporting Club and at the Mena Hotel.
>
> After a brief delay, Don and our crew left as passengers on a Pan American DC2 bound for West Africa *en route* back to England to pick up another Wellington for Egypt.

At Lagos Don and his crew met up with other 458 Squadron crews awaiting a ship to return them to England for the second trip out to Egypt with much-needed Wellingtons. The town was more pleasant than anticipated and the white population lived very well in the hot, humid conditions. The squadron officers were comfortably accommodated at an officers' mess. Many of the sergeant aircrew members were housed at the Ritz Hotel, where they discovered a novel way of creating havoc on the road beneath the hotel windows. The natives carried their gear on top of their heads and a penny tossed down caused a delightful (to the sergeants) scramble with head-loads flying in all directions.

S/Ldr Jim Sargeaunt, the newly appointed flight commander of B Flight, a British RAF officer in his early thirties and a close friend of Don Saville, now arrived with his crew to join the transit aircrews. Like Don, he was a very experienced pilot who had given up a squadron leader post as a test pilot with Vickers-Armstrong to become a flight lieutenant bomber pilot in 12 Squadron and 458 Squadron.

Eventually the 458 aircrews embarked on a ship, ostensibly for the United Kingdom. It was a former Irish packet steamer converted to a naval auxiliary and now known as HMS *Ulster Monarch*. In the hot equatorial conditions it was hellish, particularly for the NCOs who had overcrowded accommodation below and terrible food. Most of the sergeants were friends of Eric Lloyd from training days and they asked him to put their case to the ship's captain. Don arranged the meeting but the captain was not responsive. In fact Don told Eric that the captain had threatened to put Lloyd in irons for the rest of the voyage if he caused any more trouble. Eric was not sure if his leg was being pulled but a few days later the aircrews were off-loaded at Freetown to await more congenial shipping.

S/Ldr Sargeaunt, who could be guaranteed to be up to some fun whenever possible, now set about composing a squadron song, later to become famous as 'Lagos Lagoon'. Eric Lloyd admits that he and Don helped with the words, which like most service ditties were unfit for publication. The song deals with the sexual activities of a squadron crew condemned to a long wait in Lagos for sea transport to Britain – rather like the position of the 458 Squadron crews, known cheerfully to each other as the 'Savillians' after their Officer Commanding, found themselves in.

I believe that these following three verses can now be printed without much fear of offence except perhaps in the racial overtones – which were not thought of as such in 1942.

Lagos Lagoon

Verse 1. In the year Anno Domini 1942
In the city of Lagos there landed a crew
They stayed at the Grande and they drank at the Ritz
And amused themselves pulling the native girls' tits.

Chorus: Lagos Lagoon, Lagos Lagoon, they're belting black velvet round Lagos Lagoon.

Verse 2. They stayed there some time
And in spite of the heat
Refrained from inserting their sexual meat
Until at last – the whole aircrew got pissed
And the black beauties' wiles could no longer resist.

Chorus:

Verse 7. The rear gunner's patience by waiting was marred
The size of the target made range judgement hard
The whole silhouette appeared to him strange
And he fired all his ammo while well out of range.

Chorus:

The other verses describe the amorous efforts of other crew members including the skipper. The last verse starts: 'They went back to England and sent for the Doc!'

One night at Freetown Jim Sargeaunt and Don went out on the town and arrived back late. That same night someone blocked the local railway line and a train was derailed. The connection was never admitted – nor denied.

S/Ldr Sargeaunt and P/O Lloyd left Freetown on a Dutch luxury liner, the SS *Dempo*, which was carrying some wealthy escapees from Singapore, including members of a famous banking family who not long before had left the blitz in England for the 'safe haven' of Singapore. Don remained behind in Freetown to organise shipping for the other 458 crews. And so the Saville legend was extended by the story of the Sunderland flying boats.

Don was not one for slow passages on ships in convoy when there was a possibility of flying. By some means he discovered that Sunderlands were flying regularly between Bathurst, farther up the West African coast, and Britain via Gibraltar. He quickly arranged a flight by Pan American Airways from Freetown to Bathurst. By 18 March he had organised a trip back to Britain as a crew member on a 95 Squadron Sunderland. The flying boat duly took off but after some hours' flying, one engine failed and they returned to base. The next seven days were spent in unsuccessful attempts to repair the engine and test flights to check its performance in the air.

On 26 March the impatient Don set off again, this time in a Sunderland of 210 Squadron. It must be remembered that he had considerable experience of flying boats and was a test pilot with some thousands of flying hours so that he was well aware of problems such as fuel consumption in adverse wind conditions. His log book records that this flight was the longest he had ever flown – fifteen hours and forty five minutes – and that he found that the captain showed very little knowledge of flying. As the senior officer and most experienced pilot on board, he intervened to make the captain come down to almost sea level to make Gibraltar.

After two days' delay in Gibraltar owing to bad weather on the English coast, they left on 31 March. They arrived at Mt Batten in daylight, refuelled and arrived at Calshot at 12.00 hours. Don caught the first available train to London.

Early in April Don, Jim Sargeaunt and Eric Lloyd were reunited in London, and Don booked an apartment with a bedroom, lounge and kitchen at the Mount Royal Hotel near Hyde Park. One particular early morning was somewhat hilarious. The friends came back at different times, Eric first, then Jim. They were wakened by Don pouring water over them and pulling the bedclothes onto the floor, demanding that they get up and eat olives and drink Scotch. He had with him a Canadian army private, a machine gunner, who proceeded to get out on the narrow catwalk outside their window and give a series of wild Indian war cries, trying to attract the attention of the air-raid wardens on duty. Jim and Don engaged in a wrestling match which ended with Don falling to the carpet, looking up grinning and saying, 'I'sh spun in!'

Don slammed the door of the apartment and broke the handle, so that the four were confined to two single beds and the floor, until they were let out by the maid next morning. The Canadian departed and Jim and Eric went down to breakfast, but Don was still asleep when the maid came back again to tidy the room and make the beds. She was a big buxom Irish lass and had more trouble with Don. He looked up at last and said, 'Make my bath, woman!' She did just that but then came back into the bedroom, lifted Don bodily out of bed and dumped him into the bath. It was no trouble at all for her, as the slim little Australian would not have weighed more than 57kg (9 stone). Jim and Eric were back in time to enjoy the splash!

Following leave in London the squadron crews were to re-form under the CO, W/Cdr Johnston, at the Air Delivery Overseas Unit at Moreton-in-the-Marsh, in preparation for the second delivery flight out to Egypt. The other 458 Squadron aircrews duly went to Moreton but Don somehow or other organised his own crew to divert to Bassingbourn, one of his former ferry pool stations. With hindsight it may have been a little demonstration of independence, showing that he did not entirely approve of Johnston's appointment – and of course he was not exactly in favour at Moreton-in-the-Marsh after his run in at 21 OTU in 1941.

On 1 May he and his crew flew to Portreath to prepare for the flight to Egypt via Gibraltar. This time they had extra tanks to enable them to fly direct from Gibraltar to Egypt, thus avoiding the danger of damage to aircraft and crew at Malta. At Portreath instructions were waiting for Don to return immediately to the Air Delivery Overseas Unit at Moreton to fulfil the requirement for night-flying training. S/Ldr Jim Sargeaunt acted as go-between for Don and the station commander at Moreton. The conversation is reported to have gone something like this:

'Has he done his two hours' night-flying training?' asked the Moreton CO.

'No sir,' replied Sargeaunt.

'Who does he think he is? How many night flying hours has he got?'

'Three thousand hours, sir.'

'I asked for night hours, not total flying,' said the CO.

'Yes sir. Three thousand night – ten thousand hours total.'

'Good God!' came the CO's responses.

Needless to say, Don and crew took off next afternoon for Gibraltar, landing after a flight of seven hours and forty minutes. It was uneventful this time and Eric Lloyd was allowed to fly the plane for forty minutes. After one night at the Rock they took off on the long haul to Kilo 17 on the Cairo-Alexandria road. The Wellington IC was equipped with three overload petrol tanks carried in the bomb compartment and very little ammunition. The all-up weight was over the permitted capacity, which meant a hazardous take-off on the short Gibraltar runway and flying over enemy territory with only the rear gun turret in operation. Without headwinds they could expect to be near the battle line just after dawn.

The planned route took them across Tunis from Cape de Garde to Sousse in darkness but they ran into headwinds and it became apparent that they would be off Cyrenaica in daylight. At Sousse the harbour was brilliantly lit and a ship was being unloaded.

Over Cyrenaica at dawn a dust storm blew up and with his usual flair Don reduced height and took cover in the dust until they reached friendlier air space.

They landed at Kilo 17 after fifteen hours and fifty minutes' flying time, with thirty minutes' petrol in the tanks. Eric Lloyd offers some interesting comments on his captain. He says that in those days there were some senior officers who accused him of being reckless, but during Eric's eight months as his navigator he never found him to be so. Reducing height over France and Germany away from enemy night fighters and below flak level somehow made sense, just as the approach to Malta at 150 metres (500 ft) did, and seeking the protection of the dust storm at Cyrenaica. Eric concludes:

> As his crew, we always felt safe with him at the controls. As a pilot he was one of the 'greats' and it is a pity he was lost to the world of aviation. In my experience he never at any time indulged in unnecessary low flying or exhibitionism. Throughout a long flight he took careful note of all instrument readings and weather conditions. The safety factor always dominated his flying.

May, June, July and August 1942 were months of confusion and hard work for 458 Squadron aircrews and ground staff. It was a time of great tension and adjustment for Allied army units, the Royal Navy and the RAF because in May, while they were preparing to mount another push westward from the Gazala line, Rommel struck first and began a series of attacks which brought the enemy to the natural emergency defence line for Egypt between El Alamein and the Qattara Depression to the south. Tobruk was captured by the Germans – a severe shock to the Allied forces, particularly to Australians.

Don was CO of the 458 Squadron aircrews and ground staff, who now met up together at RAF Station Fayid. In view of the urgent need for reinforcement aircrews for the battle-worn Wellington squadrons of 205 Group, and the pressing need for servicing groundcrews for the Liberators of American units reaching the Middle East, it is a miracle that 458 Squadron eventually survived as a unit.

Aircrews were posted to various squadrons on detachment and parties of 458's ground staff went to Lydda, St Jean near Haifa, and Aqir in Palestine, while men of a servicing flight remained at Fayid under Don's command.

Finally, 458 Squadron was re-formed between August and October 1942 as a torpedo bomber squadron at Shallufa Egypt, under the command of W/Cdr Johnston, largely owing to his own determination to keep it intact.

Don did not rejoin 458 Squadron, as he had been posted on the 4 August 1942 to command No. 104 Wellington Bomber Squadron, RAF, at RAF Station Kabrit.

Air Commodore A. E. ('Mick') Mather, DFC, AFC (RAAF Retired) was a captain-pilot in 458 Squadron at this time and he has provided several interesting and important pieces of information about Don's appointment to command No. 104 Wellington Bomber Squadron. He and his crew had been employed on ferry flight duties at Fayid after arriving with their second delivery Wellington from the UK via Gibraltar.

Early in July Don apparently knew that he was to become CO of 104 Squadron because he asked Mick Mather, 'What about getting back on ops with me?' Mather said, 'Beaut!' and within days was posted to 104 Squadron. On 16 July he did his first operation with the squadron, to attack Tobruk. Don himself duly arrived at Kabrit to take over command on 4 August and brought with him several of the crews from 458 Squadron.

Other 458 Squadron crews went to 108 and 148 Squadrons, also at Kabrit, while some joined 37 and 70 Squadrons at Abu Sueir. S/Ldr Jim Sargeaunt from 458 had earlier been appointed flight commander of A Flight, 104 Squadron.

Who arranged this? Mick Mather recalls that Don always appeared to be on first-name terms with very senior RAAF and RAF officers at headquarters and to be capable of arranging and altering postings if necessary on behalf of his subordinates.

With regard to the transfer of 458 Squadron crews to the RAF squadrons at Kabrit there is an amusing story of confrontation at Shallufa between W/Cdr Saville and W/Cdr Johnston. They got on well together but on this occasion Johnston told Saville to go away. 'Get out of here, son, you've pinched enough of my good crews already!'

104 Squadron certainly benefited from this process.

CHAPTER THIRTEEN

Commanding Officer, No. 104 Wellington Bomber Squadron in Africa (1942–3)

I myself was a member of No. 104 Wellington Bomber Squadron when W/Cdr D. T. Saville assumed command on 4 August 1942. As squadron intelligence officer I was soon introduced to him and made this note in my diary: 'The new Wing Commander, an Australian W/Cdr D. T. Saville, arrived today and seems O.K. He's one of those smaller, very sharp and alert type of Australians.'

He was taking over his first operational bomber squadron at a highly critical stage of the war in the Middle East. The front was only 100 km (60 miles) from Alexandria and not yet stabilised. It was expected that Rommel would make further probes and thrusts to try to get through to the delta and the cities of Cairo and Alexandria. The 8th Army had suffered a major defeat, ending in a confused retreat to the Alamein defences. New generals were about to take over; General Alexander arrived in Egypt on 8 August and General Montgomery on the 12th. Everyone seemed to be changing places.

However, RAF and other Allied air units had not been defeated in the retreat and leadership remained in the steady hands of Air Chief Marshal Tedder and Air Vice Marshal Coningham. At RAF Station Kabrit on the Great Bitter Lake three Wellington squadrons (104, 108 and 148) of the enlarged 236 Wing (205 Group RAF-ME) maintained intensive operations against the enemy in the battle area, his supply bases and landing grounds. In the RAF vernacular of the time it was a case of 'withdrawing the finger and keeping it well out'!

No. 104 Wellington Bomber Squadron had operated against Germany in 1941 from Driffield, Yorkshire, until it was sent to Malta in

October under W/Cdr 'Teddy' Beare, DFC to attack targets in Libya, Sicily and Italy. It moved on to Egypt in January 1942 and had been welded by W/Cdr Beare and W/Cdr Blackburn into an excellent, respected unit of 205 Group – itself a smaller Bomber Command. Both commanding officers received the DSO for their brave leadership, W/Cdr Beare's on Malta in November 1941.

Like all the night bomber wings and squadrons, 104 Squadron had become a mobile unit and moved forward to advanced landing grounds in the Daba area during 1942, only to return to the Canal Zone during the retreat while continuing maximum bombing operations to save the army from being completely overrun.

In the welter of operations in May, June and July 1942 the Wellington squadrons had suffered serious losses and crews had had to be retained after completing their tours; some were even brought back from ships that were about to take them back to the UK for rest periods in Training Command. Now in August, Don was dealing with a mixture of tired experienced crews and raw new ones replacing surviving tour-expired crews who had at last been released. He also had new and untried flight commanders so that the squadron required rebuilding back to maximum efficiency.

To my surprise the new CO appeared to have no decorations attached to his name, although rumour had it that he had been a test pilot and aviator of great experience as well as a flight commander on 458 Squadron, RAAF. He quickly settled in and was immediately on good terms with the group captain (G/Capt. Simpson, DSO, DFC) and W/Cdr Roger Maw, DFC, the CO of 108 Squadron, with whom he had served in Bomber Command on 12 Squadron. The new A Flight commander, S/Ldr Jim Sargeaunt was also an old friend, of course, but unhappily he and his crew went missing on a Tobruk raid only three days after Don took command. They survived to become PoWs.

The new CO showed his style at once – he operated on the second night after his arrival, taking Sgt Manning and his crew in Z for Zebra to Tobruk, now the most heavily defended target in the Middle East, because it was Rommel's best port and the nearest to the front. In August Don operated himself with different squadron crews on the 6th, 9th, 12, 17th, 20th, 23rd and 31st, demonstrating his clear intention to lead by example and his wish to get to know his captains and crews as quickly as possible. We all recognised that a very active and confident man had taken command of our squadron.

He was friendly and pleasant to me personally. Several times in the first week he came into Intelligence during mornings to discuss the individual bombing reports from our crews and any new information available about the war situation. At briefing he took my contribution seriously and listened intently to details about the target and how our bombing of it contributed to the war effort. In his briefing he was decisive in his language and bearing and made some use of the 104 Squadron motto, 'Strike hard!' – a very suitable phrase for a bomber squadron, and one which the CO interpreted as giving our crews the incentive to make each bomb hit and hurt the enemy. He portrayed our squadron and crews as the executive arm of the RAF, carrying out the orders of our leaders and the policies of our government. It made good sense and the captains and crews reacted well to this CO, who was so keen to operate himself and go with them. In war, example is the best form of leadership.

If he was not operating himself he always went to the flarepath to see the crews off and often asked me to accompany him. Take-off, with the bulky Wellingtons heavily loaded with bombs, fuel and their six-man crews, was always thrilling – sometimes too much so, with various incidents and accidents. We stood in dusk or darkness amidst a small crowd of well-wishers, usually including the group captain, several squadron officers and some groundcrews, near to the Chance Light which was used to project a beam down the runway, which was marked by two rows of only low-intensity lights to avoid attracting possible enemy attention.

With three squadrons operating we might have from twenty-five to forty bombers lining up on the taxiing paths after leaving the relative safety of their sand-bagged dispersals. Take-off was the most dangerous time on a bomber station for both accidents and enemy attack. The long row of lumbering aircraft with engines and propellers roaring and whirring, flames spitting from exhaust ports, was a stirring sight for any observer but particularly emotional when one knew most of the crews and could wave to them high above you in their cockpits and turrets as they took their turn on the end of the runway to await the green light from control. To me all aircrew were heroes and take-off was a crisis point in an operation starting at briefing and ending the following day in intelligence at tables set up for the interrogation of the crews.

Then with an ear-splitting roar from the twin motors as the revs were put to maximum the plane slowly gathered speed and sped away into the darkness before almost imperceptibly lifting off and disappearing out over the Bitter Lake with the navigation lights visible for a short while. The main Kabrit runway ended at the lake's edge and in recent weeks several of our Wellingtons had crashed and exploded in the lake, with disastrous loss of young lives. On the first night I accompanied Don the take-off was interrupted by engine trouble on one plane, which came round in a low circuit to land heavily and bumpily before stopping near the end of the flarepath. One of the crew must have thought the plane was about to crash and blow up because he threw himself out of the astro-hatch and was severely injured.

On 13 August I asked Don about a trip to Tobruk, pointing out that it was important for an intelligence officer to experience conditions over a target. He agreed and said he would take me on a suitable occasion. He and I seemed to be developing a closer personal relationship than I had had with my previous commanding officers. I thought about this and made a note in my diary that it was probably because he was my third CO and I was now not quite such a beginner as I had been with the other two. Or was it because he was Australian?

Another Australian in 104 Squadron was in the news at Kabrit, as a result of an incident in the officers' mess. F/O Mick Mather, who had also come from 458 Squadron, got into an argument with the squadron leader administration and hit him a beauty on the chin. His victim was not much liked by any of us so we hoped Mather would escape punishment.

The wing commander was away bombing Tobruk at the time but next morning took immediate and effective action to support Mather. As I heard the story later from Mick Mather the trouble occurred over some tins of asparagus sent by Australian Comforts which he wished to have served up on toast for his crew, using the services of the cooks in the officers' mess kitchen. All went well until Mick was leaving the kitchen with a tray and met the squadron leader administration, who was showing some visitors over the mess – a WAAF officer, a group captain and the station orderly officer for the day. The squadron leader said, 'get out of my mess and put those rations down!' Mather continued on his way and the squadron leader lunged at his arm and roared: 'Put those rations down or I'll have you arrested!' He rushed at Mather, who let him have the tray and plates fair in the face.

The squadron leader, a large man and former wrestler, tried to wrestle Mather to the ground so Mather stood him off with a couple of straight lefts and dropped him with a right cross to the jaw. He left the scene with the squadron leader, screaming at the poor orderly officer to arrest him.

Next day Don called Mather to his office and told him he was to appear before the 236 Wing commander, G/Capt. Simpson. He told him to say nothing and take a dressing down entirely without comment. He said, 'He'll say a lot of rude things he doesn't mean, so just go quietly and say nothing.' The group captain duly tore several strips off Mather and informed him that if it wasn't for the good operational reports he had had there would have been further action. There was no doubt in Mather's mind that his escape was due to good defensive spade work by his squadron commander.

The same evening I experienced and witnessed further examples of our wing commander's kindness and interest in the welfare of his squadron personnel. After the briefing I told him I intended writing some letters and he immediately offered me his room and desk. With three squadrons RAF Kabrit was overcrowded and most personnel like myself were accommodated in tents pitched on the desert sand. I settled down in comfort with an electric fan to cool me and had just told my wife about two friends, Basil Blogg and Charles Stotesbury, when Don came in quickly and said, 'Blogg has crashed in the lake and the navigator is killed – coming?'

We dashed off in his car with the doctor and found that it was all too true. We could see the burning aircraft on the shore of the lake near Deversoir about 15 km (10 miles) away and heard some of the bombs explode before we reached the scene. Basil Blogg, the pilot, was marvellously composed and looking after his crew. Five were safe but my other friend, F/O Charles Stotesbury, the navigator, had been killed with a fractured skull. O for Orange had had an engine cut after take-off and could not maintain height to get back to Kabrit. Knowing that they would have to crash land, Charles had gone to defuse the bombs or make sure they could be jettisoned safely, so he was at the bomb panel when they made what was really a good belly landing on the beach. The aircraft caught fire but they got Charles out. His body was covered and lying at one side of a large tent while outside the flames still burned at the base of a billowing pyre of oily black smoke with occasional explosions and pyrotechnics soaring from the wreck. The doctor did his examination, Don talked to the crew and I felt grief-stricken and later went to bed in complete misery. I had become almost used to losing my friends in planes shot down over distant targets but this accident was terribly personal and shattering.

On 19 August big administrative changes took place at Kabrit. 236 Wing and the squadrons 108 (W/Cdr Maw) and 148 (W/Cdr Kerr) moved out to L.G. 237 (Kilo 40) an airfield on the Cairo-Alexandria Road. A new 238 Wing took over Kabrit and a new squadron, No. 40 Wellington Bomber Squadron from Malta moved in to join 104 Squadron. The new Officer Commanding 238 Wing was G/Capt. J. A. P. Harrison, DFC, who arrived with wing commander stripes and was soon on very friendly terms with his squadron officers, W/Cdr Saville of 104 Squadron and W/Cdr Ridgway, DFC of 40 Squadron.

The reorganisation of 205 Group resulted in the Wellington squadrons being based in three wings of two squadrons situated at Abu Sueir (231 Wing with 37 and 70 Squadrons), Kabrit (238 Wing with 40 and 104 Squadrons), and L.G. 237 (236 Wing with 108 and 148 Squadrons). The group also controlled two Liberator squadrons and a

Halifax squadron as heavy bombers. These changes were completed without delay to the bombing operations and in good time before the coming Battle of Alam el Halfa in the desert close to Alamein.

On 20 August my diary reads: 'Charles was buried this morning at Geneifa. At briefing we had twenty American intelligence officers to listen and watch our methods. The AOC and our new G/Capt also came but fortunately they arrived late, just after my piece!'

I wrote next day to Mrs Stotesbury and I also wrote a special letter to my wife on matters in the event of my own death on operations or in some other way. Somehow with Charles being killed and so many of our crews shot down or missing recently, death seemed unpleasantly close and possible. This was the first time I had felt like this in my year of service in the RAF and I made up my mind to forget the matter as quickly as possible.

Don, of course, had the dreadful job of writing a letter of condolence to the next of kin of anyone killed or missing from 104 Squadron. With his sincere interest in and concern for his squadron personnel I felt sure that he would write genuine and comforting letters.

About this time Don revealed an odd sense of humour and perhaps a typically Australian view of aristocracy and authority. Not only did he fly with as many different crews as possible but he checked out each of his two new flight commanders by taking them to Tobruk.

On 17 August he took Wellington R for Robert with S/Ldr Leggate, Sgt Barnard, Sgt Wastney and Sgt Murray as crew, to bomb the town. It was a long flight of eight hours and forty-five minutes, but I cannot recall hearing any details about the result, or about flak over the target. I think it can be safely assumed that they were taken right over the harbour and its defences.

On the 20th he took S/Ldr Strutt, P/O Manfield (the squadron navigation officer), Sgt Jenkins, Sgt Sparksman and P/O Dodd to the same target. This time I do know what happened, and why! Don had asked me a few days earlier if I knew we had a member of the aristocracy in the squadron. He explained that our new flight commander, S/Ldr Strutt, was entitled to be called the Honourable Ivan Strutt; he came from some aristocratic English family in Somerset. He also said that Strutt had been in an RAF training unit in South Africa and was now joining 205 Group and 104 Squadron for operational experience. I gathered that our Wing Commander intended that he should receive this experience straight away over Tobruk! He gave a wicked grin, as though he relished the opportunity of providing the British aristocracy with a suitable example of enemy defences.

Also on that flight was S/Ldr Les Manfield, a Welsh rugby international and navigation officer of 104 Squadron. Les, who was also known as 'Baldie' for obvious reasons, referred to W/Cdr. Saville as 'the Mad Aussie' wrote in 1982:

> Apart from the 'op' to Tobruk on 20/21 August 1942, when I was his navigator/bomb aimer and Struttie was his 'second dickie', I had very little to do with him during the six or seven weeks I served under him as navigation officer. I remember that he was very critical of officers like F/Lt Strutt, who had had a rather 'cushy' time at some training establishment or other during the earlier part of the war and it was typical of him to try to take Struttie back and forth over the Tobruk guns to give him 'flak experience' (and hopefully to scare him a bit). As it turned out he was a bit worried himself on the last run when a piece of flak which had hit the buckle of my chute harness where I crouched in the bombing compartment rebounded and took a piece out of the welt of his desert boot. I can remember him telling me to drop the rest of the bloody bombs and get to hell out of here.
>
> Of course Struttie turned out to be a first-class bomber pilot, although I did not know much about his later career until I read your book. But I do know that he was a very nice chap and I was grieved when I heard of his death while I was flying with 267 Squadron. I believe he was the 'Hon. Ivan C. Strutt', was he not? All I can remember about W/Cdr Saville apart from that trip was that he seemed a very dynamic character, a good mixer in the mess and intolerant of people who did not do their job properly.

The Wellington E for Edward had forty-eight holes from flak over Tobruk on that memorable occasion but returned safely with the crew unharmed. I interrogated the wing commander and his crew at Kabrit base.

On 22 August Don took Wellington G for George on a non-operational flight to nearby RAF Station Abu Sueir with a specially chosen representative party from our squadron to attend a Middle East RAF parade for the prime minister, Winston Churchill. The chosen few were four officers and four sergeants, all aircrew; W/Cdr Saville, F/Lt Watkins (New Zealand), F/O Gray (New Zealand), P/O Proctor (Canada), Sgt Cairns, Sgt Staib, F/Sgt Redwood and Sgt Gill.

Neil Watkins recalls that the V.I.P. arrived in an RAF Liberator while a standing patrol of fighters kept guard overhead. Where the Liberator stopped there was a small party of RAF personnel on parade while groups of visitors like the 104 Squadron representatives were marshalled along a taxiing strip nearby. Churchill alighted finally after much saluting and hand shaking from a top brass welcoming committee. He boarded a jeep and was driven past the parade giving the 'V' sign and waving. The parade presented arms and then all the visiting groups were collected in a small hangar where things were more informal. The great man, however, was still surrounded by high-ranking officers and security men.

Churchill gave a short speech, waved his cigar, again made the famous 'V' sign and was duly spirited away in a convoy of army vehicles. It was probable that he had quite a number of units to visit that day. Neil reports that one thing he remembers well was that although Churchill was small in stature he had a tremendous aura about him which everyone felt. He was confidence personified!

Don and his air crew group were not presented to the prime minister and were later refused permission to look over the Liberator in which he had travelled. However, the squadron team returned to Kabrit well pleased with their close-up view of the war leader and perhaps more than a little inspired by the occasion. It is interesting to note that Churchill's encouraging air of happy confidence in his armed services occurred two months before the vital Battle of El Alamein.

This fortunate group had seen the famous wartime leader who was able to inspire a nation near defeat by his own confidence. On our squadron our own small but very confident and aggressive wing commander gave the same sort of leadership to a select group of highly trained men who needed all the dash and daring they possessed to continue brave attacks on enemy targets over a long, tense and dangerous tour of operations.

In August 104 Squadron, with its Wellington IIs and Merlin engines was the only squadron in the Middle East able to carry 4,000 lb blast bombs. Two of our aircraft had been modified to carry these bombs by removing the bomb doors. HQ-RAF-ME and 205 Group were anxious to be able to drop this type of bomb on the enemy, if and when the *Afrika Korps* made its anticipated thrust through the Alamein defences. Don naturally decided that he would drop one of them.

Wellington L for London was one of the modified aircraft and Don tested it without a crew on 24 August and then flew on the 26th also alone as he had done in the ferry pool, to L.G. 226 to pick up a 4,000 lb bomb and return to base. On the 29th he took off from Kabrit with Sgt Anderson as second pilot, Sgt Sills as navigator, F/Sgt Peters as wireless operator and Sgt Smith as gunner. (Anderson and Peters had been in his crew on 458 Squadron). The intention was to fly to L.G. 237 (Kilo 40), refuel and proceed to the target in the battle area.

The plane developed engine trouble immediately after take-off in the late afternoon. There was not enough time or height to jettison the bomb and Don performed the almost incredible feat of landing the heavily laden plane with one engine, on its wheels in the open desert near Fayid. A belly landing would almost certainly have exploded the bomb and destroyed the aircraft and crew instantly.

In the 458 Squadron history, *We Find and Destroy* the story is told of their former flight commander, now CO of 104 Squadron, appearing at the Fayid bar to drink a couple of beers after a long walk from his aircraft. No one believed that he had landed a Wellington in the desert with a 4,000 lb bomb on board so they got a gharry (truck) and took him back to his aircraft to find it was true! Don's log book tells the rest of the story.

Next morning he got both engines working again and took off from the bumpy desert (still with the bomb and fuel load) to return to Kabrit. The engines were rechecked and Don took off again for Kilo 40, only to have the operation itself cancelled because of further trouble with a serious oil leak in one engine.

On the 31st they returned to base at Kabrit for engine repairs. They then again took off on the same day for Kilo 40. There Don apologised for the delays caused by their several mishaps. They had a meal, the Wellington was topped up with fuel and finally on the evening of the 31st L for London slowly rose off the end of the L.G. 237 flarepath and went off to make a major contribution to the Battle of Alam el Halfa, which was then in progress.

In *The Desert Rats* by Major-General G. L. Verney, Major H. Woods describes the bombing of the Afrika Korps on the night of 31 August 1942:

> There were seldom less than 20 flares in the air at any one time and the whole valley with its mass of the *Afrika Korps* stationary was lit up like a huge fairyland. All the time, red-orange, white-green tracer was darting hither and thither like little 100 mile an hour [160 k.p.h.] coloured fairies. The huge flash of the bombs, which included two of 4,000 lb also inspired the whole thoroughly warlike scene, with little figures silhouetted against their vehicles as they tried to find cover from our bombs.

Those two 4,000 lb bombs went down with the compliments of 104 Squadron and the one dropped from L for London by our wing commander and his steadfast crew was the climax of their brave and determined efforts of the last three days. Don had made seven take-offs and six landings with the heavy and dangerous bomb before successfully unloading it close to Alam al Halfa ridge on enemy troops, vehicles and armour at their furthest point of penetration towards Alexandria. In order to complete what counted only as a single bombing operation the captain and crew of L for London had endured engine failures, a forced landing and nerve-shattering take-offs and landings with a full operational bomb load on a Wellington II in high temperatures when Merlin engines were known to be subject to overheating and loss of power. Only a pilot of outstanding experience and immense flying skills could have survived the trials and emergencies encountered in the seven hours and fifty minutes of what was Don's twenty-first operational flight.

In retrospect it seems that his landing in the desert on one engine and with a 4,000 lb bomb on board – and subsequently taking off again fully laden – was a highly admired part of the Saville legend. It was regarded as an unbelievable feat by fellow pilots in the 205 Group squadrons, who knew the chances. In their opinion at the time, Don should have received an immediate decoration for exceptional skill and bravery.

After the successful Battle of Alam el Halfa the morale of the Allied forces continued to rise under the new leadership of Generals Montgomery and Alexander. At Kabrit we were encouraged by seeing large numbers of ships unloading in the Bitter Lakes and Suez area. We knew that the Scottish 51st Division was in Egypt and that supplies of new equipment included the U.S. Sherman tanks said to be equal to the best German tanks.

In September and early October our bombing operations were at a steady level, which seemed relatively comfortable after the furious pace of May to August. Tobruk, enemy landing grounds and the battle area were the main targets and the intensity of operations rose again sharply before the opening of the Battle of El Alamein on 23 October. My diary entry for 12 September reads:

> On this evening of 12 September the wing commander told me that I can go with him tomorrow on my first operation. I've already practised in a rear gun turret with Stan Dodd the gunnery officer and Johnny Johnston, pilot, who started up his engines so that I could operate the turret and guns. There are three controls to operate, one for hydraulic pressure – a twist grip control for turret movement – and the other is the gun trigger. It is jolly nice how anyone in the squadron will take up his own time to show me a gadget on an aircraft – and there is a purpose behind this practice.

On this occasion Don took X for X-ray (modified to carry a 4,000 lb bomb) and F/O Mather's crew without the captain, who was suffering from 'gippy tummy' – a nasty form of dysentery which attacked everyone in Egypt and the desert at irregular intervals. The crew was:

W/Cdr Saville as captain, Sgt Lynch as second pilot, Sgt Corten as observer (navigator), Sgt Hayes as wireless operator, F/O Chappell as front gunner and Sgt Symonds as rear gunner. We also had on board two passengers, an intelligence clerk and a fitter being transferred to 236 Wing at L.G. 237.

Take-off at 17.20 hours was excellent and I travelled as tail gunner to manipulate the turret and get used to it. The delta looked green and luxuriant with muddy water filling all canals and drains and overflowing from the River Nile onto the adjacent fields. The Nile was in full flood and we had a wonderful view of the delta barrage, with twin walls across the Rosetta and Damietta distributaries.

The landing at L.G. 237 was so smooth that in the rear turret I felt no jolting or jarring at all – very different from some landings I had endured with young and inexperienced pilots. S/Ldr Le Grand and F/Lt Read of Intelligence entertained me at the officer's mess for dinner and then in the darkness we went to our place by truck.

At 21.30 hours we took off smoothly into the night and after half an hour I was told to go into the front turret, entering a dark but just visible world of stars above and incendiaries like stars on the ground; these were thrown out by the aircraft ahead of us to enable us to estimate wind drift by the aircraft ahead of us. I put Le Grand's blanket around my legs and made myself as comfortable as possible. Everything in the plane was very orderly and comforting. I had not the slightest qualm because of the wing commander and what seemed like a good crew – all Australians except me! I had observed the navigator working hard at his desk, the wireless operator recording messages and tinkering with his set, the rear gunner giving wind-drift information and the captain and second pilot busy up front in the cockpit – only the front gunner was clueless!

Before Sollum we could see the flash of guns at Tobruk. Later, as we approached the target area I could see that the flak was formidable – bursts well above us up to 4,500 or 5,000 metres (15,000–16,000 ft) at least. We were then flying at 2,500 metres (8,000 ft) and I thought I could make out the dark line of the coast. Several bombers were caught in searchlights and flak and I noticed one aircraft flying around outside the flak with a strong downward light on as if to identify itself to the gunners and searchlights. This was probably a night fighter and I reported it to the captain, he had already seen it.

We searched for our own target – a gun control position near the Tobruk-Derna road which was believed to have radar equipment feeding information to the AA batteries of the port. I could see the roads as dark lines through the lighter-coloured sand, revealed by the light of flares dropped by our aircraft and others. Wadis were defined clearly and I also saw numbers of bomb bursts, and craters in the sand which looked like wasted efforts.

We eventually dropped our single 4,000 lb bomb but our bomb aimer, Sgt Corten, afterwards said he was disappointed that he had not been allowed to drop it earlier when he thought he had identified the target. Our bomb was supposed to go down at a particular time to fit in with plans for the whole operation which included attacks by naval parties coming ashore and army units attacking the defences from inland. The bomb was dropped on time but it seemed doubtful that it was on target.

In the clear conditions our navigator took us home accurately on track to various beacons and so to our Kabrit flarepath and Chance Light.

There was quite a crowd in the intelligence room when I filled in the sortie report for our crew and assisted with some other interrogations. It had been a special operation, with the bombing of Tobruk forming part of a combined land-sea-air operation. Unhappily the enemy seemed to have been alerted by the unusually heavy air attacks by a hundred bombers and the landing parties met severe opposition and failed to take their objectives. Two destroyers and one light cruiser were said to have been lost by the Royal Navy and our air losses included the senior air staff officer, G/Capt. R. Kellett, who planned the air operation and was forced down and taken prisoner.

The operation was not a true example of the real thing for me because our Wellington did not enter the flak zone over the town and harbour. However, it confirmed my view of the dangers, anxieties and boredom of night bombing and I mentally took my hat off to the aircrews even more than before.

And what did I learn about W/Cdr Saville? The flying skills were very evident and his strong confidence somehow enveloped the rest of us in the crew, making it easier for us to cope with the circumstances; we kept fully alert because it was expected of us. Don kept intercom talk to a minimum and strictly to business. There was no idle chatter – it was business only all the time or silence.

On 17 September I was up at 02.30 hours to meet returning crews and after interrogations had a long talk with the wing commander and the A flight commander (Struttie) about recent operations and future possibilities here and in the war generally. It was a very interesting conversation and as a result we didn't breakfast until 06.00 hours. Don was always articulate about the war situation and war policy.

In September the two squadrons, 40 and 104, operated almost every night but each squadron had one or two 'stand downs' so the pressure of work at Intelligence was not as severe as for the previous four months.

I remember one night which was notable for great events in the bar, where the group captain was celebrating his fourth stripe. He quietly and very firmly refused to let two visitors go who were from the ME Target Section and had been at our briefing. They were very late in leaving by car for Cairo. I had an excuse to leave early because an aircraft had come back, so I had to go off to interview the crew as it was my duty night. Don, who was not on duty, was having a wonderful time with G/Capt Harrison, and both were very merry. Next morning there were some thick heads and short tempers at breakfast, and Don tore someone off a wizard strip, obviously giving vent to his morning-after feelings.

The 30th was a full day, with a most interesting lunchtime talk with Don about aircraft in general. He had stories about New Guinea Airways, Short Brothers aircraft factory, Lerwick flying boats, maintenance units etc. He was a most experienced airman with a fund of information and many stories of exciting incidents, which he told very well.

After the evening briefing I had dinner with him and we went out to the flarepath to see the take-off at 21.00 hours. Soon after our arrival at the Chance Light an aircraft of 40 Squadron shot off red Very lights and came round immediately after take-off to make an emergency landing. After recent experiences there was a little natural excitement and people got ready to get behind the Chance Light or trucks in case of a crash. The Wellington came in fast and nearly hit the ground with its port wing tip, bounced off the port wheel onto the starboard wheel and hurtled down the runway, bouncing about in a most frightening manner. Just as it appeared it would crash into the lake, it took-off again. It was now identified as M for Mother, captained by Sgt Perry. In it came again with everyone taking cover and praying hard, but Perry made a reasonable landing this time. A fabric patch had come off the starboard wing and removed the I.F.F. aerial, and both had wound themselves round the elevator plane, preventing the Wellington from climbing properly.

As a result of this incident our squadron aircraft were late on target and we lost F for Freddie with Sgt Hunt and P/O Ramage pilots, Sgt Gillis and others. Two planes were seen to be shot down over Tobruk.

About this time, at the end of September, we learned of the loss of W/Cdr Roger Maw of 108 Squadron to the very sincere regret of us all. He was a most popular wing commander, grey haired but jolly – and the originator of the 'Maw Plan' for attacking a strongly defended target like Tobruk. By this plan all planes were given a time and heading for going over the target more or less together so that the flak and searchlights could not easily concentrate on one aircraft to destroy it. Some time later we heard that he and his crew were PoWs. On 3 October we had a stand down and it was like a glorious week's holiday in peace time. Kabrit, with its sandy beaches along the Bitter Lake could briefly give a holiday feeling, with crews able to enjoy swimming and sailing, play tennis or go off by transport to Suez or Ismailia. In the evening I was invited to go with Don, Bob Ginn, the engineer officer, and Charles Baker, the adjutant of our squadron to visit HQ 205 Group at Ismailia. We had a very convivial evening, and at about 01.30 hours got ready to depart after prawns and beer. Don decided that I was the most sober and ordered me to drive them home. I thoroughly enjoyed myself driving the Humber staff car along the road by the Suez Canal back to Geneifa and Kabrit.

On the 9th Don took G/Capt Harrison on 'ops' to bomb two adjacent landing grounds – L.G. 17 and L.G. 18, formerly ours but now occupied by enemy fighters. It turned out to be a very good operation, with plenty of fires started by bombing. But our H for Harry was missing. The crew including P/O Penman on his first operation as a captain, Sgt Govett, navigation NCO, and F/Sgt Peters, signals NCO – nice chaps all of them and F/Sgt Peters was formerly in Don's crew on 458 Squadron.

During October the pace of our bombing operations increased and it was obvious that the expected battle to drive Rommel out of Egypt was about to commence. We were attacking Tobruk as the chief enemy supply base and now also enemy landing grounds and enemy troop concentrations in the battle area.

On the 20th, after briefing and dinner I went out to the take-off with Don. The usual incidents occurred. X for X-ray of 40 Squadron swung right off the runway and then proceeded to taxi back up the runway as another 40 Squadron Wellington was returning with engine trouble. X for X-ray moved off just in time and then took off again, still off the runway. Next, one of our 104 Squadron Wellingtons had a defective artificial horizon or some such instrument. The pilot had it changed and the second one was also defective. Don became impatient and took the pilot to task. The pilot reacted indignantly and offered to take the matter to higher authority. There was quite a little altercation for a time, with tempers roused, but Don did not scrub as I expected. Instead he ordered the captain to get out and he himself took over and went on the operation with the rest of the crew!

I was up early for interrogations and then had breakfast and went back to the office. S/Ldr Strutt came and told me he was without a second pilot for the night's operation and asked me if I would like to go with him. It was a useful opportunity to see a new target so I accepted and spent the early afternoon learning to log engine details, pump oil to both engines, turn on the nacelle tanks and let the front gunner in and out of his turret. Don had agreed quite readily that I should go – red tape did not worry him! Then I played tennis and later assisted with the briefing on the target, Fuka (L.G. 16) – an enemy fighter airfield. We had dinner and got ready for take-off at 20.30 hours.

Struttie was a good pilot and D for Donald took off safely and climbed steadily. Nothing of importance occurred *en route* and we pinpointed on Ras el Kenayis, a prominent cape, and set course into the target. I was sent to the astro-hatch while we were over the target and saw flares, photo-flashes galore, and many other Wimpys flashing past, feeling their turbulence. Plenty of light flak was coming up very slowly at first then faster and flashing by us without hitting our aircraft, which was lucky, in view of our fourteen runs over the landing ground, dropping single bombs and taking several photographs. On the ground beneath I could see many bomb flashes and several fires which, with the coloured flak, made a very warlike scene. We came away after an hour and set course for base on the first leg.

Our navigator, P/O Tommy Lonsdale, was excellent and we had no difficulties – in fact the whole crew worked together like a good team.

The group captain was at interrogation and seemed pleasantly amused at my having been on a second 'op'. He evidently agreed with Don that it was a good thing for an intelligence officer to have operational experience. I interrogated Basil Blogg's crew, who were in just after us. Don had also been to Fuka and we all went off to breakfast together – Don, Struttie P/O Tommy Lonsdale, P/O Basil Blogg and myself. I must admit that it felt rather wonderful that we had all been over that target together, and we now had a good talk about the war situation, from Pearl Harbor to Stalingrad. For the operation, P/O Morrison had lent me his flying kit and I had Bob Ginn's helmet – the *esprit de corps* in 104 Squadron was warm and comforting indeed.

There was a 'stand down' for 104 Squadron on 22 October, but 40 Squadron were operating and an important visitor, 'Boom' Trenchard, attended their briefing. Later our group captain and the two squadron commanders entertained the great man in the mess.

The morning of the 23rd was busy, as was the evening, with briefings on the Alamein battle area. The business was about to begin and I watched our crews off from the lake shore; as always it was a stirring sight. In the morning 'Boom' paid us a visit but unfortunately I was too busy to attend his talk to the aircrews. Don was there, of course.

Next morning I was interrogating with Tom Allen the intelligence officer of 40 Squadron, and we found that our crews were all excited about the terrific artillery ground barrage to be seen all along the line from our side firing into enemy held territory. 104 Squadron's F/Lt Harry Beale and F/O Mather dropped the two 4,000 lb bombs on the opening night of the Alamein campaign to shake up the enemy troops.

The next few days were extremely hectic as our bombers were operating at maximum effort in support of the army by bombing enemy tanks, transport and troops close up to the front.

On the 25th briefing was at 18.00 hours and after dinner I went out to dispersals and take-off to check that each navigator knew the exact target area on the battlefield. I watched the take-off and saw Johnny Martin, one of my tennis friends, make a good start on his first trip as captain. My diary also records that the flies had been devilish for the last two days! We had had one or two hot moist days earlier when all the insects in the Middle East appeared in plague numbers including ladybirds, wasp-like flies and cockroaches. The ladybirds were very annoying as they gave a nasty bite when they landed on human flesh.

The night's previous operation was very successful, with an unbeatable record. We received a personal message from the AOC congratulating all squadrons in 205 Group. Seventy-one aircraft had been ordered, 71 operated and 71 returned. Sixteen double sorties were ordered, sixteen aircraft operated double sorties and sixteen returned safe.

What a relief it was to have operated without loss.

The briefing on the afternoon of the 26th was for our squadron to attack an enemy landing ground while 40 Squadron were on the battle area again. Interrogation and summaries took from 01.00 to 05.00 hours on the 27th and my interrogations included S/Ldr Strutt and crew who had put up a fine effort after being hit over the target. The hydraulics failed but they got the undercarriage down by violent manoeuvres and hand operation and then landed safely, thank goodness. I went to bed during the morning and then received news of a 'stand down' at night. In the afternoon our Australian navigation officer, Tom Howes, showed me a butterfly anti-personnel bomb which he said he had defused – I was not amused and left as hurriedly as possible with dignity!

That night Tom Allen kindly invited me over to 40 Squadron to dinner, where the group captain and Don were also guests. It proved a jolly evening with a very fine dinner. We left at 00.15 in the group captain's car with Don and a stray dog which he insisted on taking back to sleep in his room! I thought of rabies!

On the 28th the AOC came to our briefing in the evening and things went reasonably well to the relief and pleasure of Don and myself!

The night of the 29th and 30th was a very good operation but P/O Johnny Martin, an Irishman and a good friend of mine, was missing with his crew on only their second trip together, in P for Peter. A telltale fire with Very lights was seen at 01.30 hours in the target area. Some photographs taken with bombing showed many blast shelters erected for trucks and slit trenches for individuals. Our bombing was evidently worrying the enemy. Little flak was reported but one or two crews thought they saw a Ju.88 night fighter. This probably accounted for the loss of our squadron crew.

During the busy morning of the 30th the group captain and Don came into Intelligence and were interested in everything. After dinner I had another intriguing talk this time with Tommy Howes, the Australian navigation officer who had frightened me with the butterfly bomb, about Australia and the prospects out there. Tom and Don were both very strong advocates for their country and its future and I found their arguments interesting and persuasive. Don told me that I should seriously consider emigrating with my family after the war to one of the Dominions – preferably Australia!

On 3 November the whole of 238 Wing including the two squadrons and the Wing HQ unit was thrown into delight by the news from the front that the enemy was at last cracking at Alamein – and our 104 Squadron was to move to Malta to attack the *Afrika Korps* from the rear.

During the day briefings were held at all sorts of times and I went to the flarepath in the evening with Don to see eleven of our 104 Squadron crews off to attack the battle area and the coastal road behind the front. Seven of these crews did a double sortie that night. Everyone was full of excitement and enthusiasm at taking part in a major victory, which had been so long awaited.

The news was confirmed next day that the front was now fluid and the enemy were withdrawing from Egypt along the coastal road and through the Sollum Pass – and that on 5 November a detachment of 104 Squadron under the leadership of W/Cdr Saville would fly to Malta to attack Rommel's supply routes from Italy to Tunis, Tripoli and Benghazi. At last things were moving fast in our favour.

Chapter Fourteen

104 Squadron at Luqa (1942–3)

The strategic position of the island base of Malta must have been a constant worry to Rommel in 1942. Throughout the long retreat from Alamein to Tunis, the *Afrika Korps* and their Italian allies knew that behind them their supply ships, aircraft, airfields and ports were under constant attack from the RAF and Royal Navy operating from there.

On the other hand, Malta and its people, the garrison and resident air and naval units were frequently attacked by enemy bombers and were sometimes near starvation when convoys could not get through. The Maltese deserved the George Cross they were awarded in 1942.

On 5 November 1942 there was something of a holiday mood at Kabrit as the chosen 104 Squadron detachment crews loaded up their Wellingtons for the long flight to Luqa. The afternoon take-off was quite an event, with G/Capt Harrison and a small crowd of us to wave them off.

When I shook hands with Don I told him I took a poor view of the fact that he was not taking me! Of course I knew the reason – there was a resident intelligence section on Malta and squadron intelligence officers were not required. However, I felt rather forlorn at being left behind; the friendship links within the squadron were temporarily broken.

One by one the Wellingtons moved up to the end of the runway and with smiles, thumbs up and waves from the crews, set off down the narrow black track across the brown sand surface of the airfield and out across the Bitter Lake, leaving two trails of disturbed water from the propellers until the pilot eased the aircraft higher. I noticed that D for Donald, piloted by Laurie Page, took an exceptionally long run right to the edge of the lake before lifting off.

The other crews for Malta included Don's and those of F/Lt Dallas, F/Lt Mercer, Sgt Craig with P/O Morrison as second pilot, S/Ldr Leggate, F/O Jack Parker, Sgt Harris and Sgt Lynch with Sgt Corten and the other Australians who had been with Mather, who had completed a tour of thirty-eight operations with 104 Squadron and was on his way back to Australia.

Don had earlier called Mick Mather to one side and told him that if he did not get away immediately it was likely that he would be returned to the UK and not Australia. The words used were: 'I'm getting you out of here now, Cocky, otherwise once the push starts you'll be caught up indefinitely. You want to get at the yellow bastards, I know, and this is your chance to get back to Australia.'

My diary entry for 6 November 'The place is rather lonely but we shall be moving off soon. Squadron Leader Strutt has been awarded an immediate DFC – good work – he deserves it because he and the whole crew are a very determined and accurate bombing team.' I couldn't help thinking that Don should also have had a decoration and wondered if he might not feel a little hurt because Struttie had got his before him.

The Wellingtons arriving on Malta were immediately put to work but their campaign opened tragically on 7 November: with crews briefed for attacks on two Sardinian airfields D for Donald (Sgt Craig) crashed on take-off at Luqa; the bombs and fuel exploded, killing all the crew.

Don and his crew in M for Mother, plus five other Wellingtons, attacked the targets and returned safely. Subsequently Don sent a signal to the squadron party in Egypt requesting a replacement for D for Donald, which was to bring spares, six fitters – and F/O Chappell.

I dashed into Cairo to collect stationery, a typewriter, maps etc. among other stores required. P/O Tony Crockford was captain with Sgt Rogers as navigator in a scratch crew to fly L for London to Malta. We left L.G. 224 on 12 November, refuelled at L.G. 106 and were supplied with a meal before taking off into a very black night with a poor weather forecast.

After an unpleasant flight through rain and turbulence we arrived safely at Luqa to be welcomed by Don and S/Ldr Leggate, both of whom had just returned from double sorties on El Aouina aerodrome at Tunis, where they had started fires and silenced a gun site.

We learned that the crew of D for Donald had been buried, on 11 November at Bighi Cemetery, Valletta, attended by W/Cdr Saville and members of other crews from 104 Squadron. S/Ldr Leggate also told me that the squadron detachment Wellingtons and crews had been extremely busy since landing on Malta on 6 November. A detachment from 40 Squadron was also with our 104 crews on the island and operations had been mounted each night – 7, 8, 9, 10, 11 and 12 November, including some nights with double-sorties. The wing commander had already operated four times, including one very successful raid on Elmas aerodrome on the southern coast of Sardinia, close to Cagliari.

F/Lt 'Tich' Showell, DFC has provided a detailed account of this raid in which, as a flight sergeant he was rear gunner in Don's crew. There had been two previous raids on Elmas, both abortive, and the CO decided he would show the way. The following is an extract from a letter from him in 1982.

> I was only fortunate enough to fly once with W/Cdr Saville as a substitute for Sgt Stanley, and I must say it was an experience never to be forgotten! I had flown on 8-11-42 as front gunner with Sgt Roscoe to Elmas, Sardinia, but having failed to locate the target we bombed a secondary target.
>
> On 10-11-42 I met W/Cdr Saville for the first time and immediately felt the vitality of the man. At briefing he stressed that the target must be found and every bomb had to count – and on no account must any Wimpy attempt to strafe the target!
>
> Although our observer was 'green' to 'ops' we found the target without difficulty and immediately ringed it with flares. Elmas was a combined sea-plane and land plane aerodrome. Our first bomb fell short and hit a seaplane! We dropped every bomb singly and each started a fire. Whilst all this was going on we were in the midst of light and heavy flak and a lone searchlight kept picking us up. When W/Cdr Saville heard that all the bombs had gone he uttered a few Aussie 'unusables' and told the front gunner and myself to get ready to put the xxxxx thing out! He dived down the beam and the front gunner extinguished the 'flame' – I then strafed the buildings and parked aircraft and the source of light flak – by this time we were flying at about 300–500 ft [90–150 metres]. Just as we crossed the drome, someone hit the bomb dump.
>
> What a night! I could see the fires for over 80 miles [130 km] after leaving the target, and what a leader! I would have flown to any target with him in any old kite but unfortunately I never got the chance again. The memory of this brave man is something which I can cherish for all my days!

I saw more of the island, from a bus to Luqa on 14 November and then from the air as I went on an air test with Don, Charles Dallas and some local fitters in our L for London which had just been fitted with a new main port wing. Another aircraft had taxied into the wing, causing severe damage, so it had to be replaced. Fortunately for all of us the new one proved fine in fifteen minutes of strenuous test flying, including some tight vertical turns! I felt sure that the Maltese fitters were, like me, praying that they had made a thorough job of putting on the new wing! Don really threw that plane around! From the air there were superb views of Valletta Harbour, the bays, cliffs and smaller islands – and of the main island with its dense population, many towns, villages and churches.

I felt very unhappy internally all day with 'Malta dog' – the local name for 'gippy tummy', the diarrhoea and sickness which was so common in the Middle East and Mediterranean area.

In the evening at Luqa I met the famous S/Ldr Warburton, DFC and two bars, who flew photo reconnaissance Spitfires to locate our targets and to check afterwards whether we had used our bombs accurately. The Luqa intelligence office was extremely busy and the vital centre for a variety of air operations. The phones were constantly ringing, different people were coming in and out, individual pilots and crews were being briefed or interrogated. Those intelligence officers certainly worked hard, and their methods were sometimes different from 205 Group practices. Luqa Intelligence handled shipping strikes, night fighters, photo reconnaissance Spitfires, met flights, mine laying, bombers and torpedo bombers, plus some naval aircraft. The intelligence officers were pleased to have my help in dealing with the bomber operations.

Heavy rain caused the cancellation of the operations for 15 November. S/Ldr Warburton, who had gone out earlier to photograph the results of the previous night's bombing did not return and there were fears for his safety.

On the 16th it rained again and operations were again cancelled. Don had a remarkable ability to relax on a stand down or cancellation of operations. This time he collected S/Ldr Leggate and myself and took us back to the billets for dinner, then for an evening at the cinema to see a film *These Glamour Girls*. Afterwards two young local 'glamour girls' tried to attract us as we left the cinema – quite young girls between fifteen and eighteen. But prostitutes didn't interest us – Don wanted to visit Malta's bars. I thought we would go back to Sliema after the film but Don had other ideas. We went on to the Chocolate Box and Charlie's Bar and I had more drinks than ever before in my life, owing to Don insisting on 'another one for the road' about seven or eight times. We talked as coherently as we could to two English girls at one of the bars, who were married to civilians on the island and they told us the truth of the food situation. They were allowed one tin of bully beef and one of sardines per fortnight and lived mainly on bread. This diet explained the nasty blotches on the legs and arms of many civilians. We walked back to the mess with the girls and gave them a tin of bully, a tin of sardines and a tin of the squadron leader's cigarettes.

On the night of 17/18 November two naval Albacores went flare-dropping with a torpedo bomber and sank a large enemy tanker, causing great explosions. The oil on the water caught fire. On the same night a Beaufighter pilot shot down a Ju.88 and damaged another.

However, on the operational side things were not always easy at Malta, particularly in winter. On 12, 14, 17 and 18 November 104 Squadron bombers were sent to Tunis on double sorties using four Wellingtons to bomb the main aerodrome, El Aouina. This was an important target because it was used by transport aircraft bringing supplies and troops from Italy for the *Afrika Korps* and the German forces opposing the American-British forces in Algeria and Tunisia to the west. Unfortunately the cloud cover on the 17th was complete over the Tunisian coast and down to about 600 metres (2,000 ft) base so that it was extremely dangerous for the crews, knowing that nearby mountains came up to 1,200 metres (4,000 ft). All crews that night failed to locate El Aouina and, being unable to bomb in the area because Tunisia was French, they eventually jettisoned their bombs in the sea and returned to Luqa. Jettisoning was done deliberately because they understood that a crash landing with bombs at Luqa could have put the only base on Malta for bombers and transport aircraft out of operation.

Air Vice Marshal Sir Keith Park at Air HQ Malta, however, was furious when he heard reports of bombs being jettisoned. Don received a severe blast from the AOC and in turn the squadron crews the next night were shocked at his language, and the inferences against them at briefing. He told them that the squadron was accused of lack of morale in not bombing the target. Air Vice Marshal Park was disgusted with their conduct in jettisoning bombs that the Merchant Navy had risked their lives in bringing to Malta. 'Tonight, I don't care if I lose every aircraft but that target must be bombed!' he said.

Sgt Corten, a navigator, wrote in a letter later that the boys were reaching for their revolvers after that, but they had to take the medicine. Many of the crew members were worn out from the constant operations of the last few months and felt operationally tired. They knew, however, that on Malta a very tough line was taken over any matter involving morale. The medical officer at Luqa was reported to have told a New Zealander who complained that he was operationally tired. 'On this island you are not operationally tired until you have been unconscious for twenty-four hours.'

Sgt (later F/Lt) Corten remembers that no aircrew member of 104 Squadron was accused of 'lack of moral fibre' or put on a charge during Don's period in command. He says that he thought his bark was worse than his bite and that he preferred to deal with pilots as the captains of their aircraft and had less time for or interest in the other crew members. Corten himself, while on Malta, eventually asked Don if he might be taken off operations because he realised that he was becoming inefficient in the air and was making mistakes with navigational calculations and in bombing. Don knew that this request was completely genuine, and acted accordingly. Corten and the rest of Mather's old crew were taken off operations after having completed well over the usual thirty operations recommended for a first tour. In fact they completed forty, which was known as an 'extended tour'. As intelligence officer, I knew that our surviving experienced crews had been severely drained by the long Alamein period of maximum effort and some were only kept going by the drive, energy and inspiring leadership of our CO. I thought it remarkable that Don himself was able to stand up to the strain of operational command while doing as many operations as his captains and their crews. I also saw the reason behind the occasional drinking binges on 'stand down' evenings.

Don was aware of the strains among his crews and sometimes discussed individuals and crews with the squadron doctor and me. But he also appreciated the need for the mad rush of operations to upset Rommel's supplies and communications. It had to be that way, with double and even triple sorties to make best use of the limited number of Wellingtons and crews available to us. On Malta he followed up his own fifteen operations from Kabrit with twelve from Luqa in fifteen days including three double sorties against El Aouina and a triple sortie on 19 November against three Sicilian airfields used by the *Luftwaffe*.

Was it necessary to operate so frequently while in command? Was it a natural and reasonable response to the pressures and demands of the war as viewed from Malta in November and December 1942? I think the answer was 'Yes' for Don, because he was so totally dedicated to the war effort. He was perhaps also driven to some extent by his own desire for recognition as a successful squadron commander – and this could be interpreted by cynics as an ambition to achieve a DFC or DSO-DFC. I felt at the time, as did other officers in the squadron and wing, (and we talked about it frequently), that no one was more deserving of gallantry awards than our wing commander – yet he remained undecorated while many young pilots in his own and other squadrons, particularly at Malta, had DFCs, some with bars, DFMs and, of course, DSOs among his fellow squadron commanders. This must have hurt Don a little, or he would not have been human. He was doing gallant deeds regularly, and he was keeping up the spirit of his captains and crews – what more could he do? In my opinion the Elmas raid itself was worthy of an immediate decoration for valour, yet it was overlooked.

As if once again to demonstrate his ability to match anyone in the game, on 19 November he took Wellington E for Edward on a triple sortie to the Sicilian airfields at Catania, Gerbini and Comiso. It was to some degree a special operation to prevent enemy air interference with a small convoy of four or five merchant vessels which was now nearing Malta from Alexandria (No convoy supplies had reached Malta since July when five ships got in out of fourteen). He bombed Catania airfield on the first sortie and Comiso on the second. For some reason he then changed to M for Mother, one of his favourite Wellingtons, for the third sortie again against Catania. E for Edward was taken on that sortie by F/Lt 'Shag' Mercer and his crew. Sadly, it was seen to be shot down over Catania.

I was on duty that night and morning and it was my job to go out to the flarepath and interview each crew in their aircraft or in a bus nearby while the Wellingtons were refuelled from bowsers and rearmed with bombs and ammunition after the first and second sorties. Walking from aircraft to aircraft on the tarmac apron so frequently bombed by the Germans and Italians was a strangely exciting and heart-pumping experience. Wellingtons, bowsers, bomb trolleys, gharries, and armourers, drivers, fitters, AA personnel and aircrews working or relaxing and smoking – which always worried me because of the strong smell of 100 octane everywhere. People spoke rather quietly on the whole as if not to disturb any enemy within earshot and all of us looked up frequently at the stars and the clouds and listened for the throb of enemy engines. If they came it was a long run to a shelter – probably the quarry at the end of the runway. There was always some apprehension in the air out on the runway!

Don and his crew would cluster around cheerfully and tell me their story for the bombing report. Don was at ease in his aircraft or close to it on the ground. He was usually cheery and good tempered after an operation whereas earlier at briefing he might have been aggressive and tense while getting across the importance of the timing and the target. It was good to sense the understanding between members of a crew – experienced crews seemed like a devoted family or a group of close friends, as indeed they usually were. Don, of course, captained scratch crews or some other captain's, but his own aura of confidence would envelop the whole group. In a way I felt it, too – nothing was going to happen to me in that rather scary situation because of his presence!

There is no doubt in my mind that Don made a great personal contribution on Malta, apart from his bombing of enemy targets – he inspired us all by his own persistent example of courage and determination.

Later on the morning of the 20th while completing the final summaries about 07.00 hours I became aware of a sense of bustle and excitement outside. There was distant hooting of ships and the sounds of traffic – the convoy was in! On the way back to the mess we heard cheering and saw some merchant ships and naval vessels in Valletta harbour. I was so tired and sleepy that I fell asleep listening on my radio to the news at 09.00 hours.

I was wakened at 15.00 hours by Don and had a meal with him on the balcony overlooking the garden of the hotel we occupied. It was truly amazing how he could recover so quickly – the previous night he had been piloting a Wellington bomber for almost nine hours' flying with three take-offs and three landings, yet he was bright and cheerful and talking about Australia and his family.

He talked freely and easily about his brother's station in a well-watered valley in New South Wales and of his father's cement works at Portland. He referred to the land they had bought near Bathurst. Then, politely remembering my own background and interest in schools and education, he turned to discuss some of his own ideas on education. Among his suggestions were three which struck me as so simple yet sensible that I wrote them down afterwards in my diary.

1. That every boy and girl should be able to write a conversational and interesting letter as a vital means of communication and a social asset. (I think he realised from his experience in censorship that few men wrote good letters to their wives and families.)

2. That all children should be taught to use a typewriter, so useful in commerce and letter writing. (today that applies to computers).

3. That sex education should be part of the curriculum and that boys and girls should be educated together in co-educational schools.

I thoroughly enjoyed talking to Don and the feeling seemed to be mutual. He would always discuss squadron problems with me and perhaps this eased some of the tremendous pressures of operational command. He also enjoyed discussing the war situation on various fronts and put forward stimulating ideas for present and future campaigns.

We went up to Luqa together at 17.00 hours and I tried to sort out matters and make things ready for S/Ldr Leggate who had kindly offered to do my job that night. Then Don drove the bus back to Sliema, as the driver had cut off the top of his finger. He drove it well and we told him that he should remuster as a driver-M.T. The pleasant informality in our squadron allowed a little light-hearted banter like that.

And so I had a quiet evening and early night, but in an emergency Don went off on operations again to pilot a Wellington with a 4,000 lb bomb which had been requested at the very last minute by AHQ. He ought to have had a good night's rest but typically did the job himself, knowing that all the crews were as tired as he was. The target was at Bizerta.

Several notable things happened on 22 November. First, the rest of 104 Squadron arrived under the command of S/Ldr Strutt, and they brought three sacks of mail. Tour-expired and operationally tired crews had been sent away for rest periods and new crews had taken their place.

I also saw S/Ldr, now W/Cdr Warburton as perky as ever and about to return to his photographic reconnaissance work by going off in his Spitfire to photograph Bizerta, Tunis and Tripoli. He had scared us by not coming back on the 15th from a similar trip and I now heard the story. He had been shot-up over Bizerta and had made a forced landing at Bone aerodrome. Then he had made his way to Gibraltar, collected a delivery Spitfire and on the way back to Malta shot down a Ju.88! He joked about his batman, who he found had made off with all his clothes but now said he would get them back from the laundry!

Finally, the 22nd saw Don operating again in a double-sortie attack on Sidi Ahmed and Trapani aerodromes in conjunction with Beaufighter attacks on the same targets.

We had a stand down on the night of the 23rd and on the 24th came a double sortie on Bizerta docks. I was on duty at Luqa and worked all night, returning to Sliema very tired and sleepy. At 15.30 hours the next day I got up and had some bully beef with my tea, as I had missed lunch. It was a good job I had it for at 17.15 hours Don dashed in to say he was leaving for Egypt immediately and I was to go with him. We picked up a few clothes and dashed off in a car to Luqa. There we met Sgt Setterfield and crew from 40 Squadron and got a very hurried briefing on the weather, beacons *en route*, etc. I could not get a parachute or Mae West. Wellington 1C B for Bertie was still in a pen and had not been touched for a fortnight. It had been condemned as 'unfit for operations' by S/Ldr Booth of 40 Squadron on the main grounds of excessive oil consumption.

I knew that operational aircraft were not condemned light heartedly, but nothing like that stopped our Wing Commander. He had extra cans of oil put in, then started the engines and taxied out. And so off along the flarepath and into the night. I was none too happy about a trip in an unserviceable Wellington 1C and had anyone else been piloting I would have been really nervous. We met heavy cumulus and cumulo-nimbus clouds and Don called me up front to look at the lovely sight with the moon peeping over the tops and lighting up the cloud hills and valleys.

Three hours out from Malta we hit some bumps and lost height in a series of drops through sleet and hail, which rattled on the astrodome and fabric of the surging aircraft. After five hours the sea was covered by mist and the moon by alto-stratus. We seemed lost in mid-air – isolated. After six hours the navigator seemed puzzled at the non-appearance of the African coast and the cloud increased. Oil was being pumped manually into the engines and the main tank of 64 litres (14 gals) was dry. We put in another 73 litres (16 gals) from cans – a messy business. Don turned south and eventually we sighted the dark outline of the coast and later the reassuring shape of Ras el Kenayis and a beacon. At this point one of the engines ran very roughly and the whole aircraft vibrated. Oil was pumped manually again and very gradually the vibration lessened.

Soon afterwards I saw a flarepath and was extremely thankful. So too obviously were some of the crew, who had begun to expect some hours in a dinghy on their last flight – they had finished their tour of operations and were probably to return to the UK.

We even had a welcoming party to meet us on L.G. 106, including G/Capt Harrison, S/Ldr Carter and F/Lt Kuziar. It was cheering to be welcomed in such a way and we enjoyed a good chat and had beer, cheese, bread and butter, biscuits and pickles, which revived us considerably before we went to bed.

The reason for this hurried flight back to Egypt in a discarded Wellington with two worn-out engines was that Don was dissatisfied with the bomber strength on Malta. He wanted to arrange for another squadron and 238 Wing HQ staff to join us at Luqa. It seemed to be a piece of outrageous Saville diplomacy, unsurping Air HQ Malta, but he may have been acting for Air Vice Marshal Park.

In the morning the adjutant told me that my promotion to flight lieutenant rank had come through along with his own and Stan Dodd's. We then borrowed transport and toured the local battlefield, seeing many enemy tanks and trucks destroyed by fire and high explosive – some probably from our bombing. I felt that the bombing had been very effective because of the numerous slit trenches constructed alongside each vehicle. The afternoon made me feel melancholy at the futility of war – I picked up a *Panzer Gruppe* diary, an Italian propaganda booklet, two enemy identity cards and a ship recognition pamphlet.

At tea we found that the squadron was moving back to re-equip. I was to move off at midnight in the ambulance with the doctor.

We journeyed for some hours seeing occasional small German cemeteries by the roadside and burned-out vehicles and tanks from both armies. The Germans seemed to bury their dead at or near to the place where they were killed, while our dead were transferred to big cemeteries at central points such as El Alamein.

The next day or so was spent pitching and repitching tents at L.G. 237, and on visits to Cairo for shopping. Don visited HQ RAF-ME and presumably presented his plea for reinforcement of the Malta bombers.

On the evening of the 29th Don wanted to hear Winston Churchill's speech. My wireless set was the only one available and I could not get it to work, to the great annoyance of Don and others in the mess. 'Chappie, you've had your time!' he said. 'What incompetence, unable to work your own wireless set when I want to hear a vital and informative speech from Mr Churchill!'

On the 30th we went shopping and, after dealing with purchases for the mess at the NAAFI. we cleaned up at Wellington House and made for Jacques, the Cairo fashion shop de luxe. Don astonished the girls by buying a large supply of ladies' night dresses, pyjamas, slips, knickers, stockings etc. We all clustered round to help him choose the delectable garments and some of us, including myself bought a few for sending back to England. Don certainly knew how to look after his girlfriend or friends.

We had dinner together at the Bar Restaurant and then spent the evening at Groppis. Our transport had been parked in the army barracks and when we left there was an enjoyable altercation between Don and the Military Police at the gate over our failure to adhere to correct checking-out procedures. Don always appeared to have scant regard for RAF regulations if they inconvenienced him at all, so army regulations were paid no respect. After some shouting and rank-pulling, in which the rest of us took no active part, we were eventually able to make our getaway, but the M.P.s were far from amused!

Then it was back to camp at high speed and more fun with the group captain and Don trying to compose a signal calculated to satisfy 205 Group. Don had obviously succeeded in his mission and 238 Wing HQ and the remainder of 40 Squadron would join 104 Squadron on Malta to form a more formidable bomber force. Whether he had gone behind the back of 205 Group, or was acting with or without the support of AHQ Malta, we never found out, but G/Capt Harrison was in it with Don and enjoyed it thoroughly. It looked like a conspiracy of some sort.

While Don and squadron personnel flew back to Malta I was to proceed with the 238 Wing HQ party to Alexandria and return by sea. Who arranged this I do not know but I can believe that Don thought it would be more fun for me to travel by sea with the group captain and his staff. And so it was – a quite thrilling experience, for we travelled as guests of the Royal Navy on board HMS *Welshman*, a very fast minelayer, capable of 75 k.p.h. (40 knots). We saluted the quarter deck as we went on board and were very well received. The ship sailed at dusk.

I noticed how alert the gun crews were – scanning the sky constantly. This ship and its fine company had run the gauntlet a number of times between Alexandria and Malta, having been used to take essentials to the island when convoys failed to get through. So far it had survived attacks by aircraft and submarines largely because of its high speed. Tragically, however, it was sunk 90 km (40 miles) east of Tobruk by torpedoes from U 617 on 1 February 1943, with heavy loss of life.

The next day we joined a convoy and sailed past some coastal places known to us previously only as targets. Later we increased speed to something about the maximum and left the convoy behind as we went to the wardroom for drinks and dinner.

I felt the slowing down at dawn and on getting up saw land ahead. As we entered the magnificent harbour, with its off-shoot creeks there was much evidence of bomb damage on shore and wrecks in the water. We went alongside amidst hand-clapping and cheering and I saw the governor, Lord Gort, among the welcoming people on the quay. We went ashore and to AHQ and almost immediately there was an air-raid warning. Later I took the bus to the airfield and was on duty for the night. So was Don – he went off on a double sortie operation to bomb ships and harbour facilities at La Goulette, a good operation.

He had arrived back on the island a day or so before the *Welshman* and I gathered from Luqa Intelligence that he had had a hazardous trip (far worse than the flight to Egypt on B for Beer), arriving with only one engine functioning. The true story of the flight eventually came to me not from Don but from F/Lt Bob Ginn, our squadron engineer officer, who had flown with him and had been allowed to pilot the plane on part of the journey.

The flight was something of an epic and deserves a detailed account because it reveals different aspects of Don Saville's complex character. Bob Ginn had been with 104 Squadron from the earliest days at Driffield, and he had served under W/Cdr Beare, W/Cdr Blackburn and now Don. He found Don somewhat abrasive but in retrospect thinks that he was the right man for that time and probably as awkward a character for his seniors as he was for the squadron personnel!

There are two interesting insights into Don which are revealed in letters from Ginn. The first is that he obviously understood the engineering problems which arose with the Merlin engines of the Wellington IIs in the high temperatures of the desert and he fully backed his engineer officer when the latter made some careful experiments with oil-pressure relief-valve limits, adjusting the relationship between temperature and pressure. The alteration was subsequently endorsed by a Rolls Royce representative to the great satisfaction of both Don and Bob Ginn. The latter had been threatened with dire penalties by his senior engineer officers at wing and group. His experiment substantially reduced the number of Wellington IIs returning early with low oil pressure and high oil temperatures during the Alamein campaign.

The second insight came in what Bob describes as 'the only time we ever talked on a personal basis, and Don told me that he was determined to go back home with a DSO, DFC or not at all.' This fitted in with my own impression that Don did not like being the only undecorated wing commander on Malta.

The flight from Egypt to Luqa was described in a letter from Bob Ginn in 1985.

> I was at Kilo 40 (L.G. 237) on the Cairo-Alexandria Road with an aircraft which had had a major overhaul in Cairo, waiting for a pilot to ferry us to Malta. Out of the blue, Saville, in his best uniform but slightly the worse for wear alcohol-wise, arrived with a three-tonner loaded up with cardboard boxes of choc bars and the like – he'd spent about £400 on goodies for the troops.
>
> Loading this lot was a nightmare and he just told me to get on with it and went back to Cairo. He got back about 3.00 p.m. and said we would take-off in an hour for L.G. 104 where the R.S.U. [Repair and Salvage Unit] had settled with that alcoholic CO of theirs where we'd refuel and take off after dark for Malta. I had two fitters and he'd scared up a ground signals flight lieutenant and a sergeant navigator who'd got left at Durban, sick, and had just reached the Middle East. One of the fitters volunteered to go into the rear turret and I think the other occupied the front turret. As I had to stack all the goodies within the fuselage and as near as possible to the main spar (for trim), it was with great difficulty that anyone could have got either to the astrodome, the Elsan or down the catwalk.
>
> Saville had no flying gear but I had a Mae West and a helmet with intercom. Oh yes – we collected enough chutes and harnesses.
>
> The wing commander borrowed my helmet for take-off; we flew up to L.G. 104, landed and he disappeared into the mess with the R.S.U. fellow. I got the aircraft topped up and asked them to lay a flarepath. After dark we went out and found they'd laid the flarepath alongside the road – all of 500 yards! Saville just turned round and said (to me), 'You know this airfield – lay out a useful flarepath.'
>
> Well, I knew that if you started at a wrecked Ju.88 and went diagonally across to a couple of wrecked Me.109s that was the

longest run. So, with an ambulance (the only vehicle with a searchlight) I laid out the flarepath on which my neck depended. The Wingco had been drinking with the R.S.U. chap and frankly I was scared witless. However, he donned my helmet and we took off to Ras something or other. [Ras el Kenayis] just up the coast where the beacon was. He obviously was talking to the navigator who'd scrounged a Dalton [a navigation instrument] and charts and a ruler from somewhere, because he put a course on the compass and turned out over the Med. We went about twenty minutes and then he did no more than climb out of the seat, give me the helmet and indicate I was to fly the thing!

O.K., I'd had a lot of time at the controls and I had a private pilot's licence (he knew all this) but I'd done precious little instrument flying. However, I settled down and we went along. I checked with the signals type who was having difficulty finding anything on the radio and asked him at least to get the D.F. gear working. I wanted to see those little fingers pointing the way, especially because the course, around 300°, seemed to be more for Crete than Malta. I also tried to get the fitter in the rear turret – he had a helmet on and was on the intercom – to drop a floater and get a drift, but this was beyond him.

I think we had been out about one and a half hours when the signals guy got the D.F. working and got us on the Malta beam. The two little fingers on the instrument sprang to life and went hard to port. I gingerly turned and when they were balanced in the inverted vee I was on the heading of 270° i.e. due west. So we had been heading for the Greek mainland at least.

Soon after, the port glycol gauge went crazy – internal coolant leak. I hadn't seen Saville since he'd handed over. I asked where he was and the navigator told me he was asleep on the chart table. I told him to wake the wing commander and tell him we'd lost the port engine. The CO appeared, put on my helmet and after that I could only gather what was going on by sign language. Afterwards I found he told the wireless operator to send out maydays. I was concerned about ditching with all that gear aboard but there was no real way of getting rid of it. A few boxes might have gone down the flare chute but you couldn't get to it. The thought of dumping all that stuff through the front hatch was daunting but when I managed to get Saville to understand what I proposed I got a firm and definite No!

We started at about 8,000 ft [2,500 metres] and after twenty minutes the port engine was losing power and leaving a trail of molten metal astern. We had maintained height so far and he told me to feather and I punched the fire extinguisher button as well. I found out afterwards that he reckoned we'd ditch just off the island – however we carried on losing height (with all that weight) and were down to about 2,500 ft [750 metres] when I saw a beacon flashing just north of the track. It was the correct letters but I was painfully aware that Jerry often duplicated the beacon at Catania so I wasn't that happy until I suddenly saw that the beacon was on a little island – Gozo. We turned and came back straight over Grand Harbour and nothing shot at us – and he made a beautiful one-engined landing at Luqa.

That's how the troops got their Christmas 1942 goodies. He never referred to this incident but there was a distinct change in his attitude to me – certainly a lot more respect seemed to be there – it was as if I had qualified in some way or another.

Don's brilliant airmanship is obvious through the eccentricities of behaviour, which could be put down to human reaction to the intense pressures of operational command. He seemed to be wanting to win the war on his own in addition to organising his squadron crews and influencing the commanders above him. The sheer bravery and utter determination of the man were respected by everyone who came into contact with him. Those were my feelings in 1942–3 under his command, and they are just as strong as I consider the thoughts and comments of others, forty-five years later.

Interrogations and summary were finished at 07.30 hours on 5 December and I returned to the mess by bus. The convoy that HMS *Welshman* had left on the 3rd was now in harbour and again one could sense the excitement and happiness of the Maltese people. There was a hooting of sirens from the dockyard area and some distant cheering.

I spent the day in bed until 16.00 hours and then went up to Luqa with Don to do another night's duty – this time with F/Lt Aubyn James, intelligence officer of 40 Squadron, to help me. The target was Bizerta docks and another double sortie.

Don was with us all night in Intelligence and out on the runway apron when we interrogated our crews after the first sortie and again in the briefing room after the second sortie. We had an early-morning breakfast together at the Luqa mess and then I went back with him to Sliema. He was in a very good mood.

In the afternoon I went up to work at Luqa and did the briefing for 40 Squadron – 104 Squadron had a 'stand down'. Don and S/Ldr Strutt were at Luqa and at 17.00 hours I went off with them in an old Vauxhall car allotted to our squadron, expecting to be taken back to Sliema and our mess. Instead we called first at the British Institute, a well-equipped building with a bar and a library. We had some rum at the bar and Don introduced us to a little seventeen-year-old Maltese-English girl Liliana – a pleasant and attractive lass. She acted as our guide and took us to Monica's Bar and then went home 'because Mama is strict' – like so many wise Maltese parents, as our young aircrews were finding out. We went back to the institute for more drinks before eventually persuading Don to take us 'home' for dinner.

I wrote letters and then went to bed but Don, the adjutant and S/Ldr Leggate went off to Charlie's Bar and later returned about midnight in somewhat boisterous good spirits. I was wakened by the noise of an argument between the mess secretary and Don over the closing of the bar. The noise became a terrific din downstairs, with demands for our bar to be reopened. Don by this time was almost inarticulate but still very forceful and determined.

I dropped off again but was wakened later by Don, S/Ldr Leggate and the adjutant, all very merry and practically out for the count, but trying to turn me out of bed to join the party. What a night! It was all very funny actually and they were not nasty or violent – just very merry. They deserved, and perhaps needed such binges as a break, particularly Don. Eventually he shut himself up in a toilet and passed out while the adjutant did likewise on his bed. I can't remember what happened to the flight commander – he disappeared. In retrospect it appears possible that they were celebrating because of advance knowledge of an event that was not made public until two days later.

The 7th was a normal Malta day, with a double sortie to Bizerta docks. Don was at briefing and take-off, as was usual if he was not operating himself, and he came with me out to the flarepath to collect navigators' logs and interrogate the crews on the success of the first sortie. It was while we were doing this and talking to one of our squadron crews under the wings of their Wellington just off the runway that we witnessed a spectacular and horrifying crash. A replacement Wellington from Egypt came into land and hit the ground on the wrong side of the Chance Light. It bounced 18 metres (50 ft) or more into the air with engines roaring – in an effort, presumably, to take off again. Then it stalled and fell into an aircraft pen at the eastern end of the runway. It immediately burst into fire, became a roaring furnace, giving off dense black smoke. It seemed impossible that there could be any survivors but we could see men running towards the plane and a hose playing on the flames. Apparently in the impact the Wellington had broken its back and some of the crew and passengers were thrown out. Others were dragged out but four people were killed and seven seriously injured.

Other aircraft landing or taking off had problems because of the smoke, but Don got our second sortie crews away safely in spite of that.

The next day, 8 December was a great day for 104 Squadron, for it was announced that Wing Commander D. T. Saville had been awarded an immediate DFC for courage and devotion to duty. This thoroughly deserved – in fact extremely belated – decoration gave a lot of satisfaction to all who had worked under his leadership.

The *Malta Times* had a series of headlines and this citation:

Immediate Awards
For Brilliant Leadership
DFC W/C Donald Teale Saville

W/C Saville carried out eleven bombing raids within two weeks of bringing his squadron to Malta, and it is due to his leadership and energy, both in the air and on the ground, that his squadron has achieved such good results. Once he was the captain of the only aircraft to locate a North African target, which he bombed from low level in spite of heavy opposition and very bad weather conditions. Another time, he carried out three sorties in one night against a Sicilian aerodrome, starting a fire. His personal example and outstanding ability have enabled his squadron to strike hard at the enemy in Tunisia and Sicily at a vital time. He is a brilliant squadron commander, who by his determination and courage, has inspired in his pilots an unflagging devotion to their present tasks.

Those of us who knew the facts could only add 'Hear! Hear!' and hasten to congratulate our CO.

Life went on, however, and on the 10th Don and seven other 104 Squadron crews operated against Tunis docks and then flew on to Gibraltar to collect personnel for the Malta photographic reconnaissance unit. Our crews also managed to squeeze in some food and drink specialities to bring back.

Operations continued during December with both good and bad results for the Wellingtons of the two squadrons. On the 13th our bombers set a tanker on fire at La Goulette and on the next night crews reported a direct hit on a ship in the same harbour during a double-sortie attack.

On the 15th S/Ldr Leggate told me he was leaving the squadron shortly to go via Egypt back to the UK on two months' sick leave. On the 17th with Tunis and La Goulette as targets for a double sortie, F for Freddie, captained by F/Lt Charles Dallas, went missing and the whole night became a disaster. This was one of our most experienced crews. F/Lt Dallas, P/O Silver as second pilot F/O Coulter as navigator, Sgt Lines and Sgt Booth. It is still not clear who the rear gunner was. The name on the battle order as given by S/Ldr Strutt was that of Sgt Stanley but there was some confusion. Sgt Showell and Sgt Stanley were good friends and both were rear gunners on 104 Squadron. S/Ldr Strutt always confused the two men's names and often called Sgt Showell Sgt Stanley. Dallas had recently lost his rear gunner and Showell had permission from S/Ldr Strutt to join the crew as rear gunner. However, on that day a newcomer was detailed to go instead, while Showell was promised he would go on the following trip and become the regular rear gunner. However, Sgt Stanley's name was on the list because Strutt thought he was Showell. Next morning when the RAF Police arrived at his billet in Sliema to collect his kit, they took some convincing that he was not in fact missing. There is still some confusion as to who the unfortunate gunner was on the plane.

Three rescue aircraft were sent from Malta to search for the missing plane or locate a dinghy, as it was believed it had ditched between Tunis and Malta. They returned safely but without finding any trace. However, the pilot and some of the crew survived as PoWs.

There were enemy fighters on the prowl that night and A for Apple under Sgt Webb was shot up and his wireless operator wounded. R for Robert and F/O Tony Crockford was also attacked and came back dripping petrol from two big holes in one wing. His gunner was slightly wounded and the hydraulics and turret were damaged.

Worst of all on that fateful night a Halifax with a Polish crew and a total of sixteen men on board, including F/Lt Len Vaughan gunnery officer of 40 Squadron, crashed at Luqa with everyone killed. They were all tour-expired men returning to England, and Len, a tail gunner of great experience and a real character in the mess, had survived a hundred operations. There was consternation and gloom in the mess over this cruel accident. This fine officer was posthumously awarded the DSO on 21 December.

To add to the misery of the period, on the night of the 18th Luqa was dive bombed by over thirty enemy aircraft and we lost seven aircraft destroyed and three damaged. Wellingtons just back from their first sortie to Tunis and refuelling and rearming for a second were caught in the open alongside the runway. One enemy plane was shot down. Luckily for me I was not on duty, but I heard and watched the raid from Sliema. It was exactly the scenario that I had often pictured while out on the Luqa runway – Malta at its worst, and Don was in the thick of it!

About 20th a new wing commander arrived for our squadron – W/Cdr G. H. N. Gibson, DFC was to take over from Don. At the same time S/Ldr J. F. Newman DFC arrived to take over B Flight from S/Ldr Leggate. W/Cdr Morton, DFC took over 40 Squadron from W/Cdr Ridgeway, DFC.

The new wing commander was a complete change from our Australian officer. He was a tall, slim Englishman and rather quiet in manner. We liked the fact that he had done two tours of operations and was accustomed to Wellington bombers.

Don remained on Malta and continued to take an active interest in the squadron. I saw him on Christmas Day happily celebrating with F/Lt Baker, our squadron adjutant.

Operations continued on a nightly basis, except for an occasional cancellation due to bad weather. The night of 6/7 January 1943, with Sousse and Tunis docks as targets, produced another sad loss for 104 Squadron. F for Freddie under S/Ldr Strutt did not return from the night's operation when they were flare dropping over Sousse. Other crews reported seeing an explosion at 2,100 metres (7,000 ft) over the harbour amidst intense heavy flak and then an aircraft fire with Very lights and small explosions on the ground 5–8 km (3–5 miles) south south-west of Sousse. It was a rotten blow for the squadron; they were a good crew – brave, keen and competent. S/Ldr Strutt had proved himself a daring bomber captain and a splendid flight commander, respected and well liked throughout the entire squadron. Even Don, who had at first been critical of him as a member of the British aristocracy, had become a close friend. I knew all the crew and 'Struttie' was also a personal friend of mine.

We were now approaching the end of our duty period on Malta, although we did not know it ourselves. Don was still appearing occasionally at briefings and take-offs, and was to make one more characteristic and highly irregular contribution to the Saville legend.

On the night of 14/15 January the target was Tripoli docks and F/O 'Ham' Fuller and his crew were taken out to their aircraft 'Q' for Queenie by F/Lt Ted Stewart and Don. The former CO was apparently having a last look at a squadron take-off. However, the truck stopped first at the Wellington next to Q for Queenie and Don in his blue uniform and not attired in any way for flying, got out to talk to an inexperienced crew whom he must have known needed encouragement. Fuller said afterwards that he apparently sensed some nervousness in the pilot, so then and there he very diplomatically climbed the ladder and took over as captain.

With him on board the Wellington later taxied out for a successful operation and returned safely to Luqa. This operation, unrecorded in Don's log book brought the number of missions he completed while with 104 Squadron to 32. One wonders whether W/Cdr Gibson ever knew about that incident. As an understanding CO who had met Don previously in the UK I suspect that he would have been amused and put it down to his unorthodoxy and enthusiasm for flying – or just another example of the independent streak in those from down under! In effect, this unusual and 'off the cuff' incident illustrates something of his leadership while with 104 Squadron.

On 19 January we were told that 238 Wing and the two Wellington bomber squadrons were moving back to Egypt and torpedo bombers were to take our place to deal with enemy shipping. A message to 238 Wing from AHQ Malta dated the 21st was a pleasant farewell.

> A.C.C. sends farewell message to 238 Wing and wishes to thank them and 40 and 104 Squadrons for their fine bombing efforts during the past two and a half months. Malta is proud to have had the Wellington bomber squadrons join their team and hopes to have them back later in the year. Meanwhile we all wish you the best of luck.

CHAPTER FIFTEEN

Commanding Officer, No. 218 (Gold Coast) Stirling Bomber Squadron (1943)

Don left Malta for Cairo in February 1943, following closely upon the heels of his former command. From September 1941, when he had joined No. 12 Wellington Bomber Squadron at Binbrook, he had served on operational squadrons, mainly in command as flight commander or squadron commander level, without any significant break from the tensions of air warfare.

After handing over command of 104 Squadron to W/Cdr Gibson, he relaxed in his own way, by taking part in almost nightly drinking parties. Cairo was full of service personnel exuberant in the aftermath of the Alamein victory and Don had plenty of friends eager to celebrate with him.

His record of service shows that he was posted to No. 1 Personnel Dispersal Unit on 14 February, pending posting to the U.K. Some of 104 Squadron remember seeing him in Cairo during February, enjoying the fleshpots. The general feeling was that he would soon be back on a squadron because of his love of flying. We could not picture him chained to a desk in an administrative position at the Air Ministry or Command or Group HQ. Yet we knew the extreme pressures under which he had worked for so long and all thought that he needed and deserved a long rest from operational command.

Within a few weeks of returning to England, on 28 March, Don was posted to take over command of No. 218 (Gold Coast) Stirling Bomber Squadron from W/Cdr O. A. Morris, DSO. Some RAF squadrons were supported financially by member states of the British Commonwealth. The Gold Coast Government paid some of the costs of 218 Squadron –

hence the name. It was based at Downham Market, Norfolk, a 3 Group station and part of the main force of Bomber Command. It is certain that this immediate return to squadron command was at his own request – or even insistence.

On the night of his arrival Don operated with S/Ldr Beck and crew. Beck was one of three flight commanders on the squadron, the others being S/Ldr Spry and S/Ldr Hiles. The target was St Nazaire and the crew of O for Orange was: S/Ldr A. Beck, captain; W/Cdr D. T. Saville, second pilot; Sgt H. H. B. Barrett, Navigator; P/O L. G. Flynn, wireless operator; Sgt E. Quigley mid-upper, (M.U.) gunner; P/O E. J. McLennan, rear gunner; and Sgt S. G. Garbett, flight engineer.

On the same day a new station commander arrived to assume command at Downham Market. He was the well-known wing commander from the RAF film *Target for Tonight*, now 'Speedy' Powell, and he took over from the acting OC, W/Cdr O. A. Morris and the former OC, G/Capt A. McKee.

It is probable that Powell and Don, both men of outstanding courage and daring, got on extremely well together, but the group captain was almost immediately posted to North Africa to lead 330 Wing and the two Wellington squadrons which were supporting the First Army campaign in Tunisia. G/Capt D. Barnes became station commander at Downham Market with effect from 24 April, and he and Don were soon on the best of terms.

It is necessary at this point to stand back from this account of new people and postings to consider the position of Bomber Command in 1943, and the problems with the Stirling bomber, which was the main aircraft used by No. 3 Group, with HQ at Newmarket. It was a bad year for Bomber Command, in spite of the bombing offensives against the Ruhr, Hamburg and Berlin. Max Hastings, in *Bomber Command*, states that at the end of the Battle of the Ruhr from March to July, the losses were 872 aircraft missing over Germany from 18,506 sorties with a further 16 per cent damaged – a loss rate of 4.7 per cent per sortie. Stirling losses were almost always heavier than those of Lancaster and Halifax squadrons, mainly because the operating ceiling height for the Stirling was considerably lower at 4,250–5,000 metres (14,000–16,000 ft).

With the known operational strains on aircrews in Bomber Command in March 1943 one might think that Don was taking over a squadron with morale problems linked to dislike of the Stirling bomber – an aircraft subject to heavy losses from flak and night fighters, in danger of receiving bombs and incendiaries from bombers above them over the target, and with an undercarriage prone to collapse under stress in landing. And losses on 218 Squadron were indeed serious, both before and during Don's term of office – four in March, five in April, nine in May, seven in June and four in July – a total of twenty-nine four-engined aircraft in five months and over two hundred crew members killed, missing or taken prisoner.

However, all the evidence from flight commanders, the chief flying control officer at Downham Market and several other correspondents indicates that morale was good, even high, in spite of these losses. An examination of station medical records shows that cases of flying stress occurred at a rate of some four a month – not high for a three-flight squadron but enough to indicate the strain on men's nerves of operating over heavily defended German targets and knowing that few crews succeeded in surviving the thirty operations of a full tour.

Perhaps it was his recognition of the existence of flying stress that caused the senior medical officer (SMO) of 3 Group, W/Cdr Huins, to fly on operations with 218 Squadron on a number of occasions, as revealed by the squadron records. The official reason given was to test the effects of benzidrine tablets which were issued to aircrew, but one would surmise that he was also able to sample and assess the background to flying stress. On 17 January, he went as passenger with S/Ldr Hiles and crew on a mining operation, and on a second with F/Lt Pettit on 10 March. On 29 March and 14 April he accompanied F/Lt Becroft and crew to Berlin and Stuttgart. After bombing Stuttgart, the captain took the aircraft low to shoot up a marshalling yard and received some light flak at 60–150 metres (200–500 ft). Remembering Don's own effort to 'initiate' S/Ldr Strutt on 104 Squadron it is easy to imagine him commending both F/Lt Becroft and the SMO.

Bomber Command crews in 1943 knew that the odds were heavily against their survival – particularly as second and even third operational tours could be expected if they survived the first. It is a sobering thought that the *Luftwaffe* was then capable of putting up a force of over 500 night fighters against Bomber Command.

Max Hastings, *Bomber Command*, gives an example of a Halifax squadron operating in 1943 from Holme upon Spalding Moor, which was described as a bleak unfriendly place where it was widely felt by aircrew that the village had turned its back on the war. Locals seemed to resent the RAF's domination of the local bowling alley, and wives and girlfriends who lodged nearby were treated with disdain. Morale was more likely to be strained under these circumstances but, of course, the decisive factor was leadership.

Downham Market was a complete contrast to Holme although it was at first a satellite to Marham and was always a wartime emergency airfield without the comforts of a permanent RAF base. The RAF station was only a mile away from the pleasant market town, where there were several hotels and pubs, and the local people were well disposed towards the RAF personnel after the first shock of having the new airfield amidst farmland but very close to the town. The station was regarded as a happy one and aircrew officers speak warmly of the fun they had at the Bexwell Rectory which had been turned into the officers' mess. Airmen were often made welcome in civilian homes in Downham and the townsfolk frequently lined the airfield boundaries to watch the Stirlings take off for an operation.

S/Ldr Geoffrey Rothwell arrived in April for his second tour and says in answer to the question, 'What was your reaction to having an Australian CO?'

> Overjoyed! The lack of bull and friendliness to all were features which endeared Don to all who served under him. We got on extremely well from the start and I remember how I admired the way he was able to run the squadron so effectively without relying on tight discipline as many others in his position did. It was the free and easy atmosphere which brought out the best in the crews.
>
> He was always ready for a bit of fun, whether it was sticking a potato up the exhaust pipe of the car of an unpopular squadron leader administration and hiding in the rhododendron bushes to witness the joke to the end, or joining the boys in the local in Downham.

S/Ldr Ian Ryall, another flight commander, commented in a letter in 1985:

> Don was a great chap and I remember him as a good friend. He was a good CO – the sort of chap that made Bomber Command tick by giving the lead both on and off duty. He liked his pint and was always there with the boys when there was a night off.

He said in an interview with me in 1986:

> I did three tours in my time in the war and I had lots of commanding officers. Quite honestly, he [Don] was the most outstanding, without a shadow of doubt! My only regret is that I only knew him for that short time of about eight weeks. I was just beginning to know him well and felt that we would become close friends.

It is clear that 218 Squadron experienced the Mark II Saville, with some improvements on the 104 Squadron Mark I model. Don now had nothing to prove to himself or to the RAF. He had his well-deserved

DFC and a wealth of flying achievements behind him to give him the easy confidence which is so valuable in command. His toughness of mind and body had allowed him to recover from the strains of his command in the Middle East and Malta. He was now in his fortieth year and still keen to fly on operations over Germany.

In 1943, squadron commanders in Bomber Command were, it is said, supposed to restrict themselves to one operational flight per month. Don had clearly not read this instruction or, if he had, he ignored it with an Australian imitation of Nelson's blind eye. He settled into squadron life at Downham Market with ease and speed. He accepted the Stirling as an improvement on the Wellington and enjoyed flying the new Stirling IIIs which were now entering squadron service. The Battle of the Ruhr was in progress, which meant that all targets were heavily defended by searchlights, flak and the deadly night fighters.

Former members of 218 Squadron remember many details of the Saville regime. The Wing Commander was always smartly dressed; he talked easily with crews; everybody liked him; he had a presence, perhaps because he was much older and more experienced than the rest, he always had a joke or a cheerful remark for everybody.

The squadron briefings were well organised, with the usual contributions by the CO, the meteorological spokesman, the intelligence officer, the various technical officers and frequently a few words from the station commander. Don's own briefing was always concise, encouraging and efficient – designed to send the crews out in cheerful and determined spirit to attack their targets.

In April Don went on five operations and acquired his own crew of F/Sgt Beckworth (navigator), F/Sgt Moroney (wireless operator/A.G.) Sgt Foster (bomb aimer), Sgt Heath (M.U. gunner), Sgt Farmer (flight engineer) and P/O Nuttall (rear gunner). On the 6th he took Sgt Hoey, a new pilot, as second pilot and the above crew on an operation to lay mines off the Bay of Biscay ports. Three Stirlings from 218 Squadron operated and the mines were laid successfully.

On the 8th the target was Duisburg in the Ruhr and Don went on his third operation, bombing on flak concentrations visible through cloud cover. Of thirteen crews sent, two jettisoned and returned, one attacked a last-resort target and P for Peter, piloted by Sgt Tomkins, was missing. Bomber Command sent 392 aircraft to Duisburg and lost 19 (4.8 per cent).

On the 10th, RAF Downham Market was visited by the Secretary of State for Air, the Right Hon. Sir Archibald Sinclair, accompanied by the AOC No. 3 Group, Air Vice Marshal R. Harrison. They attended Don's briefing for an attack on Frankfurt. This operation was a failure owing to 10/10 cloud over the target. There were no losses for 218 Squadron but four Stirlings returned early. On the 11th three squadron crews were required for an air sea rescue operation and Don and his crew went. There were no losses.

On the 16th, seventeen crews, including Don again, were briefed for Mannheim. His aircraft, U for Uncle, was hit by light flak over the target and Sgt Heath the M.U. gunner was wounded. Two other 218 Squadron Stirlings were damaged by flak and X captained by P/O Howlett, did not return. This raid was in full moon conditions and eighteen aircraft were shot down out of 271 sent. A raid on Pilsen by 327 aircraft lost thirty-six Lancasters and Halifaxes. Total losses that night were fifty-four or 8.9 per cent.

On the 20th, fifteen squadron crews were sent to Rostock, including Don and his crew, with F/Lt Birbeck as M.U. gunner in place of Sgt Heath. Eighty-six Stirlings of 3 Group were to bomb the Heinkel factory near the town but were hindered by a smokescreen. Eight Stirlings were lost including B from 218 Squadron, with Sgt Jobling and crew – an overall loss rate of 9.3 per cent, again very heavy

On the 27th and 28th Bomber Command attempted the largest mine-laying operations so far carried out. On the 27th 160 aircraft laid mines off the Biscay and Brittany ports and in the Frisian Islands. One Lancaster was lost. On the 28th the process was repeated by 207 aircraft laying mines off Heligoland, in the Elbe estuary and in the Great and Little Belts – the channels to and from the Baltic Sea on both sides of Funen Island, Denmark. A study of a map of the Jutland Peninsula and the entrance to the Baltic immediately reveals how dangerous these missions could be for aircraft coming low to identify the mine-laying areas. Low cloud over the German and Danish coasts forced the minelayers to fly low and much German light flak activity was seen. Twenty-two bombers were lost: seven Lancasters, seven Stirlings, six Wellingtons and two Halifaxes. Mine laying or 'gardening' operations were usually considered to be relatively safe operations and this was the heaviest loss of mine-laying aircraft experienced during the war (over 10 per cent). The number of mines laid, however, was the greatest in one night. No. 218 Stirling Squadron had a disastrous night, losing three out of eight aircraft operating: F under P/O D. J. Brown N under F/Lt G. F. Berridge and O under Sgt K. S. Hailey, a squadron loss rate of 37.5 per cent.

This brought the losses during April to five Stirlings and their crews. Don, as commanding officer, was responsible for sending a personal letter to next of kin of thirty-five crewmen. This traumatic task was common for squadron commanders and their staffs and must have been an emotional strain and a time-consuming duty in times of heavy losses.

The first few days of May were spent in air tests and training. On the 4th eleven crews were detailed for an attack on Dortmund, a heavy raid by 596 aircraft altogether. It did some serious damage but thirty-one bombers were lost, including Z captained by F/Lt Turner, of 218 Squadron. A further seven aircraft crashed in bad weather on return to the bomber bases.

On the 5th the squadron supplied four Stirlings for mine laying around the Frisian Islands, out of a force of 21 Stirlings from 3 Group. One aircraft was lost but all 218 Squadron planes returned safely. The Stirling appears to have been used for mining more than the Lancasters and Halifaxes. The Stirling could carry six mines but division of the bomb bay into three sections prevented the loading of blockbusters and other larger bombs.

The weather was bad for some days early in May, preventing large-scale operations. However, the squadron records show that on most days there were practice cross-country flights, night-flying exercises, beam-flying exercises, etc. Don encouraged his crews to do as much flying as possible, believing that thorough knowledge of one's aircraft was a safety factor.

On 'stand downs' Don would always join in the fun in the mess or arrange a meeting with some of his crews at the Crown, the Castle or another of the pubs in Downham Market. He enjoyed life to the full, knowing perfectly well that it was likely to be short. He wanted his crews – officers and sergeants alike – to enjoy their lives while they could. When one of his crews got into trouble with the military police he would call them in and listen to their story – then tear up the provost marshal's complaint and throw the pieces into his waste paper basket. He firmly refused to take any action against his crews for small misdemeanours and told the provost marshal and civilian police that his crews were liable to be killed on any operation and as long as he was in command he wanted them to be happy and have a good time while they could.

This attitude to minor complaints endeared him to the crews, particularly to the sergeants, and of course they all knew that he went himself on the most difficult trips. That was leadership which was effective in binding the squadron together.

It would be wrong to give the impression that everyone associated with 218 Squadron was entirely enamoured of the Australian wing commander. The senior flying control officer, S/Ldr L. E. Skan at Downham Market accepted that he was a wonderful pilot and skipper and respected him for that. However, he thought that Don had a slightly condescending attitude to the 'Poms'. While he knew Don and spoke to him a little in the mess he felt that he was not altogether a friendly man and seemed to regard flying control officers as a necessary evil rather than, like most aircrew, as one of themselves. S/Ldr Rothwell, also a 'Pom', however disagrees with this sentiment.

Skan also confirmed that, in his opinion, morale was never low at 218 Squadron – and he was in a good position to know as he was with the squadron from August 1941 to October 1944. He has also given some useful comments on the Stirling. He believed that most pilots developed real affection for the aircraft they flew and did not think that having to fly it on 'ops' affected morale. He thought that apart from some lack of power for fully loaded take-off and its ceiling, the aircraft performed well in the air. On take-off it had a tendency to swing and the undercarriage was suspect if too much sideways strain was put upon it. The most telling statement from this honest and observant officer was that he had noted that fully loaded Stirlings just about scraped over the hedge at the end of the main runway while Lancasters (to which 218 Squadron converted in August 1944) became airborne more or less opposite the control tower halfway down the runway.

On 12 May, eleven crews were detailed for Duisburg including Don and his crew, with Sgt Cummins as M.U. gunner in A for Apple, S/Ldr Beck and crew, and F/Lt Saunders and crew with Sgt Aaron as second pilot. Six aircraft were coned by searchlights and five 218 Squadron Stirlings were hit and damaged by flak. It was a successful raid, with fires started and several large explosions in the target area. Don reported good visibility; he saw the bend in the river near the town and bombed on red target indicators (T.I.s) from 3,500 metres (11,500 ft). Aircraft K under P/O R.J. Bryans did not return. This raid was a major attack in which 572 bombers were used and thirty-four (5.9 per cent) lost. The river port – the largest inland port in Germany – suffered severe damage with 1,500 buildings destroyed and twenty-one barges and thirteen ships sunk, and others damaged.

The next night sixteen Stirlings were ordered to attack Bochum, another centre in the Ruhr, between Essen and Dortmund. All three flight commanders of 218 Squadron flew on this operation – S/Ldr Rothwell, S/Ldr Beck and S/Ldr Sly – as part of a force of 442 aircraft. Some damage was done but it was believed that decoy markers drew much of the bombing away from the target. A further force of 5 Group Lancasters and Pathfinder Lancasters and Halifaxes, a total of 168 aircraft, were sent to Pilsen in Czechoslovakia to bomb the Skoda armaments factory but this target was difficult to locate and the bombs mainly fell in open country.

The totals for the night were 642 sorties with thirty-four bombers lost (5.3 per cent). The trouble for 218 Squadron came on the return. Stirling G (Sgt Nicholls) crashed at Chedburgh with five killed, and at

Downham Market the brakes of I (Sgt Carney) which had been severely damaged by flak at Bochum, failed on landing. The aircraft veered off the runway and crashed into the operations block, killing two aircrew who had just been debriefed on the steps of the building. The crew in the Stirling were not seriously injured. Don was on the spot in Operations.

After a 'stand down' on 15 May, there was a small mine-laying operation by six Stirlings of 218 Squadron on 16th. During the take-off one Stirling crashed but the crew were fine. That was also the night of the famous raid by 617 Squadron Lancasters on the German dams. The Mohne and Eder Dams were breached but at a cost of eight aircraft and crews out of nineteen despatched to the targets. W/Cdr Guy Gibson was awarded the V.C. and thirty-four other men received decorations for this achievement, which damaged the water supply for the industrial Ruhr and therefore made a major contribution to the Battle of the Ruhr being fought by the Bomber Command squadrons.

The next large operation for 218 Squadron was on 23 May when seventeen crews were briefed for a major raid on Dortmund. Twelve Stirlings bombed on markers which had been well placed by Pathfinders in clear weather conditions. Large areas of the industrial centre were devastated by a total force of 826 bombers, of which thirty-eight were lost (4.6 per cent). Of the Downham Market aircraft four returned early with various troubles and aircraft Y under P/O Phillips was missing. On this very successful raid, S/Ldr Beck and S/Ldr Rothwell, with F/Lt. Ryall, the incoming flight commander, as second pilot, all took part.

By contrast the raid on 25/26 May to Dusseldorf was a failure with two layers of cloud obscuring the target from the large force of 759 bombers, of which 218 Squadron supplied fifteen. Five returned early and Z under Sgt Collins was missing. A total of twenty-two bombers were shot down (3.6 per cent) and crew reported flak defences weak but night fighters very active. The bombing appeared to be widely scattered and the target suffered little damage. All the three flight commanders of 218 Squadron again operated – F/Lt Ryall this time with F/Lt Saunders and his crew. Don would have looked carefully at the number of early returns from the Dortmund and Dusseldorf operations; Stirlings had a poor serviceability record and a number of things could go wrong, such as oil pressure, oil cooling and icing up of the airframe. One senior pilot writes:

> Pilots developed a sort of loyalty to the aircraft they were flying and, on the whole, we liked our Stirlings, once we got used to them. That is not to say we would not have been quite pleased had

> we woken up one morning and found we had been re-equipped with Lancs.

There was a royal occasion on 26 May – a visit by Their Majesties, the King and Queen.

S/Ldr Rothwell, who survived seventy-two operations and the war, remembers the occasion, which largely took the form of a tea party in the WAAF officers' mess. Don was presented to the King and Queen as squadron commander, and was asked some very pertinent questions about the Stirling by the Queen who showed a knowledge that amazed the aircrew present. S/Ldr Rothwell with some nervousness offered a plate of eclairs to Her Majesty and asked, 'Would you care for an eclair, ma'am?' The reply was, 'No thank you, squadron leader.'

Some decorations were conferred on air- and ground-crew during the brief visit. Some of the airmen were less enthusiastic afterwards, as they had been paraded to line the route and cheer the royal party.

An interesting sidelight for railway buffs is that the King and Queen were said to be scheduled to catch the *Flying Scotsman* from Peterborough but they were running late. The King reprimanded an aide for having arranged to stop the train to wait for the party. His attitude seemed to be that nothing should stop or delay the *Flying Scotsman*.

A puzzling question is whether Don ever took leave from Downham Market. S/Ldr Ryall says that Don was always on the station as far as he can remember. S/Ldr Rothwell thinks that Don might have had a lady friend among the WAAFs of flying control which, if true, might offer some explanation for his apparent devotion to duty. However, the general opinion is that he was always too busy for any girl to assume much importance in his life at Downham Market. S/Ldr Skan has pointed out that his WAAF watch-keepers were sergeants not officers. He cannot remember any affair.

The next large-scale operation against the Ruhr was against Wuppertal on 29 May, when fifteen crews were required and Don operated with his crew in D for Donald with G/Capt. E. D. Barnes as second pilot and the gunnery officer, F/Lt J. Birbeck, as M. U. gunner. This was a massive attack by Bomber Command, using 719 aircraft and is claimed as the outstanding success of the Battle of the Ruhr. Marking and bombing were accurate and a huge fire started – possibly a 'firestorm.' Don attacked from 4,250 metres (14,000 ft), bombing on red T.I.s and saw fires and smoke at the target. It was an excellent experience for the group captain and for thirteen Stirling crews from 218 Squadron, but two aircraft, A (F/Sgt Davis) and H (P/O Allan) did not return. The total Bomber Command losses amounted to thirty-three (4.6 per cent).

During May nine Stirlings and most of eight crews were lost from

Downham Market – almost one-third of the normal number of aircraft on the station.

June started well, with minor mine-laying operations until the 11th when fourteen crews were detailed to attack Düsseldorf, including S/Ldr Rothwell and S/Ldr Ryall. Only one Stirling returned early and the thirteen others reached and successfully bombed the target, returning without loss. It was a near-maximum Bomber Command attack by 783 aircraft, with losses of thirty-eight (4.9 per cent), and proved to be the most damaging raid of the war on this city.

On the 18th Don lost four tour-expired members of his crew, who were posted out to O.T.U.s and conversion units. F/Sgt Beckwith, F/Sgt Moroney, Sgt Farmer and Sgt Foster.

The next heavy raid was on the 19th against Le Creusot in eastern France to attack the Schneider armaments factory and Breuil steelworks. Twelve crews were briefed, including Don who took S/Ldr Beck's crew, with a few alterations, in U for Uncle. This was largely the crew with whom he had flown his first operation on 28 March. Because of commissioning of some crew members it resulted in an all-officer crew of eight men: W/Cdr Saville as captain, P/O White as second pilot, P/O Barrett as navigator, F/O Flynn as wireless operator/gunner, P/O Hopkins as bomb-aimer, F/Lt Birbeck as M.U. gunner, F/O Nuttall as rear gunner and P/O Fairgrieve as flight engineer. The operation was reasonably successful, with Don's crew bombing from 1,100 metres (3,500 ft) in good visibility, seeing their bursts across the Schneider factory. S/Ldr Ryall attacking from 1,400 metres (4,500 ft) saw the factory and holes in its roof. All 218 Squadron Stirlings returned safely and Bomber Command losses were, for once, only two Halifaxes out of 290 aircraft sent to the target.

On the 21st fourteen crews were required from the squadron to attack Krefeld in the Rhine-Ruhr industrial area. This was an attack by 705 bombers in good visibility and moonlight. The raid was successful in getting fire to the centre of the city but heavy casualties were caused by night fighters. Forty-four aircraft were lost (6.2 per cent of the force), including 218 Squadron's G, captained by P/O Rich, and D, captained by P/O Shillinglaw. It is now known that D was shot down by an Me.110 night fighter near Aarschot, Belgium. The brief period without operational losses had come to an end. Both the young captains lost were Australians – like most crews, these were mixed British and overseas representatives from the Empire Training Scheme.

On the 22nd, fourteen crews were detailed, six for mine laying and eight for an attack on Mulheim. S/Ldr D. Maw, who had been posted to 218 Squadron on the 19th, operated successfully in laying mines. S/Ldr Ryall attacked Mulheim and reported many good fires and smoke to a great height. In fact Bomber Command achieved an excellent result on this medium-sized town, destroying 60 per cent of the built-up area. Some 557 aircraft took part and the losses were thirty-five (6.3 per cent of the force). Now 218 Squadron lost K under F/Sgt Smith.

On the 23rd, Don and G/Capt Barnes entertained the AOC of 3 Group, Air Vice Marshal R. Harrison and Air Commodore Runciman in the officers' mess after they had inspected the station and squadron and watched the take-off of six Stirlings for mine laying. All aircraft returned safely.

On the 24th fourteen crews briefed for Eberfeld. S/Ldr Rothwell took S/Ldr Maw as second pilot and reported that it was quite an initiation because the aircraft was coned for five minutes in about twenty-five searchlights and intense flak, and suffered fifteen holes. He noted huge fires in the target area. This was another successful large-scale attack using 630 aircraft, of which thirty-four were lost (5.4 per cent of the force). For 218 Squadron it was another bad night, for S/Ldr Beck and crew in U for Uncle and Sgt Hoey and crew in N for Nuts did not return. S/Ldr Beck and his crew were near the end of their tour of operations.

At this point, it is worth mentioning the effects of losses on personnel at an RAF station. These men had been in the officers' or sergeants' mess for some months and would be sadly missed by their friends – including WAAF friends. The groundcrews allotted to the Stirlings also had deep feelings for their own aircraft and for the aircrews who flew them over Germany. Don would recall that he himself had flown on operations twice with S/Ldr Beck's crew; that Sgt Hoey had flown with him on 6 April as second pilot, while F/O Nuttall, the rear gunner lost with Beck had flown on eight operations with him. The emotional strain of living on a bomber station in wartime and in particular in being part of a squadron, was at times extreme.

The next night brought more losses. Seven crews were detailed to attack Gelsenkirchen including S/Ldr Maw in W for William. Five aircraft bombed on markers and reported fires beneath clouds. Two did not return to Downham Market – G for George under Sgt Hughes and W for William under S/Ldr Maw. Maw had been on the squadron for less than a week after posting in from 1657 Conversion Unit. Two flight commanders of 218 Squadron had been lost in two nights. Bomber Command lost thirty aircraft from a force of 473 (6.3 per cent) and the raid was not considered successful. The squadron's loss of two aircraft from seven was heavy.

The 28th saw a major raid on Cologne using 608 aircraft with twenty-five lost (4.1 per cent). Ten went from 218 Squadron and nine took part in a very successful attack; one returned early. In June the squadron had lost seven aircraft and their crews of seven or eight men. The weather had been poor, with rain causing the cancellation of some operations. The Ruhr was still the main target, and with its heavy defences was bound to exact a nearly intolerable toll on the attacking force. Nevertheless the people of the friendly, small but busy town of Downham Market, and the personnel of the active RAF station on the low ridge above it all faced the warm summer month of July with optimism. The relaxed and cheerful leadership of Don made a big contribution to the resilience of the aircrews.

The evidence from those who were there at the time indicates that this Mark II Don Saville was well suited to the hour. The atmosphere engendered by his friendly but vital and daring personality was one in which courage and bravery were encouraged and determination flourished. Cowardice and half-heartedness were not thought of in spite of the loss of friends and companions. The squadron morale must have helped the young aircrew to face their slim chances more bravely and go on accepting the nightly demands of Bomber Command. For example, F/Sgt A. L. Aaron and his all-sergeant crew were on the squadron at this time and under Don's inspiring influence. Three weeks after Don and crew were shot down over Hamburg F/Sgt Aaron's Stirling Q for Queenie was hit by air-to-air machine-gun fire near Turin. Aaron was terribly wounded in the face, chest and right arm, the navigator was killed and several other crew members were also struck by bullets. The bomb aimer and flight engineer managed to fly the damaged Stirling to North Africa under the guidance of the pilot and made a safe crash landing at Bone. Aaron died in hospital shortly afterwards. He was awarded the V.C. the bomb-aimer the GCM and the wireless operator and the flight engineer the DFM.

The first large-scale raid by Bomber Command in July was on the 3rd when 653 aircraft were again sent to Cologne, with 218 Squadron contributing thirteen Stirlings. S/Ldr Saunders, who was now in charge of B flight, bombed from 4,750 metres (15,500 ft) and reported that a large proportion of the bombs were bursting on the eastern side of the river, which was the target. Fires were started in industrial sections and adjacent houses. The attacking force lost thirty aircraft (4.6 per cent) but 218 Squadron had no losses. This raid was notable for the deployment by the *Luftwaffe* of single-engined fighters using only the visual illumination of the flares, searchlights and the ground fires to pick up the bombers. The concept was termed 'wild boars' by the Germans.

S/Ldr Rothwell was posted to No. 11 OTU on the 10th, after a brave and efficient tour as flight commander with 218 Squadron.

For the week following the Cologne raid, the squadron was called upon only for small numbers of Stirlings to undertake mine-laying operations. However, Bomber Command used other groups to continue operations against Europe with attacks on Cologne on the 8th, Gelsenkirchen on the 9th and Turin on the 12th.

On the 13th Don briefed ten crews for a raid on Aachen in which 374 aircraft made a successful attack, starting a large fire in the city and damaging much property and eight industrial premises for the loss of twenty bombers (5.3 per cent). The squadron crews bombed on red T.I.s and noted many fighters and heavy flak. One Stirling returned early and there were no squadron losses.

Don himself had not operated over Germany so far in July but had kept various crews active by taking part in night-flying 'bullseye' exercises on the 5th and the 17th and daylight formation flying with other squadron aircraft on the 15th. He and a scratch crew also did air tests on the 19th and the 24th to make sure that they were prepared as a team for an impending major attack on 'a very important German city'. He and his station commander, G/Capt Barnes, would have been aware of the identity of this target because at the end of May 1943 Sir Arthur Harris had circulated an order to his group commanders to start preparing for a series of heavy raids on it. It was Hamburg: Europe's largest port and the second largest city in Germany.

In June 1943 Bomber Command and the American 8th Air Force had received a new directive, code-named 'Pointblank', from the combined chiefs of staff for a combined bomber offensive. It was a recognition of the growing danger to both day and night bombing forces from the *Luftwaffe* fighters and the directive was for combined operations against the enemy fighter force and its manufacturing bases.

Sir Arthur Harris appeared to continue as before with his campaign for the systematic destruction of German cities. For the Battle of Hamburg, Bomber Command was able to use two new aids – H2S radar sets and 'window' (tinfoil strips dropped to confuse enemy radar). Situated on the estuary of the River Elbe, the city was particularly suitable for identification by the H2S sets of the Pathfinders, which showed up coastlines and adjacent built-up areas, docks etc. better than inland cities without recognisable shapes. In this raid, 'window' was the major innovation to be used and it did in fact disrupt the German radar defences and allow the bombers to operate with greater safety. The decision to use it is thought to have been made by Churchill himself at the request of Bomber Command and the reason was that even 'Bomber' or 'Butcher' Harris had at last realised that the losses endured by Bomber Command were now intolerable, particularly in Stirling squadrons. 'Window' had been available since 1942 but had not been used because it was felt that it would be copied by the Germans if they made further large-scale bombing attacks on Britain.

When the news came from 3 Group HQ at Newmarket of the

unusually important raid planned for Hamburg on 24/25 July a wave of excitement spread through the station. While at first the actual target was known only to Intelligence, Operations, the group captain and Don, enough of 'a big one tonight' spread to the flights and groundcrews to make the preparations memorable. Twenty crews were detailed and Don decided to go himself. He was posthumously accused by some officers of having taken a carefully chosen expert crew, including the squadron navigation officer, the signals leader and the gunnery leader. It must be remembered, however, that of the crew who had flown with Don on his first eight operations with 218 Squadron, four members had become tour-expired and been posted from Downham Market, while the rear gunner, F/O Nuttall had been lost with S/Ldr Beck and his crew on 24/25 June. Don had taken S/Ldr Beck's crew, with F/O Nuttall on his last operation on 19 June. Now, if he was to go to Hamburg, he had no alternative but to gather together a scratch crew from those who were available and in some cases who volunteered. The crew he eventually chose was: W/Cdr D. T. Saville, captain, on his fifty-seventh operation; F/Sgt N. W. Beavis, second pilot, a new pilot on 218 Squadron who was on his first operation over Germany; P/O J. Brighton, navigator, who had not flown previously with Don on operations; F/Lt T. A. Stanley, wireless operator, the 218 Squadron signals leader who had not flown previously with Don on operations; F/O H. C. Eyre, bomb aimer, who was on his second tour, but (his previous captain was tour-expired), and who had not flown before with Don on operations but was pleased when he was asked; F/Lt J. L. Birbeck, M.U. gunner the 218 Squadron gunnery leader who had flown with Saville on operations several times previously; F/Sgt A. B. Howat, rear gunner who was previously gunner with S/Ldr Rothwell who had now left the squadron and probably had a few more operations to complete his own first tour; and F/O T. Fairgrieve, flight engineer, who had flown once before with Don on 19 June. The squadron navigation leader was F/Lt Brown, and he was *not* in this crew. The crew included four very experienced officers in Don, Stanley, Birbeck and Eyre, but only Don, Birbeck and Fairgrieve had flown together previously.

The briefing room, operations room, control tower and most administrative and technical offices at Downham Market were clustered together parallel with the main east-west runway and between the taxiing path and the airfield boundary, bordering the road from Downham Market to Swaffham. The crews' living quarters and the messes were on the other side, south of the road and in the area adjacent to Bexwell Church, the Rectory and Bexwell Hall.

The crews walked or were taken by trucks to the briefing room which, with the operations room, could be considered the nerve centre of the station during operations. It contained seating for 150 men in rows facing a raised platform backed by a wall map of western Europe. This map was usually covered until the intelligence officer dramatically drew aside the curtain to reveal the route and the target.

Briefing was a formal ritual and taken seriously by everyone, although navigators and wireless operators had usually already met their respective navigation and signals leaders for their own technical briefings. The senior intelligence officer, S/Ldr Duncan, who had been an observer in the First World War, introduced the target and summarised its importance to the German war economy. It was the chief port and second largest city of Germany, with shipbuilding industries now concentrated on naval ships and submarines. Other industries were widely scattered throughout the built-up area, including some producing aircraft components.

The meteorological expert, a civilian, gave the expected weather *en route* and at the target. The skies were clear of cloud and the moon was not due to rise until after the aircraft had left the target. The moon aided bomber crews in finding a target but particularly assisted the night-fighter crews, for visual identification was always possible in such conditions.

The station navigation officer, signals officer and gunnery officer said their pieces for the general audience and then came Don. His slim, neat figure brought a noticeable increase of interest by the crews, and a warm reaction to their commander – they knew he was going with them.

He was cheerful and encouraging. Tonight was very special in that for the first time each Stirling had supplies of 'window' to be dropped *en route* from 54°34' N, 07°41' E to 54°06' N 07°22' E some distance beyond the target and on the route home. Navigators would be responsible for notifying these points and one crew member would be on duty at the flare chute to drop 'window'. This was expected to upset the enemy radar so that searchlights, flak and ground control for night fighters would probably all have difficulty in operating against the bomber forces. Don suggested that this operation would be easier than usual – or so the scientific people were saying. 'We'll wait and see!' he said with a laugh, which helped relax the group listening to him.

He reminded the crews that the route had been carefully worked out to avoid the attacking force becoming involved with the defences of Heligoland, Kiel and the Elbe estuary on the way in to the target. On the way home the route avoided Bremen, Bremerhaven, Wilhelmshaven and Cuxhaven.

> Please keep strictly to course tonight and to help you on the route in, there will be yellow T.I.s dropped at point A – the crossing point

> on the German coast in the province of Schleswig-Holstein. They will be accurate, I hope, because the crew of P for Peter have the job of dropping them for our squadron!

This caused a brief chuckle as it was his aircraft for the night's operation.

> On timing, you know the reason for its importance – for those eight minutes the sky above you should be clear of Lancasters and Halifaxes ready to unload all they've got upon innocent Stirlings as well as the target! Our time on target is zero + 18 to zero plus 26, or 01.18 to 01.26 hours.
>
> We are on the third wave of the attack – 114 Stirlings of 3 Group. There are some 230 bombers plus all the Pathfinders ahead of us and over 300 bombers in the following waves. We are to bomb on the T.I. reds if they are visible or otherwise on the centre of the pattern on T.I. Greens.
>
> There are over 700 aircraft bombing Hamburg tonight so this is a major attack which I believe may be the first of a series of raids to destroy this target entirely and thoroughly.
>
> Good luck boys! See that you get right over the target tonight!

The group captain took over to say a few words of encouragement, and the briefing was over.

The operation was now 'on in a big way' in RAF language. The crews made their way by trucks to their huge aircraft waiting at individual concrete dispersal sites distributed around the airfield perimeter. There were some thirty-six such sites and usually about thirty Stirlings were allotted to a three-flight squadron. Tonight twenty were required and these had been armed and fuelled during the afternoon from long sets of bomb trolleys drawn by tractors and by teams of men working from trucks and petrol bowsers. The groundcrews were now clustered around each plane with their duties performed but ready to check any electrical or hydraulic system with the aircrew. And each ground team wanted to wish their aircrew the best of luck and to watch the take-off.

The period between briefing and take-off was edgy for everyone, especially the aircrews. An eerie sort of semi-silence pervaded the airfield and conversation was quiet and stilted under the wings and fuselage of each aircraft. Eventually each captain said it was time to get aboard. Crew members urinated under or near their aircraft and slowly climbed up the ladder into the dark fuselage. Each man stowed his gear and settled down to his own duties.

At P for Peter Don was friendly and cheerful with the ground crew and with the scratch team who were now aboard with him. He knew that this could be one of his last operational trips because his tour as commanding officer with 218 Squadron was almost over. He had reason to believe that his period in command had been a successful one and that this was well known and appreciated at 3 Group HQ. It is possible that he also knew that his name had gone forward for the award of the DSO. He and G/Capt. Barnes were on the very best of terms and some hint of the decoration may well have been given in confidence. In fact, the award must already have been in the pipeline, as it was announced on 27 July.

He quickly put aside such thoughts and concentrated on the matter in hand, which was flying his Stirling Mark III bomber and leading nineteen other captains and crews across the North Sea to Germany.

The silent airfield came alive suddenly with the chatter of the first Hercules engines being started up. One by one each Stirling began to throb with noisy power.

In his lofty cockpit at the control, Don was perfectly at ease and looked around the field at the other Stirlings, hoping that some of the younger and less-experienced captains were as happy and confident as he was. He checked with his crew; all were ready and they sounded cheerful as they answered. But both inside the Stirlings and around the airfield and in the station buildings, tension began to build up as the aircraft slowly moved out onto the perimeter tracks and towards the end of the flarepath set along the main runway.

Take-off was always the most dangerous time on an operational bomber station. An intruder could create chaos and destroy half a squadron with one attack. An accident, a crash of one bomber on take-off, could damage others and cause delays which would be fatal to aircraft and crews late over the target. Each loaded bomber was a potential menace to its own aerodrome and neighbourhood until it was safely airborne and away on course.

That night the take-off went well and one by one the heavy Stirlings accelerated down the main runway into a light wind from the south-west and lifted off as if reluctant to leave earth. Each roared low over the northern edge of Downham Market, causing ornaments to rattle and some of the inhabitants to rush outside into their gardens to peer upwards and send their good wishes.

P for Peter took off at 22.20 hours. P/O Brighton gave a course for Cromer, the 3 Group crossing point on the English coast, as Don smoothly set the aircraft on a slow, climbing turn between Downham Market and King's Lynn – the operation was in its first stage.

Once over the North Sea and on course for the first turning point, north-west of Heligoland, Don handed over the controls to F/Sgt Beavis and went back to be sure that P/O Brighton, the young navigator, was coping. He was himself a trained navigator and thoroughly knowledgeable about the methods used. However, with light winds forecast and good fixes available from the G.E.E. radar navigation aid, navigation was not difficult for the Hamburg mission and Don noted that Brighton was obviously competent and careful. He spoke briefly to other crew members and returned to his cockpit.

After the first turning point at 54° 45′ N, 07° 00′E the next interest lay in starting the 'window' drop at 54° 34′N, 07° 41′E. Don and his crew wondered how effective it would be against the skilled radar operators of the Hamburg defences.

Point A, the point for dropping the yellow routemarkers was on the German coast at 54° 11′N, 08° 50′E. Don was satisfied that the T.I.s were dropped correctly and at the estimated time. He himself was back in the pilot's seat and flying carefully on course to aid accurate navigation, at about 3,600 metres (12,000 ft). There remained only one more route point before the target and he wanted to climb to a bombing height of 4,500 metres (15,000 ft) by the time the slight course change was made into the target area.

All went smoothly as they approached Hamburg and saw in the distance the searchlights and heavy flak. The nearer they got the more delighted they were – the searchlights were waving aimlessly about the sky and heavy and light flak was concentrated in firing barrages. No aircraft could be seen coned in the searchlights as was usual at Hamburg, when all the flak would concentrate fire upon the unfortunate bomber and usually blow it out of the sky. Bright flares illuminated the city, which was already ablaze with fires. Target indicators were visible but already a lot of smoke was rising to 1,500 metres (5,000 ft) over the burning city.

Of the twenty Stirlings that set out from Downham Market, seventeen returned safely and reported that they had bombed on T.I.s which were clearly visible; if they were correctly placed then the attack had been very successful. Among the crews over the target were those of S/Ldr Ryall and Sgt Aaron. The latter reported bombing on green T.I.s and seeing many large fires and the attack well concentrated.

The flight commander thought the raid was very successful and relatively easy because of the effects of 'window' on the enemy defences. The flak and searchlights were all over the place and he saw no fighter activity.

Of the other three crews, one had brought bombs back early owing to engine trouble and landed safely at base and another, with more serious problems, had jettisoned bombs in the North Sea and returned early. The third, however, P for Peter under W/Cdr Saville, was posted on the operations board as missing.

The group captain and others waiting up for news were puzzled and worried by the fact that no signals had been received from the aircraft, although they knew that F/Lt Stanley, the signals leader, was on board. This was not encouraging, and as time passed without news, they were left with the hope that if it had been shot down, some of the crew would survive as PoWs.

S/Ldr Ryall, who remembers waiting up for many missing aircraft says simply:

> We were, so to speak, conditioned not to expect all our aircraft to return. One waited around for a long time after there was any hope and then, with an empty feeling, gave up and went to bed.
>
> As it was one of those massive 'window' operations Don was very unlucky, since our use of 'window' practically put the enemy defences out of action, and our losses were minimal. He was sadly missed, of course he was, but we were too busy to let it get us down and there was always the hope that he had baled out and got away with it.

The Bomber Command War Diaries gives these statistics about this raid: 791 aircraft took part and 728 dropped 2,284 tons of bombs in 50 minutes. Twelve aircraft were lost – four Halifaxes, three Stirlings and one Wellington – 1.5 per cent of the attacking force (far less than the usual loss rate). Because this was the first occasion on which 'window' was dropped and Bomber Command was mounting a maximum effort, twenty-three squadron commanders and three station commanders went on the operation. The most senior officer lost that night was W/Cdr D. T. Saville, DFC of 218 Squadron.

Don had not baled out, as had been hoped by those waiting at Downham Market on the morning of 25 July 1943, but there was eventually news of one survivor from P for Peter – F/O H. C. Eyre, the bomb aimer, was reported as a PoW in Germany. He returned to Britain in 1945 and told his story. He received a partial disability pension from the RAF because of wounds and damage received in landing by parachute on the northern outskirts of Hamburg, and always had to walk with the aid of a stick. He returned to his former profession as a schoolmaster and became headmaster of a large Cardiff school, but unhappily died of a sudden heart attack at the school in 1978.

The story of the loss of Stirling P for Peter BF 567 is reconstructed here from information largely supplied by members of the Eyre family through letters and conversations. A brief Ministry of Defence statement said that it was attacked by night fighter, caught fire and went out of control. Eyre baled out and was taken prisoner. Three other crewmen also baled out but died of injuries. All other crew were killed.

Eyre returned as F/Lt Eyre. He was not given to talking much about the war but Mrs Eyre says that sometimes during a sleepless night it would come out. He told her it had been a voluntary flight for him – he was asked if he would make up a crew. As bomb aimer it was his job to get the crew out in an emergency. He had examined the emergency exit and got a member of the groundcrew to grease the hinges of the escape hatch before take-off.

When the aircraft was shot up it all happened so quickly there was no time to think. He heard Don shout 'Get away boys!' and got the escape hatch open and helped some of the crew get out. The Stirling was on fire and he shouted up to Don in the cockpit, 'It's on fire, you've got to get out!' Don shouted back, 'You get out – I'll follow you down.' Eyre said the last thing he saw as he was getting through the hatch was the glint of the captain's gold cuff links – Don wore uncut gold nuggets as cuff links. Eyre believed that he himself was the last to leave the plane. He seemed unsure of the exact number of crew who got out – it varied from four to six. As he floated down he remembers seeing two others descending by parachute.

Eyre landed on the roof of a *Luftwaffe* station building and smashed one of his knees in doing so. He found that he had a shrapnel wound in one leg. He stayed where he was until it seemed quiet, but soldiers were waiting for him and he was knocked unconscious by a blow to the head with a rifle butt. Later he was taken into a *Luftwaffe* building and made comfortable. He stayed some days at the airfield before being moved to an interrogation centre. Six armed men protected him from civilians on the way to the centre. He was told that the other crewmen had been seized by civilians and hanged from lamp posts. Eyre understood and spoke German fluently, and believed that he had escaped the same fate only because he had landed on a roof and been protected by *Luftwaffe* personnel.

He was sent to Stalag Luft III for the duration. He became education officer there and taught German to his fellow PoWs.

Mrs Eyre says that her husband had told her that 'of all the men he knew in the war he had the greatest respect for Don Saville. He didn't care for red tape and was a thoroughly honest, down-to-earth, Aussie. Saville was his own man – he didn't scrape to authority like some officers.' At another time, Eyre commented to his son-in-law: 'He was a rough diamond but a damn good pilot – I liked him both as a man and as an aircraft commander!'

The wreck of P for Peter finally crashed 70km (45 miles) north of Hamburg near Neumünster, but the parachutists are believed to have landed in the suburb of Schnelsen, today a respectable residential area of modern and prosperous buildings. Don was found burned beyond recognition, still at the controls. Like many other pilots in similar situations, he had put the safety of his crew before his own. It appears that he steered the flaming Stirling away from Hamburg. Always a courageous man, he died as he had lived. The badly burned bodies of three other crew members were found in the wreckage.

Today seven members of the crew lie together in the War Graves Commission cemetery at Ohlsdorf on the outskirts of Hamburg. They were first buried by the German authorities at Neumünster South cemetery on 27 July 1943 and subsequently moved to Ohlsdorf after an investigation by RAF No. 4 Missing Research and Enquiry Unit on 17 May 1946.

Ohlsdorf British Military Cemetery, Hamburg
Plot 4, Row B, Graves 1–6
74738 W/Cdr D. T. Saville, DSO DFC.
147921 P/O W. J. Brighton
113849 F/Lt T. A. Stanley, DFC.
116801 F/Lt J. L. Birbeck DFC.
979354 F/Sgt A. B. Howat
51686 P/O T. D. Fairgrieve
R. A. F. 25–7–43
Grave 7
417003 F/Sgt H. W. Beavis, R.N.Q.A.F.

The *London Gazette* of 27 July 1943 carried the following citation:

Distinguished Service Order

Acting Wing Commander Donald Teal SAVILLE DFC (74738) No. 218 Squadron.

This officer has completed a very large number of sorties and has displayed outstanding determination to achieve success. He is a fearless commander, who invariably chooses to participate in the more difficult sorties which have to be undergone. Whatever the opposition Wing Commander Saville endeavours to press home his attacks with accuracy and resolution. By his personal example and high qualities of leadership, this officer has contributed materially to the operational efficiency of the Squadron.

Appendix A

Memories of Don Saville

The following are extracts from letters and conversations which provide insights into his contemporaries' memories of Don Saville. They are arranged in chronological order so that it may be possible to detect change or development in the character of this intriguing and complex man.

The Tasmanian Aero Club 1935-7

Harry Whelan of Hobart:

> Don Saville was a likeable young man – a very good type of fellow – a good companion – a cheerful sort of soul – everybody loved Don Saville! He was an expert flier – an ex-air force pilot who could do spectacular aerobatics – a very accomplished pilot with all aircraft.

W/Cdr F. R. Graeme-Evans (Retired):

> When I met Don Saville as flying instructor to the Tasmanian Aero Club I was not sure at first whether he was English or Australian. He was immaculate in his dress and looked like a high-powered executive – a businessman rather than a flying instructor. I found him a charming chap and he seemed grateful to be back on flying even though the job was hardly worthy of his talents and experience.

ANA and Ansett Airlines 1937-9

Captain John Presgrave:

> One big regret I have in his passing is that I never had an opportunity to repay his many kindnesses to me personally plus the time and effort he put into working with me to assist me in establishing my career as an airline pilot. He was most generous.

Captain Arthur Lovell:

> Don was an excellent pilot, quite unflappable and always the gentleman. He was particular about his appearance and dress – really a top airline captain. His confidence was based on ability and competence – he was always correct with ground staff – friendly but never familiar. All these qualities would be those of a really good air force commanding officer.

Captain Peter Gibbes:

> Don Saville was a good friend and companion. I remember him as short and jovial – and a natural pilot. He was generous and helpful with co-pilots. He was convivial – one of the boys – he loved booze and girls! He was a great raconteur and always had a store of good stories – some of the 'tall' variety.

RAF AND RAAF 1939–43

F/Lt 'Ken' Kenton, RAF (Retired), a sergeant pilot in the ferry pool after surviving tours on Battles and Blenheims:

> Don Saville was my CO at No. 4 Ferry Pool at Hullavington. Don was always friendly and cheerful and we respected him as a pilot. I remember him as a decent quiet officer and a very competent pilot.

W/Cdr George H. N. Gibson, DFC, AFC, RAF (Retired):

> Gibson first met Don Saville in 1941 when the latter was a flight lieutenant in 12 Squadron. He noted that Don was more experienced than anyone else and 'more elderly'. Saville was perhaps inclined to be a little impatient with young pilots who seemed to be lacking in fundamental flying knowledge. He, of course, knew it all! 'Don Saville was a small very active man – someone you couldn't forget!'

Air Commodore A. E. Mather, DFC, AFC, RAAF (Retired):

> Don was a larrikin at heart, somewhat scornful of hard and fast regulations and higher brass bureaucracy, pushing and determined to get his own way on the operational scene. Yet mixed with this there was a great personal kindness to subordinates and he did many things to help many people. Don was the sponsor of my

DFC (judging from the wording of the citation) and responsible also for my return to Australia.

Peter Alexander, author of *We Find and Destroy*, a history of 458 Squadron, RAAF:

Don was a great pilot and a loss indeed . . . as were so many others who were the brightest and best of their generation.

F/Lt Eric Lloyd, DFC, RAAF (Retired), navigator in Saville's crew in 458 squadron, RAAF:

At thirty-nine years of age, Don Saville was an ancient among the operational pilots flying at that time. He was a small man, slightly built with thin features – but there were more guts and energy packed into his 130 lb [59 kg] than in a youth half his age. He was shot down over Hamburg in 1943 – a loss to the war effort and a sad loss to the world of aviation. He was a beautiful pilot with thousands of flying hours behind him. Flying was his life!

S/Ldr Leslie Manfield, DFC, RAF (Retired), navigation officer of 104 Squadron:

I remember that he was very critical of officers who had a 'cushy' time at some training establishment or other during the earlier part of the war. He was a very dynamic character, a good mixer in the mess but intolerant of people who did not do their job properly.

F/Lt Steve Boylan, RAF (Retired), a pilot in 104 Squadron:

In my opinion he was the best CO any airman could wish for, a great, inspiring leader – fearless and always took a great interest in his crews whatever their rank, and he could always get maximum effort from them. I was only a flight sergeant at the time but he treated me as an equal and always remembered even small details of our 'ops'. A great leader!

I don't think all the time I flew under two other commanders they ever spoke to me once.

F/Lt Colin E. Corten, RAAF (Retired), a navigator in 104 Squadron:

Don Saville was the only CO I ever flew with and I think it could safely be said that he was the type of leader responsible for winning the war – an RAF 'Montgomery' in a somewhat lesser role.

From recollection he was rather a small man in build and in my experience such men are not averse to addressing their subordinates in a somewhat aggressive manner when the situation appears to justify an element of disapproval. However, he confined his irascible remarks to the captains of aircraft and did not interfere with the work of other aircrew members. Don Saville was extremely keen and being an old flier he did not imagine that it would ever happen to him. He was in fact, too oblivious of the risks of operational flying to survive the war.

F/Lt W. McRae, DFC, RAAF (Retired), a pilot in 148 and 104 Squadrons:

You may recall that about a dozen aircraft from 148 Squadron joined 104 Squadron on Malta early in December 1942. The day after our arrival Don gave us a 'welcome' talk which consisted mainly of the shortcomings of crews who did not press on to the target and warning us of the consequences if we were ever among the delinquents. This did not go down very well. I also had an argument with Don one night as to the serviceability of an aircraft. He was wrong and more or less apologised next day.

F/Lt H. M. Fuller, DFC, RAAF (Retired), a pilot in 104 Squadron:

I think that Don Saville was the bravest man I ever met.

S/Ldr G. M. Rothwell, DFC and Bar, RAF (Retired), a flight commander, 218 Squadron:

The lack of bull and friendliness to all were features that endeared Don to all who served under him. I remember how I admired the way he was able to run the squadron so effectively without relying on tight discipline as many others in his position did. It was the free and easy atmosphere which brought out the best in the crews.

S/Ldr Ian Ryall, DFC and bar, RAF (Retired), a flight commander 218 Squadron:

I knew Don Saville well. I was his senior flight commander on 218 Squadron. He was a great chap and I remember him as a good friend. He was a good CO – the sort of chap that made Bomber Command tick by giving the lead both on and off duty. He liked his pint and was always there with the boys when there was a night off.

I had lots of commanding officers but quite honestly, *he* was the most outstanding, without a shadow of doubt!

S/Ldr L. E. Skan, RAF (Retired), flying control officer, Downham Market:

> W/Cdr Saville was a wonderful pilot and 'skipper' and respected for that. I have the lingering feeling that, if you will forgive me, he had what is a popular British notion of Australians, a slightly condescending attitude to the 'Poms'. I certainly knew him and spoke to him a little in the mess, but would not have described him as altogether a friendly man. I would, for example, say that, unlike most aircrew, he regarded flying control officers as a necessary evil.

F/Lt Cedric Eyre, RAF, bomb aimer (the last man to see Don alive):

F/Lt Eyre died in 1978. These comments come courtesy of Mrs Eyre and members of the family. Mrs Eyre says that 'Ced always spoke of Don Saville as someone very special and important to him. He told me that of all the men he knew during the war he had the greatest respect for Don Saville.'

F/Lt Eyre is quoted as saying,

> He was a rough diamond but a damn good pilot. I liked him both as a man and as an aircraft commander . . .
>
> Saville didn't care for red tape – he was a thoroughly honest, down to earth Aussie – and an essentially courageous man.
>
> Wing Commander Saville was a very popular commander and his crews ere happy to go with him anywhere!

Appendix B

Don Saville's Record of Service

Royal Australian Air Force

2 May 1927	Air Cadet, No. 1 Flying Training School, Point Cook
17 December 1927	Termination of period of enlistment (graduated as pilot)
1 May 1932	Flying Officer in Citizens' Air Force Reserve on return to Australia
30 April 1936	Relinquished rank of flying officer on completion of service in the reserve

Royal Air Force

14 February 1928	Granted a short-service commission in the RAF as pilot officer in the General Duties Branch
14 February 1928	Central Flying School, Wittering
2 May 1928	No. 17 Fighter squadron, Upavon
2 November 1928	Flying officer
21 January 1929	RAF Calshot for Air Pilotage Course
24 April 1929	No. 17 Fighter Squadron, Upavon
17 March 1930	Armament and Gunnery School, Eastchurch
19 May 1930	No. 17 Fighter squadron, Upavon
13 October 1930	No. 207 Bomber Squadron, Bircham Newton

5 January 1931	No. 23 Fighter Squadron, Kenley
13 January 1931	Training Squadron, RAF Calshot
13 May 1931	RAF Depot
14 February 1932	Relinquished commission on transfer to RAAF

ROYAL AIR FORCE WAR SERVICE APPOINTMENTS

27 September 1939	Commission as a pilot officer (on probation) in the General Duties Branch of the Royal Air Force Volunteer Reserve for the duration of hostilities
27 September 1940	Confirmed in appointment and promoted flying officer
9 October 1940	Appointed acting flight lieutenant
1 July 1941	Appointed acting squadron leader (paid)
27 September 1941	Promoted flight lieutenant (war substantive)
4 August 1942	Appointed acting wing commander (paid), to command
4 November 1942	Promoted squadron leader (war substantive)
13 February 1943	Relinquished acting wing commander (paid)
30 March 1943	Appointed acting wing commander (to command)

Royal Air Force War Service Postings and Attachments

27 September 1939	No. 2 Ferry Pilots' Pool, flying duties
1 May 1940	No. 4 Ferry Pilots' Pool, flying duties
1 July 1941	No. 11 Ferry Flight, flying duties
11 August 1941	No. 21 Operational Training Unit
5 September 1941	No. 12 Wellington Bomber Squadron, flying duties
2 December 1941	No. 458 Wellington Bomber Squadron RAAF flying duties
27 February 1942	RAF Station Holme upon Spalding Moor, supernumerary pending overseas posting
2 March 1942	No. 458 Bomber Squadron, RAAF, flying duties
2 May 1942	No. 2 Training School, supernumerary
14 June 1942	No. 458 Bomber Squadron, RAAF flying duties
4 August 1942	No. 104 Squadron, flying duties
14 February 1943	No. 1 Personnel Dispersal Unit, pending posting to UK
30 March 1943	No. 218 Bomber Squadron, flying duties

Honours and Awards

18 December 1942	Distinguished Flying Cross
27 July 1943	Distinguished Service Order

1939/1945 Star

Aircrew Europe Star

Africa Star

Defence Medal

War Medal 1939/1945

OPERATIONS AGAINST ENEMY TARGETS

With No. 12 Wellington Bomber Squadron, RAF (captain-pilot) over Europe	9
With No. 458 Bomber Squadron, RAAF (flight commander) over Europe and in the Mediterranean	6
With No. 104 Wellington Bomber Squadron, RAF (in command) against North African and Italian targets	32
With No. 218 (Gold Coast) Stirling Bomber Squadron, RAF (in command) over Europe	10
Total operational missions	57

From February 1943 Bomber Command recommended that a pilot's first tour should be thirty sorties and the second should normally not exceed twenty. These limits were finally laid down by an Air Ministry letter dated 8 May 1943. The Pathfinder force was on a different basis; its tours consisted of forty-five sorties but crews could be withdrawn at any time after the completion of thirty.

There is apparently no record of any directive about the number of sorties required of, or suggested for, a squadron commander. They operated as they saw fit in order to maintain good morale among their aircrews. Restraints on their operations were, however, suggested in 1943 because of losses.

Appendix C

Aircraft Types Flown by Don Saville

RAAF at Point Cook, 1927

Avro 504 K (A3)

DH9A(A1)

Royal Air Force, 1928–32

Avro 504N
Woodcock
Horsley
Bristol Bulldog
Fairey IIIF
Fairey III seaplane
Gamecock
Bristol Fighter
Siskin IIIA
Southampton flying boat
Wapiti
Grebe
Atlas

1932–5

Amateur-built planes and various other small types from Mascot at weekends – more than ten different types.

Tasmanian Aero Club, 1935–7

DH60

Australian National Airways, 1937–9

DH Moth IA
DC2
DH89
Short Scion
DH86
Lockheed 10A (Ansett Airways)
Percival Gull
DH83
DH84
Monospar
DC3

Royal Air Force 1939–43

Ferry Pool

Wellington IC and II
Hampden
Gauntlet
Henley
Hurricane I and II
Whitley
Hereford
Electra 10A
Lerwick flying boat
Sunderland flying boat
Tutor
Northrop
Leopard Moth
Piper Cub
Beaufighter
Whirlwind
Monarch
Douglas DB7
Halifax
Anson
Blenheim I and IV
Hudson
Spitfire I, II, V
Gladiator
Lysander
Oxford
Beaufort
Moth Minor
Battle
Botha
Curtis Hawk
Walrus amphibian
Defiant
Stirling
Tomahawk
Proctor
Havoc

12 Squadron, RAF

Wellington II

458 Squadron, RAAF

Wellington IV
Liberator

104 Squadron, RAF

Wellington II

218 Squadron, RAF

Stirling I and III

Appendix D

A Saville Chronology

DONALD TEALE SAVILLE	1900	WORLD EVENTS
Born	1903	Wright Brothers powered flight
Voyage to UK ended at Adelaide	1909	Bleriot flew across the English Channel
Don and John Saville visited UK with their parents. On return	1912	Titanic disaster
attended All Saints' College, Bathurst	1913	A. V. Roe built the Avro 504
Saville boys entered SCEGS (Shore)	1914	Outbreak of First World War. Point Cook flying school established
Saville children taken to Britain to be educated at the Friends School, Great Ayton, Yorkshire	1916	Naval Battle of Jutland No. 1 Squadron Australian Flying Corps formed at Point Cook
	1918	Formation of the Royal Air Force End of First World War
	1919	Alcock and Brown crossed the Atlantic (Vickers Vimy bomber) R34 first airship to cross east to west
Saville boys returned to Australia	1920	
Worked in chemist's department, Portland Cement Co. Clyde Engineering, Sydney (1920–2)	1921	Formation of the Royal Australian Air Force
Entered Sydney Grammar School to gain Leaving Certificate	1922	
Saville brothers employed by Bathurst Motors	1924	Goble and McIntyre flew around Australia (Fairey III seaplane)

DONALD TEALE SAVILLE		WORLD EVENTS
In charge of motor transport at Portland Cement Co.	1925	
Joined RAAF as air cadet at Point Cook	1927	Lindbergh flew the Atlantic (solo) to Paris
Joined RAF on short-service commission	1928	Hinkler flew solo from England to Australia Kingsford-Smith flew the Pacific with stops at Hawaii and Fiji
	1930	R101 disaster.
	1931	Final Schneider Trophy Race ANA airliner (*Southern Cloud*) lost between Sydney and Melbourne
Returned to Australia and was placed in Citizens' Air Force Reserve	1932	
Selected as pilot for all-Australian plane	1934	London–Melbourne Centenary Air Race
Flying instructor, Tasmanian Aero Club	1935	Kingsford-Smith missing in *Lady Southern Cross*
Joined Australian National Airways	1937	Hindenburg disaster
	1938	Munich Agreement
Rejoined RAF	1939	Outbreak of Second World War
Pilot officer to squadron leader in Ferry Pool	1940	Battle of France . . . Battle of Britain
Posted to 12 Squadron, Bomber Command Squadron leader and flight commander, 458 Squadron	1941	Pearl Harbor
Wing Commander and commander 104 Squadron, RAF	1942	Darwin bombed Battle of El Alamein
Commander, 218 Squadron, RAF	1943	Battle of the Ruhr Battle of Hamburg
Killed in action over Hamburg		

Appendix E

A Career Comparison

A Mid-level commander (Wing Commander D. T. Saville, DSO, DFC)		**A Top-level commander** (Air Chief Marshal Sir Frederick Scherger, KBE, CB, DSO, AFC)
	1900	
Born 22 December 1903 Portland, NSW *Education*: Private and All Saints' College, Bathurst Sydney C.E. Grammar School, 1916–20 Friends School, Great Ayton, England Bathurst High School Sydney Grammar School		Born 18 May 1904 Ararat, Victoria *Education*: State Primary School Ararat High School
		Cadet, Royal Military College, Duntroon, 1921–4
		Pilot officer, RAAF Point Cook 1925
Cadet, RAAF Point Cook 1927		Adjutant, No. 1 Squadron, Point Cook (flying officer), and flying instructor, 1927 Permanent commission in General Duties Branch RAAF, 1927
Short-service commission RAF, 1928–32. (flying officer)		
RAAF Citizens' Air Force Reserve, 1932–6 (flying officer)		RAF Staff College, 1934–6 (flight lieutenant)

A Mid-level commander (Wing Commander D. T. Saville, DSO, DFC)		**A Top-level commander** (Air Chief Marshal Sir Frederick Scherger, KBE, CB, DSO, AFC)
Flying instructor, Tasmanian Aero Club, 1935–7		
Airline pilot and captain with Australian National Airways, 1937–9		Chief flying instructor, RAAF Point Cook (squadron leader)
	1939	
Rejoined RAF as pilot officer for flying duties, 1939		Director of training at Air HQ RAAF, Melbourne, 1939 (wing commander)
Ferry-pool flying duties and command of No. 4 Ferry Pool (squadron leader), 1939–41		Air Force Cross, 1940 (group captain)
	1941	
No. 12 Bomber Squadron, operational flying, 1941		
Flight commander, No. 458 Bomber Squadron RAAF, 1941 (squadron leader)		C.O. RAAF Darwin, 1941 (group captain)
	1942	
		SASO HQ N. W. Area, Darwin, 1942
		Director of defence, Allied AHQ, Melbourne, 1942
Commander, No. 104 Bomber Squadron (wing commander), 1942		Director of training, AHQ, Melbourne
Distinguished Flying Cross, 1942		
	1943	
Commander, No. 218 Bomber Squadron, 1943		
Killed in action, 1943 Distinguished Service Order, 1943		AOC, No. 10 Group, RAAF, New Guinea, 1943

A Mid-level commander (Wing Commander D. T. Saville, DSO, DFC)		A Top-level commander (Air Chief Marshal Sir Frederick Scherger, KBE, CB, DSO, AFC)
	1944	
		Promoted to air commodore, 1944 Distinguished Service Order
	1945	
		Commander 1st Tactical Air Force, RAAF
	1946	
		Imperial Defence College Course, U.K., 1946 Deputy chief of air staff, 1947
	1950	
		Promoted to air vice-marshal, 1950 Chief of air staff (air marshal), 1957
	1960	
		Chairman, chief of staffs committee. 1965 Promoted to air chief marshal 1984 Died

It is worth noting that the separate paths taken by the careers of these two distinguished airmen were the result of decisions made by the RAAF. Scherger was offered a permanent commission, while Saville was placed on the reserve.

There were three early career differences which favoured Scherger. First, he was trained at the Royal Military College, Duntroon, where he achieved the highest marks in his class. Second, he was granted a permanent commission in the RAAF in 1927. Third, in 1934 he was posted overseas to attend an RAF Staff College course.

Scherger was appointed to a non-flying staff position at the outbreak of the Second World War and continued to rise after a temporary setback connected with the bombing of Darwin. He held high operational command as AOC of No. 10 Group, RAAF in New Guinea and was in command of the 1st Tactical Air Force, RAAF in 1945, which led naturally to the highest commands in the peace-time service and to the rank of air chief marshal.

Saville flew constantly in many types of aircraft. He forced his way into Bomber Command and quickly rose to command two operational RAF bomber squadrons. Although the same age as Scherger, he completed two operational tours as a bomber captain and made his name as a brilliant squadron commander. Scherger, on the other hand and probably to his great regret because he loved flying as much as Saville, never commanded an operational squadron.

Appendix F

Saville Family Tree

Origins: *Saville family from Yorkshire, England –* Middlesbrough area (Eston and Marton)

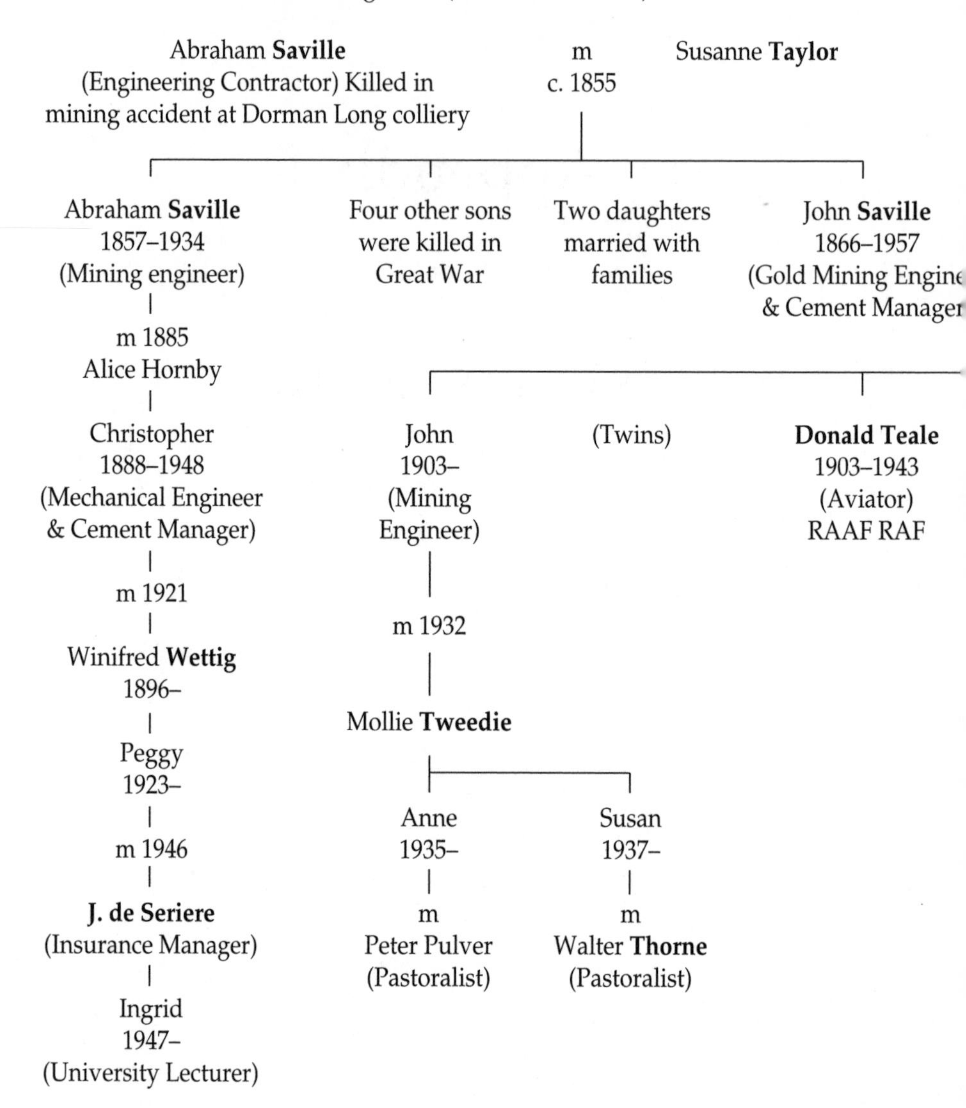

Summary:
The major family profession was engineering (various branches) among those connected with Britain. In recent times the family in Australia has become directly interested in the land and farming. Engineering has disappeared but family members show a wide spread or professional interests. Donald Saville and John de Seriere were both bomber pilots in the Second World War.

Teale family from Yorkshire, England –
Richmond, Yorkshire and Gourock, Scotland. Don's Teale grandparents both died early and the family was brought up by an uncle in Scotland

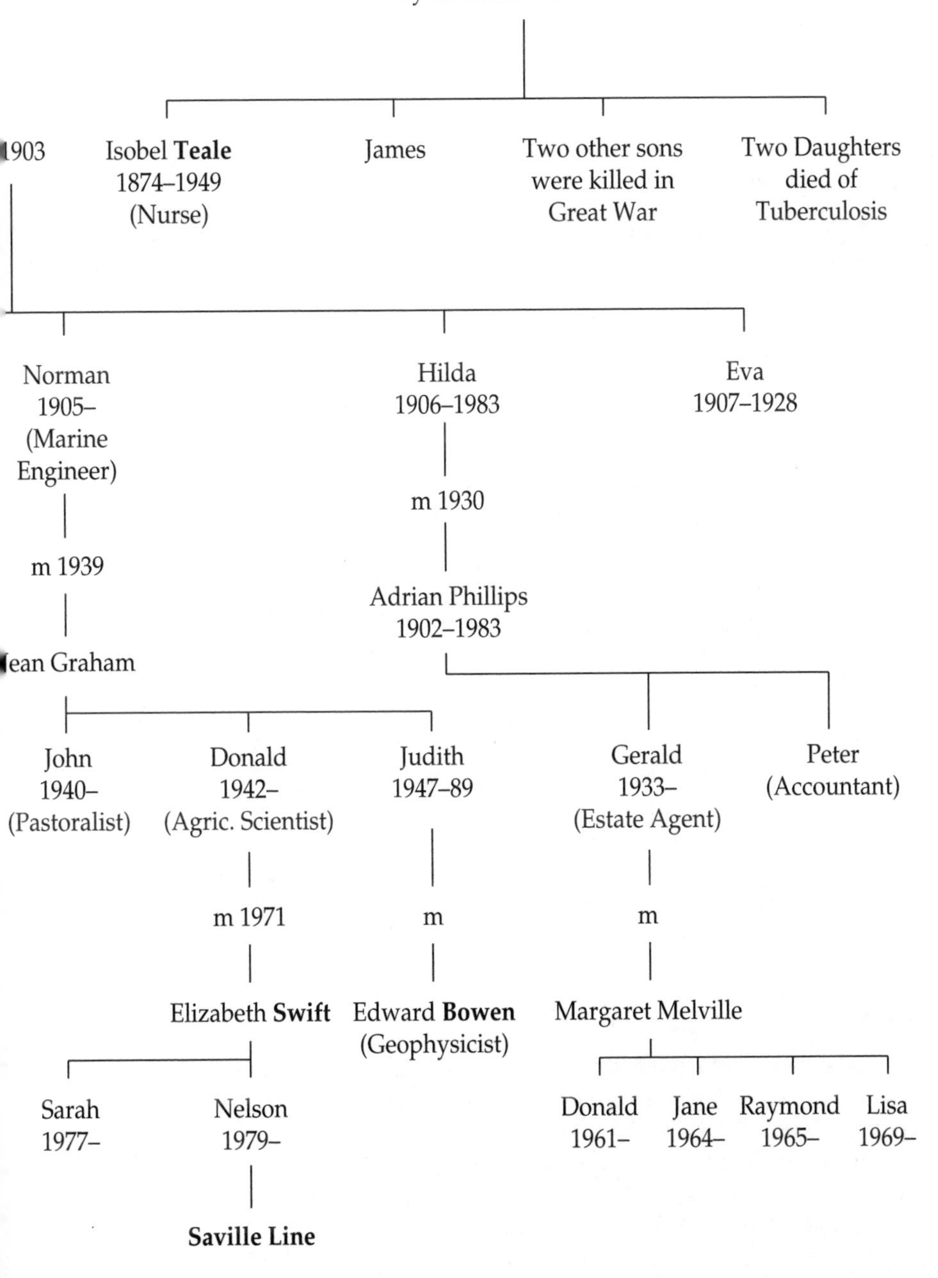

Bibliography and Sources

Other Sources

The Saville family in general and in particular Don's brothers, John and Norman, were willing to help in every possible way when research began in 1983.

Members or former members of the Tasmanian Aero Club and of Australian National Airways also provided information.

Details of RAAF and RAF service were obtained from records of service and log books.

RAAF records were examined at Point Cook RAAF Museum and Archives, the RAAF Historical Branch at Canberra and at the Australian War Memorial Library. These included records of No. 458 Squadron, RAAF for the years 1941 and 1942.

RAF records were studied at the Public Record Office, Kew. These were mainly the operational record books of squadrons, wings, stations and groups, including: Air 27 documents of 104 Squadron, 40 Squadron, 12 Squadron, 218 Squadron; Air 26 documents of 236 Wing, 238 Wing, RAF Station Holme upon Spalding Moor, RAF Station Downham Market; and Air 29 documents on Filton, Hullavington and Moreton-in-the-Marsh.

RAAF and RAF personnel who knew Don Saville were traced and information obtained through correspondence and/or personal interviews which in most cases were recorded on cassette tapes.

Visits were made to the RAF Museums and to Bomber Command Library at Hendon.

Books

Alexander, Peter. *We Find and Destroy*, 458 Association Council, 1979

Bowyer, Chaz. *Wellingtons at War*. Ian Allen, 1982

Bowyer, Chaz. *The Wellington Bomber*. Kimber, 1986

Carroll, Brian. *Australian Aviators*. Cassell, 1980

Chappell, F. R. *Wellington Wings*. Kimber, 1980

Charlwood, Don. *No Moon Tonight*. Penguin, 1987

Chorley and Bennett. *In Brave Company*. Privately published, 1979

Ginn, Robert. *Strike Hard*. 104 Squadron Association, 1990

Halley, James J. *Squadrons of the Royal Air Force*. Air Britain, 1980

Hastings, Max. *Bomber Command*. Michael Joseph, 1979
Herington, John. *Air War Against Germany and Italy 1939–1943*. Australian War Memorial, 1954
Herington, John. *Air Power over Europe 1944–1945*. Australian War Memorial, 1963
Horner, David. *The Commanders*. Allen and Unwin, 1984
Jackson, Robert. *The RAF in Action*. Blandford Press, 1985
Johnson, Frank. *RAAF Over Europe*. Eyre and Spottiswoode, 1946
Long, Gavin. *The Six Years' War*. Australian War Memorial, 1973
Middlebrook and Everitt. *The Bomber Command War Diaries*. Viking, 1985
Middlebrook, Martin. *The Battle of Hamburg*. Allen Lane, 1984
Musgrave, Gordon. *Operation Gommorah*. Jane, 1981
Odgers, George. *Pictorial History of the Royal Australian Air Force*. Ure Smith, 1977
Playfair, Molony, Flynn and Gleave. *The Mediterranean and Middle East*. HMSO, 1966
Rayner, Harry. *Scherger*. Australian War Memorial, 1984
Richards and Saunders. *The Royal Air Force 1939–1945* (3 volumes). HMSO, 1974
Robertson, John. *Australia at War 1939–1945*. Heinemann, 1981
Rumpf, Hans. *The Bombing of Germany*. Muller, 1974
Saint-Exupery, Antoine de. *Wind, Sand and Stars*. Pan, 1975
Saward, Dudley. *Bomber Harris*. Cassell, Buchan and Enright, 1984
Summers, Eric M. *Blida's Bombers*. Privately published 1943
Terraine, John. *The Right of the Line*. Hodder and Stoughton, 1985
Turner, John Frayn. *British Aircraft of World War II*. Stein and Day, 1975
Verney, G. L. *The Desert Rats*. Hutchinson, 1954
Wright, H. J. *Pathfinders Light the Way*. McCann, 1983

Index